BOOKS BY JOHN KEATS

See Europe Next Time You Go There
The New Romans
Howard Hughes
The Sheepskin Psychosis
They Fought Alone
The Insolent Chariots
Schools Without Scholars
The Crack in the Picture Window

The
Life
and Times
of
Dorothy Parker

SIMON AND SCHUSTER / NEW YORK

YOU MIGHT AS WELL LIVE

by John Keats

Third printing,

SBN 671-20660-5
Library of Congress Catalog Card Number: 70-130195
Designed by Edith Fowler
Manufactured in the United States of America

AUTHOR'S NOTE

To identify in the text or in notes all the sources of material in a book of this sort seems to the author an imposition on the reader. Yet he is eager to give credit where credit is due. Many lines, ascribed to Dorothy Parker by quotation marks, originally appeared in Wyatt Cooper's article "Remembering Dorothy Parker," which appeared in the July 1968 edition of *Esquire* magazine; in Marion Capron's interview, published in *Writers at Work, The Paris Review Interviews*, First Series (The Viking Press, 1958); in Richard E. Lauterbach's article "The Legend of Dorothy Parker," appearing in the October 1944 issue of *Esquire* magazine; in an Associated Press interview with Dorothy Parker that was teleprinted in August 23, 1963, newspapers and in a radio interview with Mrs. Parker conducted by Richard Lamparski of Radio Station WBAI, New York. In addition, material has been taken from Anita Loos's *But Gentlemen Marry Brunettes*; from Vincent Sheean's *Personal History*; from Ernest Hemingway's *Green Hills of Africa*; from Corey Ford's *The Time of Laughter*; from Nathaniel Benchley's *Robert Benchley*; from Jane Grant's *Ross, The New Yorker, and Me*; and from George Oppenheimer's play *Here Today*. Quotation from Dorothy Parker's poems and stories is by permission of The Viking Press. Permission to quote from Mrs. Parker's magazine articles and from magazine and newspaper interviews with her and from reviews of her work has been granted by *The English Journal*, *Esquire* magazine, *Vogue* magazine, *The New York Times*, and the New York *World Telegram & Sun*. Quotation from *The Merck Manual of Diagnosis and*

Therapy (11th edition, © 1966) is by permission of Merck & Co., Inc. The sources of particular items not identified in the text will be supplied on the request of any seriously interested reader.

For their hours of tape-recorded conversation, correspondence, or other special assistance, the author is particularly indebted to Beatrice Ames; Mr. and Mrs. Robeson Bailey; Dr. Alvan Barach; Mr. and Mrs. Hiram Beer; Gertrude Benchley; Mr. and Mrs. Nathaniel Benchley; Marshall A. Best; Beatrice B. Bodenstein; Elizabeth Bodine; Louis Bohlman; Joseph Bryan, III; John Collins; Mrs. George Cookinham; Wyatt Cooper; Dr. and Mrs. William S. Creighton; Charlotte Devree; John Durant; Dr. and Mrs. H. Keith Fischer; Corey Ford; Walter Fried; Arnold Gingrich; Harold Hayes; Richard Henson; Mr. and Mrs. Don Kindler; Richard Lamparski; Anita Loos; Mrs. Henry B. Luce; Joan Marlowe; Stephen Morris; Howard Moss; George Oppenheimer; Mr. and Mrs. Murdock Pemberton; Gilbert Seldes; Mr. and Mrs. Vincent Sheean; Donald Ogden Stewart; Frank Sullivan; Ursula Thebaud; and Mrs. James Thurber. The author is also indebted to several persons who asked not to be identified (and who were not) for reasons of their own.

Lillian Hellman's moving memoir, *An Unfinished Woman*, sheds valuable light on Dorothy Parker's later years. The author wishes to make clear, however, that Miss Hellman, Mrs. Parker's close friend in those years and the executrix of her estate, has chosen not to be involved in this biography in any way. Her stated reason has been Mrs. Parker's desire that she should never be the subject of a biography. With all respect for the obligations of friendship, it has seemed to the author and his publishers that Dorothy Parker is a public figure of whom biographies are bound to be written, and that an authoritative attempt should be made now to gather and present the facts as well as the legend while they are still fresh in living memories. This is, however, in no sense an authorized or definitive biography. Rather, the author has chosen to set forth certain facts and contemporary opinions that seem to him to explain a time and a woman in terms of each other, in order to suggest reasons why Mrs. Parker said and wrote what she did—and why her life took the form that it did.

FOREWORD

Once upon a time, the world was bright and new, and Dorothy Parker was one of the brightest and newest people in it. She was an elfin woman who had two kinds of magic about her. Her first magical quality was that no one could ever consider her dispassionately, and the other was that no one could precisely define her.

She was for a while rich, famous, and powerful. She had two husbands, four lovers, a mansion in Beverly Hills, a country estate in Pennsylvania, and a series of apartments in New York. She was a central figure of the celebrated Algonquin Hotel Round Table; newspaper columnists quoted her; practically every bright remark of her day was attributed to her. Two Broadway plays were written about her and she was portrayed as a character in a third; she was the most talked-about woman of her time. Her books of poems and short stories were immediate best sellers. Subscribers to *The New Yorker* would turn first of all to the column that she wrote. A college generation worshiped her, for she mirrored, expressed, and helped to establish a new style in life and art for the nation in the late nineteen-twenties and early nineteen-thirties.

That time now seems long ago and far away to most of the people who were in college then, yet if you ask any one of them today to tell you who Dorothy Parker was, he will probably grin and immediately recite:

> *Men seldom make passes*
> *At girls who wear glasses.*

Unfortunately, that may be all of her poetry he can quote. He will not mention her short stories. He will, however, gleefully recall her wit. He will tell you what Dorothy Parker said on learning that Calvin Coolidge had died:

"How could they tell?" she wondered.

Theater people still treasure her saying that Katharine Hepburn in a play "ran the whole gamut of emotions, from A to B." Literary people are fond of her observation that "Verlaine was always chasing Rimbauds," and less complicated folk relish her party line: "One more drink and I'd be under the host."

Because Dorothy Parker said and wrote so many funny lines, it was commonly presumed, by people who did not know her personally, that her life was a merry one, spent in delightful badinage with witty people. She did have a great deal of fun, but she was also a quite serious and creative artist. She was not a minor writer, nor was she a minor figure, although her literary output was quite small: two volumes of short stories and three of poetry. But she was at the very center of New York's intellectual life in the twenties and early thirties, which is to say that she was at the center of what in retrospect seems to have been America's intellectual adolescence. She seemed to know personally everyone who mattered, and certainly everyone who mattered wanted to meet *her*. Her tart reviews of plays and books were more than merely funny; they helped to create a national taste. They also helped to create a national attitude, or style—as did her poems, her stories, and what she said and did in the course of the life she led in the company of extremely intelligent, effective, and influential people. The style that she and her friends created called for one to go through life armed with a wry, hard suspicion; to be always ready to acknowledge excellence, but equally ready to express an informed contempt for all that was in any way bogus—meanwhile being just as ready to have a damned good time at every opportunity.

"Promise me," she said on her seventieth birthday, "I shall never grow old."

And she never did. She is still alive and well so far as the current college generation is concerned. Today's collegians do not know her primarily as a wit, because they know next to nothing about the twenties and the thirties. But they read her poems, as their parents no longer do. Much more important, they read her short stories, for it is on her stories that her literary reputation will rest. They find what she wrote to be as stingingly appropriate today as others found it when she wrote it. Her work does not, to the current generation, appear to be breaking new ground, but rather it seems to be in their own familiar idiom. Their professors ought to tell them how much Dorothy Parker contributed to the creation of that idiom.

Her poems and her stories are often funny, wry, and mocking —and youth will always find these qualities refreshing. But there is something else in her writing that is peculiarly her own: Dorothy Parker was forever unable to say that a human situation was either tragic or comic. Instead, she saw both elements present at once in every situation, and therefore her poems and her stories are not only youthful but poignantly so.

The magical quality she had of defying definition may have been traceable to this insistence on seeing life as an inextricable tangle of disaster and joy. Her own life was never one thing or the other, and because of this, she was a perpetual puzzle to a great many people who believed that they knew her rather well.

Her friends were afraid of her. At the same time, they wished to protect her. To this day, her friends will tell the most horrifying stories about her, immediately adding that she was never vulgar or cruel, but really was quite exquisite, honest, generous, and kind. They agree that her life was a consistent tragedy, and they recall its brilliant gaiety. This infinite woman seemed always to represent matched opposites. Shy and retiring, she dominated every room she entered. She made a great deal of money but her purse was always empty. At the time of her greatest wealth, she believed herself to be a Communist. She hugely enjoyed her fame and was bitterly derisive of it; well aware of her power, she felt herself to be utterly helpless and useless. She was unhappiest when most deeply in love; and while seeming to personify the carefree exuberance of the twenties, she tried to kill herself on at least two occasions. One of her friends said she had the mind of a man imprisoned in the body of a woman, but it is dangerous to believe whatever any one of her friends says about her, because each of the people who knew her knew a different Dorothy Parker. Perhaps this was the most magical thing about her—or the most telling truth of all.

PART
ONE

"*I was just a little Jewish girl,*
trying to be cute."

—Dorothy Parker

1

Like any well-to-do New Yorker, Mrs. J. Henry Rothschild wore six yards of clothing even in summer. Therefore, because she would be gone at least a month, a great trunk was required to contain her supply of chemises, corsets, corset covers, knickers, stockings, petticoats, and dresses. She would have to pack her shoe bags, her hatboxes, and the private bag that would contain her jewelry cases, nightcaps, nightgowns, hatpins, buttonhooks, and medicines. She would have to fill another trunk with her daughter's clothing, and pack the bags and boxes for the child's shoes and hats; she must pack for Mr. Rothschild and their son. Would a dozen collars be enough? There was the problem of the rugs. They must be taken up, cleaned, and stored for the summer. The dust covers must be got out and put on the furniture, the silver sent to the bank. The rooms must be closed one by one, their blinds drawn and the gas jets checked to be sure they had been turned off, the doors locked. Plans had to be made for the servants' summer. There were the picnic hampers to be packed. For all that she had servants to help her, Mrs. Rothschild, who was pregnant, must have found her duties tiring. No doubt she accepted them with native Scottish patience.

Yet, when at last Mrs. Rothschild stood in the gathering morning heat on the pavement outside the house on West Seventy-second Street, watching the draymen lift the trunks into the wagon and the children climbing into the Victoria, and feeling the baby kicking inside her, she must have viewed rather grimly the prospect of the slow, jolting, creaking ride downtown to the Hoboken ferry slips. After that, there would be the horror of the hot, sooty train, and then the lurching crawl across the miles of sandy roads that led from the depot to the shore. It was no great distance on the map from Manhattan to West End, New Jersey, but in the summer of 1893, no distance was covered easily. City streets were paved, but there was not a single paved highway in the United States at that time. When the horses reached the sand, it might be necessary for the Rothschilds to climb down from the stage and walk.

Possibly the fatigue of this expedition had something to do with the fact that Mrs. Rothschild was delivered two months prematurely of the child the world would one day know as Dorothy Parker. Perhaps it was the combination of the journey, middle age, and failing health. At any event, when Dorothy arrived on August 22, she arrived too soon, and although she was later to say it was the last time she was early for anything, the fact of her premature birth was important to her. Fifty years later, it would be held against her.

The family remained in West End for three weeks following her birth, at the end of which time it was believed that Mrs. Rothschild was well enough to be returned safely to New York and the comfortable house in the West Seventies where Dorothy would spend her childhood. It could be said, or sung to a nostalgic violin, that she was lucky to have known, as a child, the perfect peace of an era in which there were no telephones, no motion pictures, no radios, no television sets, no airplanes—and no Levittowns and inchworm commuter traffic. The traffic on the streets consisted of drays, delivery wagons, surreys, hansoms, Victorias, democrat wagons, and phaetons; there were no electric signs on Broadway, no skyscraper canyons in Manhattan. Butter then came to the market in tubs, and cabbages in barrels, and because there was little refrigeration, poultry was sold alive. At dusk the lamplighters would come down Manhattan's streets, carrying their little ladders, to light the gas lamps. These were the good old days that we assume to have been both placid and spacious—when men could have a free lunch with a five-cent beer, and everyone ate salmon and peas on the Fourth of July.

Moreover, Dorothy could have been considered fortunate to have been born not only in this golden age but also to a father of some means. Mr. Rothschild was not a man of great wealth, nor was he even a remote relative of the great banking family, but he had been sufficiently successful in the garment industry to be able to afford summer vacations at a time when very few Americans could do this, and to move into a quite respectable *petit bourgeois* neighborhood at a time when most American homes lacked indoor toilets. The decade of Dorothy's birth has been called the Gay Nineties, and they may well have been gay enough for Andrew Carnegie, who was then making more than $23,000,000 a year without having to pay taxes on a penny of it, but whether the nineties were in fact gay for most Americans is a serious question. The great majority of people earned less than what would be the equivalent, in purchasing power, of an income of $2,000 a year today, eking out a marginal existence under conditions we would now call insufferable. Not only was there an Oriental distance between the rich and the poor, but it was rapidly increasing. Thus, compared with all other Americans born in 1893, Dorothy Rothschild was born rich.

She was also born with a first-rate intelligence; and her large brown eyes and delicately fashioned bone structure promised the striking features that would emerge. Every auspice was propitious, and it would seem only logical to suppose that this fortunate child would have grown as gently as a flower in a well-protected garden. Instead, she was to know tragedy and horror before she learned her alphabet.

The first problem was that she arrived, almost as an afterthought, in a household that held no love for her. She was the last child; her sister was nine years older than she. The tragedy was that the one person whose presence might have made all the difference—her mother—died during Dorothy's infancy. The child never knew her. Instead she was to know only too well the second Mrs. Rothschild. She could never bring herself to call this woman "mother" or "stepmother," nor even to call her by name. She almost never referred to her family in later life, but when she did, it was with great bitterness, and then she would refer to the second Mrs. Rothschild as "the housekeeper." And as far as her father was concerned, she quite simply regarded him as a monster. She was terrified of him. She could never speak of her father without horror.

She was treated like a remittance child, if not like a child brought up in an orphanage administered by psychopaths. If the household held no love for her, neither did it have a place for her, for there was nothing she could do in the house. In the 1890s, the daughters of affluent families were most certainly not instructed in the domestic arts. Instead, they were strictly taught that housework was what servants did. She was not allowed in the kitchen; she never learned to cook. She was, however, instructed in proper manners, and this instruction took bleak forms. She was taught that it was polite to be on time; dinner was at six thirty, and if Dorothy was not there, seen but not heard, precisely at six thirty, her father would hammer her wrists with a spoon.

Her stepmother provided religious and moral instruction. One of Dorothy's earliest childhood memories was that of looking down into the street one snowing day, watching tattered old men shoveling in the blizzard. She was promptly informed that thanks were due God for sending the snow because it gave the unemployed an opportunity to work. But she wondered why God did not give men a chance to work in good weather.

The stepmother was inordinately religious. Apparently Mr. Rothschild was not, but the stepmother told the child that Dorothy was a Jew. Her mother had been Scottish, but her father was Jewish, and that meant his daughter was not a Scot, but a Jew. To save the child's soul, and to further ensure her instruction in good manners, the stepmother saw to it that when she became old enough to go to school, she was sent to a Catholic one—to a school operated by nuns from the Blessed Sacrament Convent. The school was close by. She could walk to it without having to cross any major avenues. Each afternoon, when the child returned, the stepmother would ask, "Did you love Jesus today?"

It was quite a childhood: a terrifying father hammering her wrists; a rather lunatic stepmother hammering at her mind; a sister and a brother too remote in age for any communion; the servants put out of reach by social convention. Dorothy called herself a mongrel. She hated being a Jew and began to think that her mother had deserted her by dying. She began to hate herself. She hated her very name. She thought Dorothy was a ridiculous name, and that Dottie was worse. She did not love Jesus or anybody else. She began to think that good things could never happen to her. Naïvely, she clutched at the hope that if she went to a Catholic school her name would not be held against her. But the school did nothing to give her the slightest reason to feel that she was welcome there. Her experience of the Catholic children made her wary of associating with any children. She hated being a child and she did not do the things that children do. She never flew a kite in Central Park; she never went to a skating rink. Each day she would walk to a school where she had no place, and each afternoon she would return to a house that had no love for her. She approached each new day apprehensively, and began to approach each person she met in a manner that suggested she wished to apologize for being alive.

Manners, however, provided her with armor, and her intelligence with a sword. Manners are simply a contrivance designed to permit people to conduct necessary social relationships on a mutually acceptable but impersonal plane. Good manners are a means to keep emotion from becoming involved; as Winston Churchill was to say, when you have to kill a man, it costs nothing to be polite. Dorothy clad herself in the armor of excellent manners and wore it constantly. At the same time, because it was so terribly necessary for her to do so, she used the sword of her mind to cut through toward the truth of things. Then, when she was satisfied that she had found the truth, she usually kept this discovery to herself. Yet she could not always do so, for at her birth the Devil had touched her tongue (as she said), and she fell early on into the habit of muttering, as softly as if talking only to herself, those thoughts that manners are specifically designed to conceal. "A girl's best friend is her mutter," she would one day say; but for her, this was not at all funny. For her, it was the truth.

So there were two Dorothys growing up together. One was the beautifully mannered, self-effacing, pretty little girl with the mass of dark hair and the lovely large eyes that always seemed so close to tears. That was Dorothy defensive, the feminine dissembler. Inside that one was the other, Dorothy offensive, the feminine truth-seeker, seeing everything quite clearly and coldly through those great, lambent eyes and saying, albeit to herself, exactly what she thought about the people she beheld. It was necessary to her survival to find truths to cling to in the lonely, if not downright inimical, world she inhabited as a child.

To her, the truth about her father was that he was a bombastic hypocrite. She thought the stepmother's religious enthusiasm was crazy, and she regarded all religions with profound suspicion. Her dim view of religion, compounded by feeling herself to be out of place in her Catholic school, eventually led to rebellion. By the time she was of high school age, she said she had had enough.

"I was fired from there, finally, for a lot of things," she told an interviewer many years later, "among them my insistence that the Immaculate Conception was spontaneous combustion."

"Convents," she said, "do the same things progressive schools do, only they don't know it. They don't teach you how to read; you have to find that out for yourself. At my convent we did have a textbook, one that devoted a page and a half to Adelaide Ann Proctor; but we couldn't read Dickens; he was vulgar, you know. But I read him and Thackeray, and I'm the one woman you'll ever know who's read every word of Charles Reade, the author of *The Cloister and the Hearth*. But as for helping me in the outside world, the convent taught me only that if you spit on a pencil eraser it will erase ink. And I remember the smell of the oilcloth, the smell of nuns' garb.

"All those writers who talk about their childhood!" she said bitterly. "Gentle God, if I ever wrote about mine, you wouldn't sit in the same room with me."

But she was wrong about that. She did write about her childhood. She wrote about it in her poems and in her short stories. All of her adult life, she acted out upon a more public stage the attitudes and parts perfected in lonely misery by the unhappy Dorothy Rothschild. It is true that she almost never spoke about her childhood, and then only to intimate friends, or to the rare interviewer she trusted, but if her acquaintances had had some knowledge of the child she was, they might have found more explicable the woman she became.

2

One wonders whether the word "fired" describes exactly her departure from Blessed Sacrament. The image conjured up is that of a disputatious child being booted by nuns through the door and down the steps to the street. She said she rebelled and was fired, but her statement was a self-serving one. To be sure, she disliked both the school and the religion, but she was a diffident child, not an intolerable little brat with whom nothing could be done. More likely, Dorothy Rothschild kept her rebellious thoughts to herself and was an orderly and diligent student, for the fact is that she was admitted to Miss Dana's School in Morristown, New Jersey—and Miss Dana's had no place for the slow or the unruly.

It was a first-rate private school of such excellence that the nation's leading women's colleges would waive the examination requirement for applicants who held Miss Dana's certificate. The school was set well back on spacious grounds in the best residential section of Morristown, an affluent community of some 12,000 souls. A curving carriageway led beneath huge elms, oaks, and spruces to the main building, a square, wooden, Victorian structure of four stories, festooned with second-floor porches and third-floor balconies and fire escapes that were themselves festooned with potted plants. A passageway, containing two classrooms, led to the second principal structure, a cottage where teachers lived. There were two separate buildings—a gymnasium with wood-paneled walls and ceiling, and a studio with a north skylight. Behind the main building there was the school kitchen and the bakery. There were tennis courts, and then a woods with a stream forming a boundary line; beyond the woods was a private tennis club. When Dorothy arrived in the class of 1911, the buildings were lighted by electricity.

Oriental rugs lay on the polished floors of the main building, and carpet runners climbed the twin curving staircases that led up from the front hall. A heavy velvet curtain framed the double doorway of the drawing room; there were chandeliers, overstuffed plush sofas, and on the walls, those dark allegorical etchings and prints that the Victorians collected. There was a piano in the parlor, lace curtains in the library. The convent and its oilcloth were very far away: Dorothy had entered the world of wealth and fashion. She had arrived—together with her name-taped clothing, the required twelve towels, six sheets, six pillow cases, two laundry bags, six napkins, napkin ring, umbrella, raincoat, overshoes, high shoes, tennis shoes, dark bloomers, and hot water bottle.

Her schoolmates were no longer the children of modest homes. They included cattle princesses from Colorado, heiresses from Philadelphia, belles from Southern plantations, and the debutante daughters of successful steel makers, brewers, physicians, and bankers. One girl, daughter of a Newark brewer, arrived at Miss Dana's driving her very own phaeton with her footman perched on the seat behind her. The footman found a livery stable for the horses, and lodgings for himself in the town, and brought the phaeton around for his mistress to drive in the afternoons. Another girl, daughter of the Childs restaurant chain owner, was a day student who arrived each morning in a novelty —a motorcar. It must have been an excellent vehicle for its day, because it was able each day to complete, without breakdown, the fourteen-mile round trip between the Childs' home and the school.

Miss Dana's School set out an academic bill of fare that compares favorably with many a junior college today. Two courses were required for every term of the four years at Miss Dana's: the Bible and English. In addition, each girl carried three major subjects each term and as many electives as she might wish to handle. Four years of Latin were required for the classical diploma, and all candidates for graduation were required to take a year's course in the history of art. Dorothy had instruction in these courses, plus work in required courses in history, algebra, and geometry. She also had choices among courses in botany, physiology, astronomy, music, studio art, Greek, French, logic, chemistry, physics, psychology, and (of all things) banking. To list the course offerings is not to describe them, but this was an ambitious academic menu to have set before adolescent girls, even if the portions were small and the girls might only nibble at them. The opportunity was there, and with only fifteen girls to a class, each student received considerable personal attention —and from excellent teachers. Moreover, the classes were conducted in seminar, with students and teachers sitting together at facing tables, so that learning proceeded with a kind of easy, livingroom informality.

Miss Dana's was both a finishing school and a college-preparatory one, quite progressive for its time. Neither an ivory bower for bluestockings, nor a last-minute repair shop for the gaucheries of the *nouveaux riches*, the school made serious efforts to turn out well-read, well-informed, and well-spoken young women who would be effective in the world. The senior year focused on writers and on questions and events of the day, and once a week the entire school met to discuss them. In short, the school sought to show the relevance of thought and action and, firmly believing that all thoughts can be expressed in words, bore down heavily on precision in English. "Especial attention is given to the study of Expression and to the cultivation of the speaking voice," Miss Dana's proudly said. Each student was many times required to recite before the entire school; each girl's voice was placed. Much of the material recited was poetry, for to explore the deeps of meaning in a poem's compressed imagery demands a singularly thoughtful control of body, face, and voice, not to mention a perceptive knowledge of the poem's meanings.

Dorothy said nothing about the totally new life she entered as a boarding student here, but it would seem that for once the cat, and not the Devil, had got her tongue. She never complained that the stairs to the fourth floor were rickety and that they creaked, or that the fourth floor was really an attic with tiny rooms built in dormers for the boarding students. She never complained about Miss Dana's (or about her family) to her schoolmates nor, in later years, to anyone else. But the testimony of her schoolmates indicates a quite different girl from the one that Blessed Sacrament knew.

"She was most attractive," one of her classmates said. "She was small, slender, dark-haired, and brilliant. She was in the last class that was graduated from Miss Dana's before Miss Dana died and the school went bankrupt. I admired her as being an attractive girl; she was peppy and she was never bored. She was outstanding in school work, but I can't remember her playing games."

The games were tennis, basketball, and tetherball. At no time was Dorothy an athlete. She was the epitome of the indoor, not the outdoor, girl—small, soft, and rather elegant. Athletics apart, her classmate's description implies that she certainly took part in the life of the school, including its entirely extracurricular and unofficial fun and games.

School was kept from 9:00 A.M. to 1:00 P.M.; there were no afternoon classes. After lunch, the girls were free until the 4:00 to 6:00 P.M. study period began, and they were encouraged to spend this free time by buttoning on their high shoes and going for long, chaperoned walks through the pleasant little town and its environs. They were specifically forbidden to go to the movies, which was grounds for suspension from school. Going to the movies was therefore a devilish thing to do, and the bright little girls put their quick minds to the task of finding ways and means to evade teachers and chaperones.

"It was only a mile and a half to the movie palace from school, and we would pretend we were going shopping and then skin into town the back way, and when nobody was looking, pop into the movie palace," one of Dorothy's school friends said. "For five cents, we could see the 'Perils of Pauline' and those awful things."

Then there was smoking. Very few women smoked then, except the scarlet women in French novels. Smoking was, at Miss Dana's, the unforgivable sin, punishable by immediate expulsion. Perhaps it was at Miss Dana's that Dorothy learned to smoke cigarettes. If so, she was not caught at it, but while she was there, there was a great scandal: the daughter of a wealthy and socially prominent Philadelphian was caught in the act of puffing carefully out her fourth-floor dormer window, and the next day, back she went to Philadelphia.

Then there were boys. Dorothy Parker described Dorothy Rothschild as being an irritating little girl with stringy hair, but none of her contemporaries at Miss Dana's School agree with that appraisal. She had French ankles and an Italian bosom; being just five feet tall, she was provocatively small. More than this, she had a rich mass of dark brown hair and great, dark eyes, and she was attracted by boys and was attractive to them, particularly tall, wide-shouldered and darkly handsome boys. There were dances at the school, duly chaperoned. These occasions were of course exciting, but even more exciting it was to watch the boys coming through the woods in the back of the school. The boys were members of the private tennis club, and the girls would "hang out the windows, looking at them coming through the woods, and we would flirt with them," one of Dorothy's schoolmates said.

It was all very innocent and daring, as precisely adventurous as the matter of the eclairs. The girls were strictly forbidden to eat between meals and were not allowed to have food in their rooms or to receive packages of sweets from home. Naturally, every adolescent girl has an uncontrollable passion for all that is sweet, rich and sticky, and the school's baker seems to have been a great humanitarian. The bakery faced the tennis courts, and the baker leaned on the windowframe, watching the girls very much as the girls would lean out of their windows, looking for boys; and when the girls came flushed and sweating off the tennis courts, he would defy the authorities by giving them chocolate eclairs, which they at once smuggled up the back stairs, and up that creaking flight that led to the boarding students' rooms on the fourth floor. Everyone would gobble up the eclairs and try not to giggle too loudly.

After supper they would all be decorous young ladies in their high-collared, leg-o'-mutton-sleeved dresses and their black lisle stockings, sitting thoughtfully in the school hall as they listened, perchance, to an improving lecture by the Reverend William E.

Griffis, D.D., or enjoyed an evening of music offered by the Kronold Quartet. Dorothy, who by this time had discovered La Rochefoucauld, must have been mordantly bored.

There are always students, indeed a majority, who simply attend school, do what is required of them, and go on to become the butchers, bakers, brokers, bankers, or housewives they would have become if they had not gone to school. Perhaps Dorothy Rothschild would have become Dorothy Parker in any case. But there are students who find in school something to fasten to, who in adolescence not only flirt, giggle, and eat eclairs, but are preternaturally perceptive and sensitive to human motivation and to the events taking place in the world around them. It is more than possible that Dorothy was one of those. If so, then Miss Dana's School was an excellent place for her to be, in the light of its emphasis on current thought and current events.

There was, in the early 1900s, a rather thundering and stultifying Establishment, more Victorian than Edwardian. Right was right and wrong was wrong, and there were no two ways about it, but even so, thought was changing and Victorianism was being challenged. A United States senator, raising a glass to welcome the twentieth century on New Year's Eve of 1900, said "the regeneration of the world, physical as well as moral, has begun, and revolutions never move backwards." What he had in mind was the Victorian notion of the perfectability of man, but the regeneration was about to take forms he did not imagine: the world was beginning to move toward the catastrophic years we have known since 1914.

For example, America was staunchly Christian, and most people felt that the white man must shoulder his black burden, put South Sea islanders into Mother Hubbards, and bring the blessings of Western theology and civilization to Chinese who had a theology and civilization of their own. But Darwin's theory of evolution had been brought to public attention, leading some people to question the authority of the Bible and even the existence of God. Such talk would have been both exciting and comforting to young Dorothy, who did not believe in God herself, and who at home had noticed the immense difference between the teachings of Jesus and the practices of some of his twentieth-century followers. She had been perforce a student of the New

Testament, and what she got out of that book was that if a man was truly good, he would most certainly be crucified.

Then, no matter that most people felt it was the country's duty to govern the Filipinos for their own good, the intellectual community was saying that the Spanish-American War had been a vicious fraud perpetrated upon the public by scheming capitalists, that all wars were immoral, but that imperialistic wars were more immoral than others, and that the Spanish-American War had been immoral, unnecessary, and un-American.

At the same time, the intellectuals who challenged fundamentalist theology and the legitimacy of the Spanish-American War were also challenging capitalism itself. True, the businessman was still an heroic figure; the public saw nothing simplistic in the rags-to-riches theme of the Horatio Alger books, and imagined that pluck, luck, hard work, honesty, and frugality would make anyone rich. Yet, socialism was in the air, and in 1912, the year after Dorothy left Miss Dana's, the Socialist Party drew 1,000,000 votes. A Labor Department would be established the following year, and the year after that the Clayton Act would pass, giving unions the right to bargain collectively. It was a time when the Sherman Anti-Trust Act of 1890 was first taken seriously; Theodore Roosevelt became a trust-buster—at least in public speeches.

Meantime, the first truly mass-circulation magazines had appeared, and they were rapidly increasing their circulations by printing the startling exposés of the "muckrakers." The word was Theodore Roosevelt's, and he used it pejoratively, but it was a fact that there was muck to rake. Reporters were describing the frightful living and working conditions to be found in slums, factories, and slaughterhouses, showing exactly at what human cost men like Carnegie became rich. In those days, the exploited slum dwellers were largely European immigrants, and the reports of the muckrakers had particular meaning for Dorothy, who said that in her own household, the servants were brought so fresh from Ellis Island that they were still bleeding when they arrived to do the laundry.

In that first decade of the twentieth century, changes were taking place in the economy. Henry Ford was beginning to use the methods of mass production that would later drive prices down and wages up; the Woolworth five-and-ten-cent stores were introducing the concept of national cheapjack chain stores. The era of high-volume, low-cost merchandise, national advertising, the national corporation and standard brands had now arrived, albeit in infancy. The consumer society was shortly to appear, together with the installment plan and the purchase of stock on tissue-thin margins.

The era was also pregnant with changes to come in dress and morals. The Atlantic City bathing costume, revealing ankles, was more shocking then than the bikini would be four decades later, and the most daring young men were already wearing singlets instead of half-sleeved shirts upon the beaches. The jazz band had appeared, playing at hotel tea-dances—and it was all enough to make any right-thinking citizen wonder what the world was coming to.

All of these questions and matters of the day were discussed in Miss Dana's current events classes; the young ladies' attention was directed to the explosive situation in the slums, to the reports of the muckrakers, to the increasing size of the Socialist Party. All of her mature life, Dorothy Parker sympathized with the exploited and was suspicious of the Establishment. Although she did not say so, her mature views of society may have had their genesis in Dorothy Rothschild's experience at Miss Dana's School.

During these years of her late adolescence, Dorothy began to write verse. "Like everybody else was then," she said, "I was following in the exquisite footsteps of Edna St. Vincent Millay, unhappily in my own horrible sneakers."

Not all girls who write verse grow up to be women who write poems. But some do. Moreover, some students who show a literary precocity spend their lives elaborating on their talents and elaborating on themes that captured their attention while they were in school. Dorothy could have been such a student. At least, there is nothing about the mature Dorothy Parker that is inconsistent with the Dorothy Rothschild who first attended Blessed Sacrament and then Miss Dana's School.

She did not go to college; few girls did. But by the standards of the time, she emerged from Miss Dana's a well-educated young woman—and a remarkably bright and pretty one, too, possessed of a voice surprisingly rich and full for so small a person.

3

When her formal education was completed, the acceptable thing for a young girl of Dorothy's social class to do was to sit demurely at home, waiting for Mr. Right to come along. Society then pretended there was always just one Mr. Right for each pure young girl, and that he would somehow discover her address. In those days before the first World War, no well-bred young woman was expected, or even allowed, to go to work, unless bleak fortune required her to do so. If worse came to worst, and a young woman had to work in order to eat, the most acceptable task for her was to teach music, for that would imply the dignity and cultivation to which she had been born. In such case, it was then hoped that Mr. Right (who, of course, had been saving himself for the sweet young girl he would one day marry) would shortly find her on the job and rescue her from a life of gainful employment.

Dorothy would have none of this. There was nothing about her father's house that led her to want to remain in it. More important, she was anything but typical of her social class—or of any other. She was set apart by her intelligence, by her education, and as would soon be seen, by her talent. She ardently identified with the feminists who were demanding parity with men and the right to vote, although this enthusiasm did not lead her to go out on the streets herself, carrying a placard and chaining herself to a lamppost to make a point. Nevertheless, she said she believed in rights for women, and this was enough in itself to establish her difference from the still-Victorian Establishment. She also smoked cigarettes, wrote verses about love, had opinions of her own, and wanted her own apartment and a job. In Dorothy's youth, such girls not only were rare but were also viewed with alarm. To borrow words from the time, young women with advanced ideas were suspected of being fast, chiefly by people who had not met them.

How long she sat at home, if indeed she ever did, is not clear. She left Miss Dana's School in 1911, the year she turned eighteen. She said her father died when she was nineteen, and told an interviewer, "After my father died, there wasn't any money." Inasmuch as all the members of her immediate family are now dead, we have only her word for it that Mr. Rothschild's passing left them penniless. Whether she regarded her father's death as a happy or a sad occasion, we do not know, nor do we know how long thereafter it was that, on leaving Miss Dana's, she found a room for herself in a boardinghouse. We do know that after leaving school she spent a certain amount of time writing verse ("My verses," she said, "I cannot say poems") and sent it hopefully off to magazines, but it was not until 1916 that one of her verses was accepted.

The purchaser was Frank Crowninshield, the gentle and courtly editor of the Condé Nast publications, Vogue and Vanity Fair. He bought the verse for Vogue, and according to Dorothy, it was this purchase that inspired her to leave home, now that her father was dead and she was destitute:

"I had to work, you see, and Mr. Crowninshield, God rest his soul, paid twelve dollars for a small verse of mine and gave me a job [on Vogue] at ten dollars a week. Well, I thought I was Edith Sitwell. I lived in a boardinghouse at 103rd and Broadway, paying eight dollars a week for my room and two meals, break-, fast and dinner."

Her explanation leaves four and perhaps five years of her life unaccounted for, the years between the ages of nineteen and twenty-three. If she had little to say about her childhood, and nothing to say about Miss Dana's, she had even less to say of these years. But at the time Mr. Crowninshield hired her, she was living at that boardinghouse and she was supporting herself by playing the piano for a dancing school in the evenings.

Since Vogue's ten dollars a week did not cover the cost of bed, board, clothing, and such small purchases as toothpaste, Dorothy continued to work in the evenings at the dancing school, but her life at the boardinghouse was not a gloomy struggle against poverty.

"Thorne Smith was there, and another man," she said. "We used to sit around in the evening and talk. There was no money, but Jesus we had fun."

No doubt the conversations were fun, as anyone who has read *Topper* or any other of Thorne Smith's gay, risqué little satires might well imagine. At the time Dorothy knew him in the boardinghouse, Mr. Smith's books were in his future, as Dorothy's fame lay in hers, but it is easy to believe that these two talented young people, so soon to come to the nation's attention, found each other's company delightful. It is equally easy to imagine that Mr. Smith "and another man" were not the only friends she had at this time, because she was in every way remarkable in the world of 1916, enjoying a freedom unknown to most women of that time.

Her days were full. Apart from working at her two jobs, she continued to write verse and send it to magazines, including *Vanity Fair*. The burden of her small song was that love was a game and that men were fickle. Fluffy cloudlets dotted her skies, and clustered roses climbed through her lines, otherwise replete with classical shepherds and Corydons singing to rustic lutes.

"That," she later apologized, "was the style of the day. We were all imitative. We all wandered in after Miss Millay. We were all being dashing and gallant, declaring that we weren't virgins, whether we were or not. Beautiful as she was, Miss Millay did a great deal of harm with her double-burning candles. She made poetry seem so easy that we could all do it. But, of course, we couldn't."

Derivative as her verses were, they were at least clear, technically correct, in the mood of the time, and certainly not worse than others that arrived through the mail slots of magazine offices. But if any writer may claim the right to be judged on the basis of such of his work as he, in his maturity, decides to publish as his collected work, then Dorothy was well advised not to collect these preliminary efforts. The important thing about them was not that the verses were bad, but that in writing them she was acquiring skills she would bring to poetry.

Her task at *Vogue* also helped her to acquire a literary discipline. She was set to writing captions for illustrations, and caption writing demands invention. It will not do to write beneath a picture of a horse, "This is a picture of a horse." Something else must be said, and preferably it should not include the word "horse." Next, the invention must take place within grammatical and physical form. In a fashion magazine, the whole idea is to set the tone that will cajole the reader into buying the advertised goods. Therefore, the words used must meet the general requirement of advertising: i.e., they must have what advertisers used to call "pull." To be inventive and pulling in one line of, say, thirty ems, is not easy. Dorothy Parker was to acquire a reputation as a woman who could skewer a bad play with one short sentence or deflate an ego with one appropriate word. Critics would admire her terse style and meticulous selection of words. *Vogue* certainly gave Dorothy Rothschild practice, for caption writing is nothing if not exercise in selection.

If much of the future Dorothy Parker can be seen in the girl of the convent and the finishing school, so more of her can be seen in the young woman who worked at *Vogue*, busily writing such lines as "Brevity is the soul of lingerie—as the Petticoat said to the Chemise"; "This little pink dress will win you a beau"; and "Right *Dress!* For milady's motor jaunt."

It is depressing to think that she might have been inspired to write that last caption by the military events of 1916. An insane butchery was taking place in the French mud. A tone, a style of life, and an entire European generation were being obliterated. Any connection between that military caption and the war then in progress seems downright obscene, but it is important to remember that America was then naïve about that war, that Americans would shortly go to it singing, with flowers in their rifle muzzles, and that *Vogue* existed in the world of fashion, which is a world of its own.

Dorothy delighted in her job. Ever since she had been "a woman of eleven," she said, she had read the fashion magazines.

She had been fascinated by the world of wit and fashion and desperately wished to be a part of it; at Miss Dana's School she had seen a bit of it. The fashionable world was a home away from the home she never had. And now, as a staff member of *Vogue*, she was at the very center of this world; she was one of those who, if only in a very minor way, were helping to establish new styles for the fashionable. She was living in New York, which she believed to be the most splendid of cities and the only place for a bright young person to live. New York City believed in being "smart," and so did *Vogue*, and so did she. They all used the word to imply many of its meanings—witty, rich, showy, clever, brisk, fresh, stinging, and pungent.

"Boy, did I think I was smart!" she said. Then she bitterly added, "I was just a little Jewish girl, trying to be cute."

She said this late in life, but no such thoughts bothered her in 1916. She was not trying to be cute; she *was* cute. Frank Crowninshield was fond of her and glad to have discovered her talent. She was happy at *Vogue*, and Mr. Crowninshield made her even happier when, the following year, he asked her to join *Vanity Fair*, which was far more than a fashion magazine.

Mr. Crowninshield had set *Vanity Fair*'s outlook in an editorial note that appeared in the first issue in 1914. "We, as a nation," he wrote, "have come to realize the need for more cheerfulness, for hiding a solemn face, for a fair measure of pluck, and for great good humor. *Vanity Fair* means to be as cheerful as anybody. It will print humor, it will look at the stage, at the arts, at the world of letters, at sport, and at the highly vitalized, electric, and diversified life of our day from the frankly cheerful angle of the optimist, or, which is much the same thing, from the mock-cheerful angle of the satirist." Given the stuffy Victorian atmosphere of America at the time, these words were tantamount to a declaration of independence—and *Vanity Fair* more than lived up to them.

Tacitly presuming its readers to be cosmopolitan polyglots, *Vanity Fair* printed an article in French, knowing perfectly well this presumption to be most unwarranted, but thereby informing its readers what would be expected of them. It introduced its readers to *avant-garde* painters and writers, among them Picasso, Matisse, Marie Laurencin, Raoul Dufy, Gertrude Stein, e.e. cummings, D. H. Lawrence, and T. S. Eliot. Before its course was run, Vanity Fair's printed pages and color plates would show the work of virtually every important new writer and painter of the nineteen-twenties and nineteen-thirties; it was the first magazine to recognize American Negro artists. As one of its staff members, the humorist Corey Ford, later said, Vanity Fair's approach "was witty (but never gauche), sardonic (but never unmannerly, never rude), erudite (but with perfect aplomb, never taking itself too seriously)." In this, the magazine exactly reflected the character of its editor. Mr. Ford said Vanity Fair "was more than a pur-veyor of smart table talk, a sort of Elbert Hubbard of the soigné upper crust. It created a high society of its own, sophisticated and artificial and snobbish." When Dorothy Rothschild was asked to join the staff, the magazine was already the nation's arbiter elegantiarum, and she was perfectly conscious of the high compliment Mr. Crowninshield was paying her. He was saying that she belonged in, that she was a member of, the nation's intellectual elite.

Of course she joined the magazine. She did so delightedly. Also in that year, 1917, Edwin Pond Parker, II, asked her to marry him, and she gladly and promptly did that, too.

4

Edwin Pond Parker, II, was an exceedingly handsome, lean six-footer in his early twenties who worked as a broker in Wall Street. His was an old Hartford, Connecticut, family and a religious one. His grandfather, a clergyman, was author of *The History of the Second Church of Christ in Hartford,* which was published by the Connecticut Historical Society. Eddie, as Dorothy called him, was well-dressed and well-mannered; he had a quick sense of humor and a satirical smile. He seemed to be exactly what he was: a well-to-do Anglo-Saxon Protestant of impeccable antecedents and considerable charm.

"I married him to change my name," Dorothy murmured, and her friends laughed, as she meant them to. A reason why people were finding her fun to be with was that no one could guess what outrageous thing she would say next, except that it would be clever, wry, and usually disparaging. She could be particularly funny and disparaging about herself. It was perfectly clear to her friends why she had married Eddie. The reason was that they were utterly and radiantly in love.

She told one of her friends that she and Eddie had known each other all their lives, that she had married her childhood sweetheart. She told another that she had met Eddie at a summer hotel in Branford, Connecticut. She left a third friend believing that she had met him in New York City, while a fourth friend thought the two had met while she was attending Miss Dana's School. She would tell one friend one vague thing, and say something different, but equally vague, to the next, meanwhile keeping her personal life close to herself. So none of her friends knew where or when she and Eddie met, but then, young people tend to accept each other without asking such questions, anyway. What was important to their friends was that Dorothy and Eddie were in love, and everyone agreed it was a damned shame that Eddie had to go to war, although there was nothing anyone could do about that. On March 4, 1917, the United States declared war on Germany, and naturally Eddie Parker enlisted, for it was considered shameful for a young man to wait to be drafted.

In May, Eddie joined the 33rd Ambulance Company, an organization recruited largely from the manhood of Summit, New Jersey, and for the ensuing year Dorothy followed the company as it moved from Butler, New Jersey, to Syracuse, New York; to Allentown, Pennsylvania; to Charlotte, North Carolina, where it joined the Fourth Infantry Division; to Camp Merritt, New Jersey, and then to Brooklyn where it was loaded onto an Australian Beef and Troop Service ship and sent to France in time to take part in the Allied counteroffensive of July 1918 and in all the fighting thereafter.

Dorothy worked during the week at *Vanity Fair*, to which she contributed satirical verse and prose squibs, and visited the camps on weekends, except during the time the 33rd was stationed at Syracuse. Then, Eddie spent the weekends with Dorothy in New York City. His buddies remember Dorothy as a quiet, demure, extremely pretty and expensively dressed girl, and some of them felt a little sorry for her, because their nickname for Eddie was "Spook."

The name was given him on the day he showed up at reveille pale as a ghost and still drunk. Eddie was irreligious as the proverbial minister's son, and although he was not yet in his middle twenties "he was a pretty good two-fisted drinker," as one of his Army buddies said. They liked him and thought he was good company. They liked Dorothy, too, who seemed to them to be ladylike and shy. They thought Eddie and Dorothy got on very well together, and that she was very fond of her new husband. But his drinking worried them. She did not drink, but he certainly did. He was up to a bottle a day. When he took the night train down to New York City from Syracuse, he would buy a pint of whisky, drink it and pass out, wake up in New York and buy another bottle and start drinking again. Spook's friends did not think he was an alcoholic because he could do without liquor, and in fact went without it all the time the 33rd was in action, but he impressed them as being an extremely heavy drinker, and they guessed that this might someday become a problem.

A few weekends together, scattered over nine months of a year, and then the letters, and this was the marriage. She wrote to him every day. If she had thought herself lonely before, she now knew what loneliness could be. One of her closest friends said she had looked upon Eddie as Lochinvar. He had come into her life to wipe away her memories of her father's house; to rescue her from the squalor of eight-dollar-a-week lodgings; to solve all her problems for her and love, protect, and cherish her forever—and then he had gone to war. He might at any moment be killed, and all that would be left would be the memory of a few weekends, the ruin of hope, and the telegram from the War Department expressing the government's regret to Mrs. Parker. No one could say when the war would end and when her love would return. She wrote to him out of love and aching loneliness, and she sent him poems. She was at pains to keep the letters and the poems bright and funny, as well as loving, in order to send what cheer she could to a man living in mud under shellfire.

Spook shared these letters and poems with his friends. One of his buddies remembers a poem that said, "I hate Bohemians; they shatter my morale." That is all he remembers of the poem, which may have been the first draft of the eventually published "Bohemia," but he does remember that it was written on a very long, narrow paper (probably a galley sheet) with inches of space between the lines, and that Dorothy had used that space to make dozens of corrections as she sought the right words. If the poem was "Bohemia," it would have been exactly the right kind of thing for her to have sent Edwin Parker, for it says:

Authors and actors and artists and such
Never know nothing, and never know much.
Sculptors and singers and those of their kidney.
Tell their affairs from Seattle to Sydney.
Playwrights and poets and such horse's necks
Start off from anywhere, end up at sex.
Diarists, critics, and similar roe
Never say nothing and never say no.
People Who Do Things exceed my endurance;
God, for a man that solicits insurance!

True, Parker did not sell insurance, but broker does not rhyme with endurance, and in any case the message is the same. Dorothy, as a staff member of a smart magazine, would have had one foot in Bohemia whether she liked it or not, whereas Spook, if he ever returned from France, would have one foot in Wall Street and the other in Scarsdale. No doubt they were both aware of this fact. Therefore, "Bohemia," or an early version of it, would have been a funny and comforting thing for her to have sent him.

And he had need of comfort. The Fourth Division saw a great deal of fighting and its 33rd Ambulance Company brought back the Division's dead and wounded under fire. His buddies said Spook was a good driver. They also said a shell burst in front of his ambulance, and he went into the hole, and it was a day and a half before anyone found him; when they did, the men on the four stretchers were dead and Spook, although not badly hurt, was in poor shape.

For him, there was the constant battering of shellbursts, the stench of the dead, the unending danger—and like a slender strand leading back to sanity, the letters from his funny, bright, and pretty little wife.

For Dorothy, however, not every moment was a lonely century, much as she may have felt a terrible emptiness, for otherwise she was exactly where she wanted to be, doing just what she wanted to do, and her happiness led her to play practical jokes.

Those were the days when, in a fervor of patriotism, Berlin, Ohio, was renamed Canton, and sauerkraut became Liberty

Cabbage, and when, as an added blow against Teutonic imperialism, the teaching of the German language was dropped from the public school curriculum. Even more ludicrous was the popular belief that the Germans had spies everywhere. In those days, otherwise sensible Americans were seeing as many spies under their beds as, forty years later, they would see Communists. And all of this gave Dorothy Parker an idea.

"Albert Lee," she said, "one of the editors, had a map over his desk with little flags on it to show where our troops were fighting. . . . Every day he would get the news and move the flags around. I was married, my husband was overseas, and since I didn't have anything better to do I'd get up half an hour early and go down and change his flags. Later on, Lee would come in, look at his map, and he'd get very serious about spies—shout, and spend his morning moving his little flags back into position."

Like any soldier's wife, she bent her thought upon her husband's return. She knew the 33rd Ambulance Company was in constant action. It was consoling to think that the Yanks had the Hun on the run, as the newspapers put it, although the next columns, listing the casualties, created a less sporting impression. But at last New York City exploded at the news of the Armistice —and no telegram had come from the War Department. When would he be coming home?

It presently appeared that neither the War Department nor anyone else could be sure just when the troops would return. Some would be brought back at once, and others would not. Eventually Dorothy received an answer of sorts. Eddie wrote that the 33rd had been assigned to occupation duty in the Rhineland.

5

The months stretched out through the winter, and then into the spring of 1919. The nation was demobilizing, and troops were returning from Europe and troops that had not gone to Europe were being discharged, but Spook continued to help occupy the Rhineland while Dorothy occupied *Vanity Fair*.

In May 1919, staff changes were taking place on the magazine, and a new face appeared. It was a round, benign and friendly one, wearing an expression of polite but wary bafflement; it belonged to Robert Benchley, a former president of the Harvard *Lampoon*, and until now a not particularly successful newspaperman, publicist, and free-lance writer. But Mr. Crowninshield had faith in Mr. Benchley's as yet undiscovered genius, and hired him to be managing editor at one hundred dollars a week.

He was some four years older than Dorothy, who was then twenty-five, and she thought he was one of the most charming men she had ever met—thereby agreeing with everyone else who ever had the pleasure of his company, for Mr. Benchley was one of the few people of this world for whom no one could find an unpleasant word, and not a few of his friends said that his simple presence in a room made everyone feel better. The essence of Mr. Benchley's charm lay in his delightfully oblique view of the world, through which he made his way in a kind of hopeful desperation, as the title of his first article for *Vanity Fair* may make clear. It was, "No Matter from What Angle You Looked at It, Alice Brookhansen Was a Girl Whom You Would Hesitate to Invite into Your Own Home." He was to follow this with an article called "The Social Life of the Newt," in which an ardent male newt was confused by a rubber eraser.

Two days after Mr. Benchley joined *Vanity Fair,* and while he was still somewhat uncertain as to the location of the water cooler, another veteran of the Harvard *Lampoon* arrived in *Vanity Fair's* offices—a slow-speaking young man, six feet seven inches tall, named Robert Sherwood. He had followed Mr. Benchley to Harvard at a six years' distance, and he had left college in his junior year to join the Canadian Black Watch. When he drew himself to attention, he stood with his thumbs sticking straight out, at right angles to his fingers, in memory of the days when his thumbs held flat the pleats of his kilt. He had been gassed in the war and wounded in both legs. He was now about to start on his first job, on a three-month trial basis, at twenty-five dollars a week. He seemed uncertain as to what his duties would be. He had been appointed drama editor, but this title was purely a courtesy: he was to do whatever he might be asked to do about the office.

Mr. Crowninshield would seem to have been clairvoyant in his hiring practices, for just as apparently haphazard was his assigning little Mrs. Parker the job of being *Vanity Fair's* drama critic. She was to fill in for the British writer, P. G. Wodehouse, the regular critic, who was in Europe. At this time, she had no greater knowledge of the theater than any other intelligent citizen who often goes to plays, but all that was required at *Vanity Fair* was someone who could tell the readers what the plays were about, and who was acting in them, and do this deftly. Sometimes Dorothy signed her reviews—for they were reviews more often than they were criticisms—Helène Rousseau, perhaps to make clear that it was Dorothy Parker who wrote verse.

Mr. Benchley and Mr. Sherwood and Dorothy made friends immediately. They were all struck by the incongruity of their appointments. She, with no particular qualifications, was the drama critic; Mr. Sherwood, with no qualifications whatsoever, was the drama editor; Mr. Benchley, who thought of himself in terms of mismanagement, was the managing editor. They made a grave, happy satire of calling one another by their last names. To them, she was always Mrs. Parker, and to her they were Mr. Benchley and Mr. Sherwood. There were occasional exceptions to this rule. Sometimes, for no apparent reason, she would call Mr. Benchley Fred, and sometimes the two men would call each other Rob, although no one else did. The fact that Dorothy was a woman—a strikingly obvious fact to every man who ever met her—did not prevent her from becoming a triumvir. The two Roberts accepted her, not as a girl friend, but as an equal partner in an alliance against the world. Indeed, the triumvirate was originally founded to protect Mr. Sherwood from midgets.

The magazine's offices were on Fourty-fourth Street near the now-vanished Hippodrome where, at the time, a troupe of midgets was appearing. If any of them caught sight of the gigantic Mr. Sherwood coming down the street alone, they would all come hooting and jeering out after him, squeaking up at him and clutching at his knees. There was nothing Mr. Sherwood could do about it.

"They were always sneaking up behind him and asking him how the weather was up there," Dorothy Parker said. " 'Walk down the street with me,' he'd asked, and Mr. Benchley and I would leave our jobs and guide him down the street. I can't tell you, we had more fun . . ."

It became their custom to guide Mr. Sherwood to the nearby Algonquin Hotel, where they took lunch. The Algonquin was (and is) a small and unpretentious hotel whose clientele consisted principally of actors from the adjacent theater district, and its food was by no means inexpensive. In fact, on their salaries, Dorothy and the two Roberts were indulging themselves by eating there, but the Algonquin provided a quick escape from the midgets. It was far better than any of the other restaurants in the area; the hotel's decor was comfortable and homely, and there was a kind of magic to the young people in seeing actors and actresses at other tables around them. The custom of lunching at the Algonquin's Pergola Room persisted after the midgets departed from the Hippodrome—Mrs. Parker, Mr. Benchley, and Mr. Sherwood thereby inadvertently becoming the charter members, as it were, of what would be a group of wonderfully talented young men and women who would meet informally for lunch at the Algonquin for no reason other than that they hugely enjoyed one another's company.

It was impossible for them to separate work from play, because the work done by people in the communicative arts, by those in publishing, in the theater, on the staffs of magazines and newspapers, involves the free play of ideas. This was particularly true at *Vanity Fair*, which by Mr. Crowninshield's definition looked at all of life from the cheerful point of view of the optimistic satirist. So the triumvirate's discussions in the office were scarcely different from their table talk at the Algonquin, and so happy was the ambience created whenever the three of them, or any two of them, were together that, in the evenings, they would attend the theater together on the free tickets available to them through the magazine. They each seemed to be, in his and her own way, something of an innocent in an inexplicable but fascinating wilderness, and they each found this quality in one another to be refreshing; they would happily apprise one another of the absurdities and curiosities to be found in this world.

Mr. Benchley introduced his friend Mrs. Parker to what he considered to be the lugubrious world of the undertaker. During his schooldays at Exeter, Mr. Benchley had been ordered to write an essay on a practical subject, and after giving this Puritanical assignment a moment's thought, he sought out a local undertaker and asked the man to tell him the secrets of his trade. The resulting essay startled his English master, but it could not be said that the essay was not responsive to the assignment. What could be a more practical subject than the disposal of the dead? At Harvard, Mr. Benchley elaborated on this theme for a freshman essay, after considering the likelihood that his Harvard instructor would not know enough about embalming to be able to criticize the paper.

"Mr. Benchley and I subscribed to two undertaking magazines: *The Casket* and *Sunnyside*," Mrs. Parker said. "Steel yourself: *Sunnyside* had a joke column called 'From Grave to Gay.' I cut out a picture from one of them, in color, of how and where to inject embalming fluid, and it hung over my desk until Mr. Crowninshield asked me if I could possibly take it down. Mr. Crowninshield was a lovely man, but puzzled."

Dorothy delighted in Mr. Crowninshield's puzzlement. Death could be funny, the funniest thing about it being the world's fear of it. She amused Mr. Benchley by thinking up epitaphs to embellish her own tombstone, such as "This is on me," "Excuse my dust," and "If you can read this, you are standing too close."

Dorothy and the two Roberts had even more fun when, in that same month of May 1919, another triumvirate arrived in New York to take lunch at the Algonquin. The newcomers had served together in France on the Army newspaper, *Stars and Stripes*. They were Franklin Pierce Adams, Alexander Woollcott, and Harold Ross, and each would be important to New York in general and to Dorothy Parker in particular.

Mr. Adams, an erudite and witty man who greatly resembled a narrow-shouldered moose, had before the war edited the city's most widely read and literate newspaper column, "The Conning Tower," in *The New York Tribune*, and he had come back to the city to resume his role as something of a literary guru.

Mr. Woollcott, who resembled a plump owl, was a droll, often preposterous, often sentimental, often waspish, and always flamboyantly self-dramatic theater critic, who was returning to his job at *The New York Times*.

Harold Ross was a young man who looked to be put together all wrong: he wore what looked, on him, to be a farmer's Sunday suit. His hair suggested a picket fence. He had been an itinerant newspaperman before the war; he was new to the city; he dreamed of founding a magazine, and he was regarded by his erstwhile colleagues on *Stars and Stripes* to be an editor of genius.

What drew these men together was not just their common experience in France, and a love of poker, but above all else, a passionate concern for the English language. They not only lived by words but played games with words, and delighted in the *bons mots* of others. Moreover, they shared an interest in the New York theater and in all else that had to do with the communicative and performing arts.

It was a theater press agent, Murdock Pemberton, who, knowing Mr. Woollcott's passion for sweets, had introduced Mr. Woollcott to the Algonquin's pastries. Mr. Woollcott thereafter brought his friends to the Algonquin, where they met Mr.

Benchley, whom they had known before the war. Mr. Benchley introduced them to Mr. Sherwood and to Mrs. Parker.

What the men beheld was a tiny woman who wore her hair in a kind of pile atop her head, but then parted and combed down so as to make hers seem to be a wistful face at a parting curtain. Her voice was that of a young girl gently bred, soft and deferential. When she spoke, she had a way of putting a little hand on her listener's forearm, and of looking up at him with enormous eyes that at once pleaded for his understanding and assured him that *his* understanding was the most important thing in the world to her. She wore a feather boa that was always getting into the other people's plates or was being set afire by other people's cigarettes (someone said it was the only boa that ever moulted), and this unfortunate boa, and the bows on her shoes, and the curious fact that the chic and expensive clothing she wore did not, somehow, look exactly right on her, enhanced the general impression she created. It was one of innocence, utterly feminine and utterly helpless. She was the kind of girl that any man wants to take immediately into his arms, comfort, protect, and assure that everything will be all right.

All this was sufficiently intriguing, but what really fascinated these witty and articulate men was that Mrs. Parker (as Mr. Benchley and Mr. Sherwood insisted on calling her) was in no more need of protection than a nest of hornets. There was the occasion when the men were discussing the accomplishments of a woman of considerable abilities, apparently forgetful of the fact that it is never wise to praise one woman when in the presence of another. Dorothy listened, wide-eyed, and at last joined the conversation.

"You know," she murmured, in accents that seemed to breathe nothing but the most worshipful admiration, "that woman speaks eighteen languages? And she can't say 'No' in any of them."

And when the table gossip turned to an actress who had fallen and broken a leg in London, Mrs. Parker seemed distraught.

"Oh, how terrible," she muttered to her neighbor at the table. "She must have done it sliding down a barrister."

It shortly appeared that whatever Mrs. Parker murmured was well worth listening to. When one of the men asked to be excused to go to the men's room, Mrs. Parker softly explained, as if pleading for pity for a flustered young man, "He really needs to telephone, but he's too embarrassed to say so."

When it came to word games, the gentlemen discovered they had met a master. Challenged to use the word "horticulture" in a sentence, Mrs. Parker immediately replied, "You can lead a horticulture, but you can't make her think."

Mr. Woollcott beamed fondly upon Mrs. Parker through his glasses. She was, he said, so odd a blend of Little Nell and Lady Macbeth. And FPA, as Mr. Adams was known to his thousands of readers, began to take notes for his column, "The Conning Tower."

The attention of these men had much to do with the metamorphosis of the scarcely known Mrs. Parker into the quite well-known Dorothy Parker—particularly the attention of FPA, for in those days before the arrival of radio, national picture magazines and television, people read newspapers. They did not read one, but several New York newspapers if they were seriously interested in discovering what was going on. They also read not one, but several magazines, including the old *Life*, a humor magazine; *The Smart Set*, *Vanity Fair*, and *The Literary Digest*. Anyone who read those magazines could also say what had been in "The Conning Tower" that day, because FPA's position as a littérateur was a preeminent one. His column was not read just in New York; it was sedulously studied by every exchange editor of any important newspaper in the nation and by the exchange editors of every college newspaper and humor magazine. To a word-struck college boy in the provinces, Mr. Adams' column was news from Olympus, and insofar as New York editors and journalists were concerned, mention in "The Conning Tower" was the equivalent of the accolade.

The column commented on anything and everything, and Mr. Adams did not so much write it as conduct it, printing the contributions of his readers. So high was his standard that every young person with literary aspirations wished to see his name in FPA's column. It was assumed, with reason, that anyone who contributed would be well worth any other contributor's knowing and many of those who lived in New York sought each other out on the basis of their having been fellow contributors. Mr.

Adams never paid his correspondents, but once a year he gave a dinner, and the contributor who had most often appeared in the column that year would be given a gold watch. Asked why he gave a prize for the most contributions, rather than for the best one, Mr. Adams explained, "There is no such thing as the 'best' contribution. The fact that any contribution is accepted by me means that it is peerless."

"The Conning Tower" placed a premium on puns and wit— and in the New York of that time, wit especially meant the smart, or wise, crack. This is a particular form of jest that, piercing pretense, carries a reproof, and if the wisecrack is not indigenous to New York, it is prized nowhere else so much. Since it so happened that Mrs. Parker proved to be a smartcracker *par excellence*, it was no accident that her jibes began to appear in "The Conning Tower," and therefore when FPA quoted her, and printed her verses, and wrote about her in his own parody of Samuel Pepys' style, she began to acquire a notoriety, and even an importance. Following Mr. Adams' lead, other New York columnists began to quote, misquote, or write about Dorothy Parker, with the result that she was on her way to winning a public reputation as being the wittiest woman in New York before she was twenty-seven years old and before she was published anywhere outside of *Vanity Fair*.

It soon appeared that she said so many funny things that, if the real author of a *bon mot* were unknown, the witticism would be attributed to her by default. To claim an audience at a party, all anyone had to say was, "Did you hear what Dorothy Parker said today?" and everyone else would grin expectantly. Given this situation, it is understandable that many things were attributed to her that she never said at all.

For instance, it is questionable if she really made the remark she was supposed to have made to a messenger boy sent by an editor to ask if Mrs. Parker had finished an article the editor had ordered some time ago and now urgently required. So far, so good, for she was notorious for her failure to have her work ready on time. But now:

"Tell him I've been too fucking busy—or vice versa," she is alleged to have said.

Well, perhaps. She *could* have said it. If a bawdy word was ever required, she could certainly supply it. And it would have been just the kind of remark to have made that particular editor blench. But the remark is vulgar as it stands, and little Mrs. Parker was never vulgar. She and her friends then eschewed gutter words not because they were dirty, but because they were unimaginative. The members of the Algonquin group were nothing if not stylists of language.

Moreover, the anecdote sets her up as her own straight man, and this was never her style. Her lines were invariably understated and murmured in a voice that further understated them. It would have been much more in her style if she had heard some harassed writer snarl, "Tell him I've been too fucking busy," and then for her to have muttered to herself, in accents of deepest sympathy for the poor, tired writer, "Or vice versa." *That* would have been much funnier, and it would have also carried the sting of her contempt for an unimaginative liar. Further, it would have been in keeping with the very thing for which she was becoming notable among her friends—the deflation of some pretentious person in two exquisitely apt words.

Then there is the legend of Dorothy Parker's encounter with Clare Boothe Luce. The legend is that the two ladies met at a doorway, and that Mrs. Luce said, "Age before beauty," indicating that Dorothy was to precede her, whereupon Dorothy said, "Pearls before swine," and swept triumphantly past.

There are two reasons for believing the story to be false. First, the remark attributed to Mrs. Luce is not in character. Even assuming that Mrs. Luce had reason to dislike Dorothy (which, considering the time the encounter supposedly took place, is *not* a valid assumption), Mrs. Luce would not have been so ill-mannered nor so stupid as to have given her such an opportunity. Second, the remark attributed to Dorothy Parker is not in character, either. It does not sound like her in public, although it might sound like the sort of thing she would say in private, behind someone's back.

Despite one informant's testimony that he was there, and heard the exchange, there is good reason to believe that the informant's memory was a victim of the legend. But having already come to this conclusion, the author felt that he must ask Mrs.

Luce about this, distasteful as the question would be to her. Mrs. Luce replied:

"I met her only once, perhaps thirty-five years ago, at the home of our mutual friends, Herbert and Maggie Swope. At that time I was Mrs. Clare Boothe Brokaw and an editor . . . of *Vanity Fair* magazine. Also, I was a newcomer to the New York literary scene. But many of Dorothy Parker's intimate friends and great admirers, like Alexander Woollcott, Ernest Boyd, Moss Hart, George Kaufman, and others of the famous Algonquin set, thought me an agreeable addition to their circle, whose Number One Darling was Dorothy Parker. Possibly they praised me a bit overmuch to Dorothy. I don't know. But to return to our meeting at the Swopes': Dorothy Parker was then in her prime as a young poetess and wit. All I remember of that occasion is that I was, of course, delighted to make her acquaintance. The 'Age before beauty' story is completely apocryphal. Certainly no such remark by me or rejoinder by her was made on this occasion. . . . The story probably was worked up as a suitable piece of dialogue for the two of us by some columnist."

Also apocryphal, it would seem, are two poems Dorothy was said to have written in California. One concerned an heiress who sued her mother for having had a hysterectomy performed on her. The poem made the girl out to be a nymphomaniac, and had the mother order the operation to prevent the birth of bastards. The poem was said to be Dorothy Parker's version of an actual event. The poem is funny, and the subject would have appealed to her sense of humor, but its meter is uneven and its rhyme scheme is atrocious—and therefore there is little reason to believe that a disciplined perfectionist like Dorothy Parker could have been guilty of writing it. It is much easier to believe that this anonymous poem, which for a while went the rounds in Hollywood, was attributed to her simply because it was funny and it was a poem, and she had a reputation for writing funny poems.

The second poem is placed, by legend, in the guest book at William Randolph Hearst's castle at San Simeon. She is said to have written it after having seen a shrine to the Madonna outside the bedroom door of Mr. Hearst's mistress, Marion Davies.

A reason for believing that she did not write it is that she simply was not a person given to making gratuitous insults. She was a counterpuncher whose blow was seldom felt at the time by its victim. He would be among the last to learn that Dorothy Parker had enjoyed a complete revenge.

It was perhaps inevitable that the lines most often attributed to her should have been raffish ones, for by social definition there was something raffish about Mrs. Parker. She smoked, worked for a living, took lunch and went to the theater unchaperoned in the company of other women's husbands; clearly, she was one of the New Women. But the essential Dorothy Parker was elegant, not raffish. Unfortunately, elegance is not nearly so quotable, nor so memorable, but typical of the pure, vintage Parker is a story that Arnold Gingrich, publisher of *Esquire* magazine, tells on himself.

"Once at a party," Mr. Gingrich said, "I rather fatuously described myself as being just a simple country boy from Michigan—and heard a small voice murmur, 'When convenient.' "

Of course Dorothy Parker gloried in her burgeoning notoriety on seeing her name in "The Conning Tower." She was pleased to have so quickly become the favorite moll of so bright a literary gang that had such fun with words together. Life in the spring and summer of 1919 was full for her in all regards save one: she had no husband with whom to share it.

It was August before the 33rd Ambulance Company returned to the United States to be demobilized. It had been fifteen months since she had seen her husband, a short separation as the wars of these days go, but one that raised a fear that all war brides know. She had written to Eddie every day, and at the same time she feared that she and he might discover that they were no longer the same people who had loved before. He had had one life overseas that she could never know herself, much as he might have tried to describe it in letters, and she had lived a life he could not know, much as she might have tried to tell him about it. In the event, it was not Eddie who came back to her, it was Spook. And she was no longer the girl who, only fifteen months before, had written little lines under pictures for *Vogue*.

6

On many a day in the fall and winter of 1919, she could be found at noon sitting at a table in the Algonquin Hotel with members of an ever growing group of friends. There was nothing formal about these occasions. She did not go there every day, nor did all the others. But enough of them would appear on any given day for Frank Case, manager of the Algonquin, to keep a table reserved for them, not in the small Pergola Room, but in the front center of the main dining room.

In its earliest days, the group included herself, Mr. Benchley, Mr. Sherwood, FPA, Mr. Woollcott, Mr. Ross, and Deems Taylor, Donald Ogden Stewart, Murdock Pemberton, George S. Kaufman, Marc Connelly, Heywood Broun, Charles MacArthur, Art Samuels, Peggy Wood, John P. Toohey, Howard Dietz, Beatrice Kaufman, John V. A. Weaver, Peggy Leech, Brock Pemberton, Jane Grant, David Wallace, Margalo Gillmore, Ruth Hale, Herman J. Mankiewicz, Neysa McMein, and Edna Ferber. Subsequent arrivals would include Harpo Marx, Ina Claire, Douglas Fairbanks, Jascha Heifetz, and Herbert Bayard Swope. In addition, there were peripheral members who did not regularly lunch at the Algonquin, such as Frank Sullivan and Corey Ford, but who were well acquainted with the others and joined various of them at other places on other occasions. As the years went by, this group enlarged to encompass what was virtually a talent elite of New York's practitioners of the communicative and performing arts of the nineteen-twenties. But in the beginning, most of these people, so many of whose names are now familiar, were by no means established as musicians, artists, players, producers, playwrights, and writers. Instead, most of them were then hard-working and not well-paid men and women in their middle twenties who had come from the provinces to seek their fortunes on Broadway or on New York's newspaper and magazine staffs. They were, most of them, on the way up, and what they had in common was their talent, their wit and their taste, their readiness to do at any time anything that promised to be fun, and a kind of inner certainty of their future successes. It was the latter quality, so suggestive of youthful errantry, that led Murdock Pemberton to think of them as members of a new Round Table—and in due course, Mr. Case provided them with a round table.

The group centered around Mr. Adams and Mr. Woollcott, if it was not also drawn together by them, and nothing exactly like it can be found before or since in American cultural history. The mood and style of the Round Table were somewhat akin to those of the Mermaid Tavern or of an eighteenth-century London coffeehouse, in that what counted was being well-informed, clever and amusing in conversation, and having an awfully good time. The joyous ambience of this well-met group was not sustained by alcohol—at least, not at the Algonquin, for the hotel had no bar during Prohibition.

While the group was not a consciously literary or theatrical one in the sense of a membership that discussed techniques and otherwise talked shop, it was certainly a critical one, very much concerned with the literary and theatrical values of the day. They were interested in a new elegance, a new sophistication. They were conscious of a new age; they were conscious of treading frontiers, and they were very sure that this fact would shortly become apparent.

When Edwin Parker first approached the table at the Algonquin, everyone regarded him with expectant interest. He was promptly made welcome, and made a part of what they called the goings-on. Occasionally he would come uptown from Wall Street to have lunch at the Round Table, but more frequently he would be part of the group in the evenings, when he escorted Dorothy to the theater and to after-theater parties. It presently appeared, however, that there was just a bit of a problem, which Donald Ogden Stewart subsequently defined as delicately as possible:

"Eddie was quite good-looking; very shy; he was modest; he was just a nice person to have around."

Mr. Stewart, who was then a young man from Yale who wished to be a satirist in New York instead of being a bond salesman in Ohio (as his family intended), and who had become a particular friend of Mr. Benchley, Mr. Sherwood, and Mrs. Parker, went on to explain:

"Eddie would help out. He would pass things at parties. He wasn't in the way. But there was no particular reason for anyone to pay any attention to him."

So when Eddie showed up at the Algonquin, people were embarrassed for him because he never said anything that anyone remembered. Everyone else was amusing, but Eddie just sat there and smiled his charming smile.

Perhaps Eddie sensed this. He soon stopped going to the Algonquin for lunch, and no one particularly missed him— except, perhaps, Dorothy. In his absence, she told stories about Eddie that gave him a distinct style and character.

Once she had him fall down a manhole while reading *The Wall Street Journal* on his way to the office. Somehow, he broke his arm while sharpening a pencil. Eddie was the eternally innocent and unsuspecting victim of disasters that occurred to no one else.

"Some awful things happened to Eddie all in the same day," Mr. Stewart said. "He got run over, or something—I forget what it was—but four or five absolutely terrible things happened to Eddie all in that same day, and Dottie was terribly sympathetic, but you screamed with laughter because it was such a line of continual misfortunes."

Everybody looked forward to these stories. Someone would ask where Eddie was, and Dorothy, in tones of disbelief, would say, "You didn't hear what happened to Eddie today?"

"Oh, God, what happened *now?*"

Once, she said that she and Eddie had gone to a funeral. Because she was never on time for anything, Eddie told her to be ready an hour before the funeral was actually to be held. On this occasion, however, she was only half an hour late getting dressed, with the result that they arrived at the funeral home half an hour early. No one else was there, not even the funeral director. They were alone with the body, which was to be cremated. She and Eddie peered curiously at the corpse, and then, somehow or other, Eddie began to fool around with a knob beneath the casket, and machinery began to hum, the casket began to move, a door opened—and casket and corpse went neatly and quietly into the hot little hell of the crematory. There was nothing she and Eddie could do but flee out a side door before the family came for the funeral, she said.

"I don't see why we are all laughing," she said. "It was really a terrible, terrible thing."

But after a while, the stories about Eddie stopped, and as Mr. Stewart said, "Eddie just sort of dropped out of the picture." Besides, something happened to Dorothy, and to Mr. Benchley and Mr. Sherwood, that was much more interesting to talk about than any of the mythical things that happened to Eddie.

Dorothy was fired from *Vanity Fair*. The two Roberts immediately resigned in protest. This took place on Monday, January 12, 1920, and that afternoon the trio came into the Algonquin laughing about it. But it seemed to some that the trio's hilarity was more forced than nonchalant, and everyone wanted to know exactly what had happened. Mr. Benchley said that Frank Crowninshield had called Mrs. Parker into his office that morning and told her that a suggestion had come to him from the publisher, Condé Nast, to fire her.

The reason was, Mr. Crowninshield had said, that she had panned three Broadway plays, and the producers of these plays complained to the publisher that they had been unfairly treated. Florenz Ziegfeld was particularly irate, for his wife Billie Burke had been the star in one of the plays, and Dorothy had written that "Miss Burke is at her best in her more serious moments; in her desire to convey the girlishness of the character, she plays her lighter scenes as if she were giving an impersonation of Eva Tanguay."

It is difficult now to imagine a magazine of *Vanity Fair*'s importance then truckling to Broadway producers, but the newspapers and magazines of 1920 did, and this was a sore point to the working newspapermen and theater critics at the Round Table. They believed that if an actor was guilty of overacting, it was no more and no less than a critic's duty to report that he was—producers be damned. Furthermore, in this case, *Vanity Fair*'s position seemed to be one of accepting a complaint from an advertiser as sufficient excuse to fire an employee with no questions asked, and it was the injustice of this position that led Mr. Benchley and Mr. Sherwood to tell Mr. Crowninshield that if he was going to fire Mrs. Parker, they were quitting.

The Round Tablers agreed the two men had done the only right and proper thing, but it meant far more than that to Dorothy. It was all right for the then unmarried Mr. Sherwood, she said, but Mr. Benchley had a wife and two children to support. She said that Mr. Benchley's resigning was the greatest act of friendship she had ever known.

"Oh," Mr. Benchley said, "I was getting in a rut."

He sought to wave the matter aside, in order to spare Mrs. Parker's feelings and to bring everyone else back into a happier mood. But there was more to the matter than Dorothy and the two Roberts may have known. The producers' complaints had given *Vanity Fair* a proximate cause to fire her, and when the two men threatened to quit, Mr. Crowninshield, who hated to fire anyone, gladly grasped the chance to say he was sorry to see them go.

The real problem was that the trio had been out of step with *Vanity Fair*'s management for some time. On October 14, 1919, the magazine's office manager sent around a document entitled "Forbidding Discussion Among Employees of Salary Received," the gist of which was that anyone who told anyone else how much he was being paid would be fired. Mrs. Parker and the two Roberts immediately circulated a document of their own, "Concerning the Forbidding of Discussion Among Employees," which said, "We resent being told what we may and what we may not discuss." They made signs stating what *their* salaries were, and hung them around their necks.

Later, they dimly viewed another office memorandum saying that anyone who was late to work would have to fill out a slip, explaining why. Mr. Benchley promptly filled a tardy slip with microscopic handwriting. It told how elephants at the Hippodrome had escaped that morning. Mr. Benchley's civic duty was plain: he had to help round them up, to prevent their boarding a Fall River Line steamship for Boston (which could have caused a marine disaster), and to return them to the Hippodrome. This had resulted in his being eleven minutes late to work that day.

There were other problems. Mr. Sherwood, asked to fill in for the writer of the column "What the Well-Dressed Man Will Wear," had treated the assignment as an occasion for satire, and the advertisers had complained. It was all very well for *Vanity Fair* to take a sophisticated and satiric view of the contemporary scene, but not, apparently, of the wares of its advertisers. Then, Mrs. Parker was chronically late for work. And they all took too long for lunch. Once Mrs. Parker and Mr. Benchley had spent a morning away from the office, sitting in the Algonquin's lobby, talking about writing a play about a man who left his rich, fascinating, and sexually attractive wife for a dull, poor, mousy little mistress. It seemed an awfully funny idea, but that was as far as they got with it. Mr. Crowninshield felt that this sort of fooling around should not take place during the working day at *Vanity Fair*'s expense. Nor did Mr. Crowninshield think that Mr. Benchley was the kind of managing editor the magazine needed, because Mr. Benchley was interested in suburban life, whereas Mr. Crowninshield wanted *Vanity Fair* to be exclusively concerned with the glittering world of the highest society and the most cultivated taste.

The trio put on as good a show as they could that Monday afternoon at the Algonquin, and they put on another during the next two weeks at *Vanity Fair*, where they stayed out their time, not really working, wearing red chevrons like those worn by troops mustered out of the service and on the way home. On the day they left *Vanity Fair* for the last time, Mr. Benchley placed in the lobby a sign he had made. "Contributions for Miss Billie Burke," it asked.

This having been done, the three of them wondered what to do next, and Mr. Sherwood's answer was to seek a job at *Life*, then a humor magazine. He was hired to review motion pictures, and found himself enjoying a freedom he had not known at *Vanity Fair*. At *Life,* he could get away with the kind of lines he wrote about the cowboy movie star Tom Mix: "They say he rides like part of the horse, but they don't say which part."

Mrs. Parker and Mr. Benchley opted for an even wider freedom—that of having no employer but themselves. They decided to set up shop as free-lance writers, and rented an office together.

It was a triangular sort of closet, with a window and a radiator, on the third floor of the Metropolitan Opera House studios. It rented for thirty dollars a month, and it was so small that Mr. Benchley said, "One cubic foot less of space, and it would have constituted adultery."

They made up stories about their office. One was that they had a firm name lettered on the door: "Utica Drop Forge and Tool Co., Robert Benchley, President; Dorothy Parker, President." Another was that their cable address was "Parkbench." In fact, they never had a name lettered on the door, nor could they have afforded a cable address even had there been anyone who might have wished to send them a cable. All this was just in fun, and they so much enjoyed talking together that very little writing was done. Mr. Benchley had three other mouths to feed. A few weeks later he abandoned the economically precarious existence of the free-lance to follow Mr. Sherwood to *Life,* where he was taken on as drama editor; and Mrs. Parker was left alone in the tiny office whose one window looked on the hokum of Broadway. It was said that after Mr. Benchley left she was so lonely (and so desirous of companionship that would give her an excuse not to work) that she had another sign lettered on the door: MEN.

No one can be sure whose joke this was. It could easily have been Mr. Benchley's, for some of the funniest lines attributed to Dorothy Parker were actually his. He was always saying, "Mrs. Parker said," or "According to Mrs. Parker," to introduce a joke different from his usual sort of fantasy. In any case, both he and she told the story, but the truth is that no such sign ever appeared on the door of any office occupied by Dorothy Parker, although it was fun to pretend that one did.

She was, at this time, capitalizing upon the incongruity between the modesty of her manner and the merry outrageousness

of her words. At a Hallowe'en party given by newspaper editor
Herbert Bayard Swope, she saw people gathered around a wash-
tub, and asked what in the world they were doing.

"They're ducking for apples," someone explained.

She sighed. "There," she murmured, "but for a typographical
error, is the story of my life."

"Damn it," she said years later, "it was the twenties, and we
had to be smarty. I *wanted* to be cute. That's the terrible thing.
I should have had more sense. A smartcracker, they called me. I
was the toast of two continents: Greenland and Australia."

Not everyone was equally smart. For the most part, the members of the Algonquin group were, and they vastly enjoyed the
quick and madcap things she could say. They also relished the
funny but perfectly poisonous remarks she could mutter about
someone behind that person's back. As one of her friends said,
she could turn a celebrity into a fool, or vice versa. But knowing
what bitter things she could say about absent friends made all
of her friends a bit uneasy. Some of the distaff members of the
Round Table would not leave a room while she was in it, not
even to go to the bathroom, for fear of what she might say about
them while they were gone. The men had the same fear, although Mr. Stewart spoke for the majority when he said this
was a price they were willing to pay for the pleasure of her company—and to hear what she might say about someone else. Most
of the men felt "That's our Dottie," as most of them called her,
and forgave whatever she might say about them. Moreover,
within the Algonquin group, badinage was a favorite sport;
everyone was expected to be able to take it, as well as to dish it
out, and the more truth there was in one of Dorothy Parker's
remarks, the more cutting and funnier it was.

Yet an edged wit can wound, and it occurred to a New York
gossip columnist to strike back. He publicly insinuated that Mr.
Benchley and Mrs. Parker were having an affair.

When the columnist's insinuations appeared in print, Mr.
Benchley and Mrs. Parker went immediately to Eddie Parker's
apartment, where Mr. Benchley said, "We hope you understand
that this, whoever he is, is lying."

Quite plainly, the columnist did not know his man. In time
Mr. Benchley would become a man with a bottle and something

of a *flâneur*, but in 1920 Mr. Benchley was an ardent Prohibitionist, a teetotaler, as starchy a moralist as New England ever produced, a family man whose activities apart from those at home and on the job consisted of helping slum boys and taking part in the good works of the Young Men's Christian Association. None of these attributes necessarily debars a man from adultery or the commission of other crimes, but they strongly suggest that he who possesses them is no likely candidate for the role of Don Juan.

Nor did the columnist know his woman. It is true that Dorothy had left Edwin Parker. She had taken an apartment in a building on West Fifty-seventh Street where the beautiful and somewhat Bohemian artist Neysa McMein had a studio. Miss McMein was a familiar of the Round Table, and her studio was a nocturnal headquarters for the Algonquin group. But Dorothy had taken the apartment because it was convenient to this meeting place of all her friends, and not for the purpose of sleeping with any of them.

Finally, the columnist did not understand the relationship that Dorothy Parker and Robert Benchley shared. He was her friend. He was perhaps the first and best friend she ever had. It is perfectly true that they were seen everywhere together. The nature of their friendship was one of camaraderie. Beyond this, their relationship had so much of the father-daughter, or at least of the big brother–kid sister, aura about it that an affair would have been as repellent as incest to each of them. This was so well understood between them that they used to make jokes about why they were not having an affair.

Eddie Parker said he understood. He accepted their word when they came to explain. He also understood that his marriage was at an end. The two-fisted drinking of his early Army days had, during the idle months of occupation duty in the Rhineland, become compulsive drinking. He knew he needed help. He wanted to get out of New York and away from its temptations. He wanted to go back to Hartford and dry himself out and start life over again. He loved Dorothy and asked her to move to Hartford with him. But this she could not do. Whether she had grounds for believing it or not, she believed that Eddie's religious family detested her because her father had been a Jew. She and Eddie had quarreled about this, and much else, and she left him. It was probably at the moment of her refusal to go with him to Hartford that Eddie knew his marriage was over. For him, her moving out of their apartment would have merely been an unnecessary confirmation of the fact.

Apparently, Dorothy did not part easily from Edwin Parker, but guiltily, for late in life she tried to excuse herself by saying that he had returned from Germany addicted to morphine and had to be shut up in a sanatorium. Neither her friends nor his believed this. What everyone did believe, however, was a theory that Mr. Stewart advanced.

"It was a case of incompatibility," Mr. Stewart said. "It just didn't work. When he got back from Germany, it was already over."

She had found acceptance in a New York literary and theatrical circle. She had chosen the "authors and actors and artists and such" over "the man who solicits insurance" before Eddie returned from the Rhineland. Mr. Stewart said the problem was not that she loved Eddie less, but that she loved her new life more.

"She was on her way up," one of Eddie's Wall Street friends said, "and she stayed in New York and Eddie went back to Hartford."

"What in God's name would she do in *Hartford?*" one of Dorothy's friends asked in tones of rising horror. "Can you see her going to Hartford with Eddie Parker after she had begun to meet people like Benchley and Sherwood and FPA and Woollcott?"

The situation was further complicated by the fact that, in her circle, the very mention of Hartford would have been a sick joke, for the Algonquin people knew all about small towns, many of them having come from such towns themselves. They were very sure that New York was the only place for them to be, the only place that mattered. As one observer of the Algonquin group said at the time, if they ever thought of anything else than New York, it was in terms of New York.

Yet, before Edwin Parker is dismissed as a dullard who could not compete in Dorothy's glittering group, much might be said for him. It is possible that Dorothy's friends bored him just as much as he bored them. Having been in Wall Street before the war, he might not have thought New York to be so wonderfully exciting as the newcomers thought it was. Her friends were all in one way or another clever and entertaining, but the things that interested them might not have interested a businessman —just as intelligent discussions of negotiable securities and long-term loans might not fascinate poets, playwrights, and satirists.

It was all very well for a popular singer of the day to sing, "Everything to me is just a ha, ha, ha!" and no doubt that song mirrored one prevalent mood of 1920. But in the street of the moneylenders, life is real and earnest, however life may seem to be uptown in the district of the mimes, the jugglers, and the scribblers. Everything to Edwin Parker was not a ha, ha, ha. He wanted to return to the known limits of Hartford to rebuild his life. He might very well have understood that Dorothy was on her way up, but a question in his mind could have been, "Up what?"

"I think," Mr. Stewart said, "that Eddie stayed in love with her longer than she did with him."

He said this because he perceived something about Dorothy that ought to have been more apparent to Edwin Parker than to anyone else. Of all her friends, Mr. Stewart was closer to her at this time than anyone other than Mr. Benchley, and yet Mr. Stewart could say this about her:

"Dottie was attractive to everybody—the eyes were so wonderful, and the smile. It wasn't difficult to fall in love with her. She was always ready to do anything, to take part in any party; she was ready for fun at any time when it came up, and it came up an awful lot in those days. She was fun to dance with and she danced very well, and I just felt good when I was with her, but I think if you had been married to Dottie, you would have found out, little by little, that she really wasn't there. She was in love with you, let's say, but it was *her* emotion; she was not worrying about *your* emotion.

"You couldn't put your finger on her," he said. "If you ever married her, you would find out eventually. She was both wide open and the goddamnedest fortress at the same time.

"Every girl's got her technique," Mr. Stewart said, "and shy, demure helplessness was part of Dottie's—the innocent, bright-eyed little girl that needs a male to help her across the street.

"She was so full of pretense herself that she could recognize the thing," Mr. Stewart concluded. "That doesn't mean she did not hate sham on a high level, but that she could recognize pretense because that was part of her makeup. She would get glimpses of herself doing things that would make her hate herself for that sort of pretense."

So, perhaps for both of them, it was just as well that Edwin Parker eventually went back to Hartford alone. And there, as far as Dorothy's group was concerned, he became a sort of harmless ghost. He would enter her life twice more, but only in an ectoplasmic way. In 1928, he courteously allowed her to divorce him in Connecticut on technical grounds of cruelty, and to retain his name, which she preferred to Rothschild. Years later, she wept for a moment on learning that he had died. Otherwise, he was to her what an anecdote makes clear:

Someone asked her why she was called Mrs. Parker instead of Miss Parker.

"Well, you see," she said, "there *was* a Mr. Parker."

And she said nothing more. But she subsequently put what she believed to be true of herself, of Eddie, and of their marriage into the poem she called "The Dark Girl's Rhyme":

Who was there had seen us
    Wouldn't bid him run?
Heavy lay between us
    All our sires had done.

There he was, a-springing
    Of a pious race,
Setting hags a-swinging
    In a market-place.

Sowing turnips over
    Where the poppies lay;
Looking past the clover,
    Adding up the hay;

Shouting through the Spring song,
  Clumping down the sod;
Toadying, in sing-song
  To a crabbèd god.

There I was, that came of
  Folk of mud and flame—
I that had my name of
  Them without a name.

Up and down a mountain
  Streeled my silly stock;
Passing by a fountain,
  Wringing at a rock;

Devil-gotten sinners,
  Throwing back their heads,
Fiddling for their dinners,
  Kissing for their beds.

Not a one had seen us
  Wouldn't help him flee.
Angry ran between us
  Blood of him and me.

How shall I be mating
  Who have looked above—
Living for a hating,
  Dying of a love?

The young Dorothy Parker

"Spook" Parker (second from left, top row)

Right, Mr. and Mrs. F. Scott Fitzgerald and daughter, Scottie

Robert Benchley in 1932

Hemingway in the mid-twenties

Corey Ford

Frank Sullivan

Edna St. Vincent Millay

Frank Crowninshield

FPA

Donald Ogden Stewart with his award for the screenplay of
The Philadelphia Story

Charles MacArthur and Helen Hayes

Harpo Marx

The remarriage of Alan Campbell and Dorothy Parker in 1950

John McClain

Vincent Sheean

Heywood Broun

Harold Ross

Alexander Woollcott

At 70, Dorothy Parker in Hollywood, 1963

PART
TWO

"If you don't stop this kind of thing,
you'll make yourself sick."

—Robert Benchley

1

"How is Dottie getting along?" someone would ask.

"Oh, she's all right. You don't have to worry about Dottie."

"I know, but has she any money?"

"I don't know. She seems to have."

"Well, she didn't have any for a taxi last night."

"She never has money for taxis. Anyway, somebody would drop her off at her place."

"But, my God, people need money."

"Well, maybe somebody is giving her money. Maybe Eddie is sending her some. Somebody must be giving her money."

So the conversations went, for her finances were a continuing mystery to her friends. They did not really worry about her; in the early twenties none of them worried about anybody who was having fun, and their Dottie was certainly very much a part of the fun. But they were curious. She had had no job since leaving *Vanity Fair*. She gave up the office she and Mr. Benchley had shared, not long after Mr. Benchley left it. Although she was writing verse and short stories throughout 1920 and 1921, there is no record of any sale to magazines, and at the time some of her friends wondered if she really was doing any writing. Yet she seemed to have money enough to go everywhere and do everything, and to buy perfume, handmade lingerie, and expensive dresses—but there was never any money for taxis, and whenever she would offer to pay for a drink, her purse would be empty. It was all very puzzling. It was as if she were following Oscar Wilde's dictum: Take care of the luxuries and the necessities will take care of themselves.

It is always possible that she was receiving support from her estranged husband, and she would not have needed much, for in 1921 a single person could find food, clothing, and shelter in Manhattan for twenty-five dollars a week, though this would be cutting it rather fine.

Dorothy Parker's apartment on West Fifty-seventh Street was hardly pretentious. She said that all she needed was enough space "to lay a hat—and a few friends." So it was a cheaply furnished room, utterly without taste, as anonymous as a room in a traveling salesmen's hotel. Apart from her clothing and toilet articles, the only things in the room that belonged to her were her portable typewriter and a canary she called Onan because he spilled his seed upon the ground.

Her room was just a cheap, conveniently located place to sleep. When she dined out (she did not cook for herself), it did not seem to matter to her what she ate. She would routinely order a steak and a salad, no matter how ambitious the restaurant's menu. Food was more of a humdrum necessity for her than it was a source of pleasure or recreation, and her attitude toward food would have helped to keep its cost low for her, wholly apart from the fact that many of her evening meals would be provided by her male escorts.

She went frequently to the theater, for in those days there were as many as nine openings in a single week during the season, but this cost nothing because she attended plays together with Mr. Woollcott or Mr. Benchley, and theater critics were always assigned two free seats. The books she read were review copies given her by magazine and newspaper friends. And her greatest source of amusement cost nothing at all, consisting as it did of the company of her friends.

She was so seldom home that her private life was, in a sense, nonexistent. She would wake at midmorning and at noon meet friends for lunch. The working hours of many of the Algonquin group were elastic and nocturnal; this was particularly true of the newspaper columnists FPA and Heywood Broun and of the motion picture and theater critics Sherwood, Benchley, and Woollcott. Their work required them to file a few hundred words of opinion each day, and their offices did not care where or how they spent their time so long as they met their deadlines with acceptable copy in hand. So, after a leisurely lunch, someone might propose a thing that seemed fun to do in the afternoon, such as riding along Fifth Avenue in a carriage. Mr. Woollcott loved to do this, and Dorothy was always glad to go go along.

On one of these occasions, she and Mr. Woollcott found their Victoria stopped in a snarl of traffic and surrounded, like a house in a flood, by eddying pedestrians. Mr. Woollcott adopted the mood of a Bourbon monarch bored by reports that the peasants were restless. But she, amused by Mr. Woollcott's air of refined distaste, and by that quality of desperate frustration that characterizes all who use New York's streets, began to giggle. Then, playing a role of her own, she rose, blowing kisses to the commonality, and calling out, "I promise to come back and sing Carmen again for you!"

In the late afternoon of such a day, Mrs. Parker might accompany Mr. Benchley and Mr. Stewart to a brownstone on the West Side. They would somewhat furtively descend the basement steps, and Mr. Stewart would ring for admission. A sliding panel in the steel door would snick back, revealing a peephole. Mr. Stewart, if not recognized to be a regular patron of the establishment, would have to mutter "Joe sent me," or otherwise give a password, and if all went well, there would be a noise of bolts and chains, the door would slip quickly open and be as quickly shut, chained and bolted behind them. They would find themselves in a dark room, thick with cigarette smoke and loud with drunken voices, themselves now a part of an illicit camaraderie which might very well include the cop on the beat, found drinking a large whisky and a small beer at the end of the bar.

There were many styles and sizes of Prohibition speakeasies, and it was a mark of sophistication to be able to discriminate among them. There were little holes in the wall along First Avenue that had sawdust on the floor; there were bars kept by the Irish, decorated with shillelaghs; Italian establishments with marble-topped tables, bad frescoes of the Bay of Naples, and worse red wine made by the proprietors. Close to the *Tribune* newspaper's building on West Fortieth Street there was Jack Bleeck's Artists and Writers Club, catering to the newspaper crowd. On Park Avenue, across from the Racquet Club, a genial and unlettered man named Matt Winkle served a clientele that seemed to consist almost exclusively of undergraduates from Harvard and Yale. What most of these establishments had in common, apart from an atmosphere of cosy lawbreaking, was grain alcohol imaginatively flavored and even more imaginatively labeled Rye, Bourbon, Scotch, and Gin. But the speakeasy the Algonquin group liked best, and which they patronized whenever they had the money, was Jack and Charlie's Puncheon Club at 42 West Forty-ninth Street. No rotgut alcohol or bathtub gin was served there, but genuine wines and spirits of the first quality. Instead of steak fried thin, hard and tough, Jack and Charlie's served ambrosia prepared by a chef paid twenty thousand dollars a year. It was not just locally known, but was internationally famous—and became wickedly expensive, for all the plebeian charm of its red and white check tablecloths.

Arriving at this establishment, Dorothy Parker and her escorts would be sure to find other of their friends there—as they would have if they had gone across the street to Tony Soma's, where everyone went when funds ran low, for Tony's sold suspect liquor and rather bad Italian food, but at prices more within the reach of everyone. It was at Tony's one night that Mr. Benchley fell at last from grace. Like the crushing majority of Americans, Mr. Benchley had believed in Prohibition before it became the law of the land. When he went to speakeasies with Mrs. Parker and the others, he would order soft drinks or orange juice. But one day he and Mr. Stewart emerged from Tony's to find it raining. A pedestrian carrying an umbrella came past Tony's doorway, and Mr. Stewart ducked under the man's umbrella, gripped him by the arm, said, "Yale Club, please," and steered his startled victim down the street, leaving Mr. Benchley gaping after him, lost in admiration.

"If drinking can do that for a man," Mr. Benchley mused, "there must be something in it after all."

Shortly thereafter, Mr. Benchley allowed Mr. Stewart and

Mrs. Parker to order a real drink for him at Tony's—an orange blossom. He tasted it and made a face.

"This place ought to be closed by the police," he said.

But he took another sip, and fell. He had come a bit late to the Children's Hour, but once in for a penny, Mr. Benchley thereafter went in for a pound.

To say that Dorothy Parker went frequently to speakeasies does not mean she drank frequently while there. Many of the Algonquin group began to drink like sewers during Prohibition, but just as their camaraderie at the Algonquin Hotel was not predicated on alcohol, so it was not predicated on alcohol at the speakeasies. Dorothy had not drunk much during the time she lived with Eddie Parker, nor did she now: one or two drinks would see her through an evening. Their favorite speakeasies were simply places where the Round Tablers could meet at day's end to enjoy one another's conversation—and where anyone who wished could also have a drink.

In the evening, Dorothy and her friends might eat at Tony's, or have a drink there and move the party over to Seventh Avenue where Mr. Benchley had found "a little French restaurant completely without charm," and after supper, they would go to the theater. Later, they might all go to Neysa McMein's studio, where Miss McMein made wine in the bathroom, and there discover George Gershwin, Ethel Barrymore, and Zelda and F. Scott Fitzgerald swelling the throng, all of them playing Consequences, Shedding Light, Categories, or a kind of charades that was later called The Game.

Still later, in what was now no longer the same night, but hours into the next day, the whole party might move to Polly Adler's bawdy shop for conversation with the girls and with Mrs. Adler, and for a breakfast of scrambled eggs, bacon, and black coffee. Everyone was amused by Mrs. Adler, who would one day become a writer herself, author of A House Is Not a Home. Mrs. Adler's was such a favorite haunt of the group that one of Dorothy's friends had a charge account and kept a black Japanese kimono there and, attired in this, would sit down to play backgammon with Mrs. Adler for twenty dollars a game—this being the price of the girls' favors—while everyone would crowd around to see how the game came out. On occasion, Mr. Stewart would take Dorothy to Polly's in the afternoon, and she would sit in the parlor and chat while, Mr. Stewart said, "I went upstairs to lay some lucky girl."

So for Dorothy's group, the pattern was home near dawn and up again at midmorning to begin yet another cycle of group activity. The Algonquin group were by no means alone in spending so much of their time with one another. In New York in the twenties, people tended to go about in groups, playing together, staying up all night together. They lived and worked in Manhattan, and the Algonquin group could conduct all of their social and working lives, every day, within a few blocks of Manhattan's West Side between the Forties and the Fifties.

The whole point of their lives seemed to be to have fun, to be clever, to know where the best bartenders were, to be knowledgeable about the city, to know all the latest catchwords, to be aware of the newest fashions and fads, to go to all the first nights and to all the Big Three football games, to go to Polly's and be satirical and blasé, and to do as little work as possible. Certainly no one saw any evidence that Dorothy did any work. There was no littered desk in her small apartment, no wastebasket filled with manuscript drafts. If anyone came to call, she would put a towel over her portable typewriter to prevent anyone seeing whether there was a work in progress—and to prevent anyone from discussing it.

"It was one of the things you didn't do," Mr. Stewart explained. "She and Bobbie [Benchley] and I never actually talked about our work, much as we saw of each other. I wouldn't call it an amateur spirit, but it was a little like that. I mean, we weren't professional literary people in that sense of discussing each other's work. The only discussions there would be, would be that I had a deadline to meet, and Bobbie would have to get out one of his theater reviews, and there were various jokes over the telephone about the poor editors, such as 'Hasn't that piece got there yet?' when you hadn't started to write it."

All this was very much in keeping with Ernest Hemingway's remark in *The Sun Also Rises* that it was then an important part of the ethics of journalism to pretend not to be working, but some people felt that Dorothy Parker was not just pretending. She was always available to do anything else instead, or so it seemed, and some of her friends thought that she was lazy. She chose to admit the charge, rather than refute it. Asked what inspired her to write, she replied, "Need of money, dear," as if to say that when she had money, writing was the last thing she wanted to do.

In certain respects, the pattern of her life, and that of her Algonquin friends, seemed to be remarkably superficial and in some ways similar to the kind of Bohemian life followed by many young intellectuals in any time of postwar flux when all values are in doubt, and when the young people tend to gather in some quarter of a city to flout the laws and social conventions of a society they believe to be rotten. But she and her friends were quite different from the Paris and the Greenwich Village intellectuals of the twenties, and their superficiality and their Bohemianism were far more apparent than they were real. They had fun together, yes, but as she said, they also worked hard—even if they pretended they did not. It was the nature of their work that made much of it fun to do and permitted the kind of fun they enjoyed when the work was done.

Like many Bohemians of the past and of the present day, Dorothy and her friends, most of them, came from well-to-do homes and were well-educated people. But there, most of the resemblance ends. They were not in revolt against society; they merely felt superior to it. Their point was that even if most people might pursue false values, they pursued good ones of their own. Their common attitude toward contemporary American life, arts, and letters was not precisely contemptuous, cynical, condescending, nor smartalecky—although it had some of these elements in it. Nor was that attitude joyous, forgiving, sympathetic, or urbanely tolerant—although it had these elements, too. The Algonquin group was somewhat in the position of Puck, saying, "What fools these mortals be," although they were not so far above the battle as Puck. They felt themselves to be an elite, and they had considerable reason to believe they were right. From there, they went on to set another standard for the nation, to create a different intellectual climate. But they did this *en passant*.

Much as Dorothy Parker was one of the most blithe and clever of a happy group of boon companions, and for all that she was wonderful to be with, as Mr. Stewart said, there was something about her that made her quite different from all the rest. She was a young, vibrant and desirable woman, by universal agreement the wittiest woman in New York, obviously talented and yet she was just as obviously unsure of herself. Although she could giggle like a schoolgirl, and would take a leading part in the fun and games, a quality of *Oi, weh* despair that Mr. Stewart noted became apparent to others. Another of her friends, Gilbert Seldes, critic, author of *The Seven Lively Arts*, and a close observer of the Algonquin group, thought of her as being "a sad person, unable to take real pleasure—as if being enormously satisfied with anything would not be in her character, or would have diminished her."

Her friends found this perplexing. A possible explanation of her sadness could, some thought, be a state of emotional confusion. She and Eddie had separated, but they were not divorced, and at this time it was not certain they wished their separation to be a permanent one. Their brief life together had been far from tranquil, as one of Dorothy's friends said, but there are always tender moments in the worst of marriages, and these moments are as well and as sadly remembered as the rages.

So perhaps she was sad because of Eddie; but apart from this, her friends found her lack of self-confidence difficult to explain. All during 1920 and 1921 New York editors would have been more than willing to receive poetry and prose from her, for if they had not met her personally they would certainly have heard about her from her friends and read about her in FPA's column. But she was not being published. It is one thing to amuse an editor in conversation, but quite another to get it onto the written page—yet the trick should not have been difficult for Dorothy Parker. She had, after all, done well enough at *Vogue* and *Vanity Fair*. Surely she had no objective reason to lack confidence in herself as a writer.

Mr. Seldes sensed the truth of it. "She was not the kind of person who could just sit down and write, as at a job," he said. "She was in the tradition of fiction as one of the beaux arts."

As is the case with many a literary artist, as distinguished from the professional writer who can always go to his typewriter and get work done, writing did not come easily to Dorothy Parker.

She might be lightning fast in conversation, but when she sat at her typewriter she would, as she said, write five words and erase seven. She could, and did, spend as long as six months on a single short story. She was not lazy; she was a perfectionist. Her critical sense consistently informed her that her work was not as good as it ought to be. She was frequently so depressed by being unable to create something that could stand the test of her pitiless critical judgment that there ensued periods when the towel would remain over the typewriter for weeks at a time. She suffered periodically from writer's block—a state of despair that stultifies creativity. In this, she was indeed unlike most of the Algonquin people, and she knew it.

Yet no one can say that a writer is not working if, for no matter what reason, he is not writing, nor that he is not successful if he is not being published. Another way of regarding the years 1920 and 1921, when Dorothy's friends were beginning to be a bit puzzled by her and were speculating as to her finances, is to presume that she was hard at work even while serving as a priestess of the revels. She may not have been consciously aware that she was, but surely she was absorbing experience of life and formulating a definite attitude—for the distillation of that experience, and the expression of that attitude, was shortly to appear. In the following year, 1922, she was prodigiously productive, even though the outward pattern of her life, as the belle of a sort of perpetual ball, did not change. But then, in 1922, she was in love again, and this may have made all the difference.

2

Charles MacArthur was a tall, handsome, talented, and altogether charming member of the Algonquin group. In 1922, he was a young newspaperman who dreamed of becoming a playwright, and Dorothy Parker adored him. In the minds of her friends, there was no question of his being worthy of her, as there had been in the case of Eddie Parker.

"Charley was something else," Donald Ogden Stewart said. "Charley was marvelous. He was something all his own, and she was so in love it was really a serious, desperate thing. When Dottie fell in love, my God, it was really the works. She was madly in love. She was not a slave to love, exactly; it wasn't a game, exactly; it was really for keeps. She fell in love so deeply: she was wide open to Charley."

Everyone thought that Charley and Dottie made an ideal couple, and the only question in anyone's mind was how long the affair would last. Some thought they would marry, but Mr. Stewart had his doubts. After all, he said, "Charley was Charley," by which he meant that Mr. MacArthur at that time was a womanizer, which is a bit different from being simply an extremely eligible bachelor.

But if Dorothy knew this about Charley, she seemed not to care. She was in love, and her writing began to flow. Just when she got this writing done, no one could say, for she kept owl's hours; but a logjam of sorts was over, and she was regularly selling what she wrote to the *Saturday Evening Post*'s comic page, "Short Turns and Encores."

America might not have become immediately aware of a new voice the moment Dorothy's byline first appeared over verse and little prose squibs in the *Post*, but her contributions were very different from those of others. The style of the day was for lady poets with three names to pen, on that same page in the *Post*, such lines as "What, canst not pay? Begone, thou worthless wretch!"; to sigh, "This timorous dust, this phantom that is I," or otherwise to suggest that people who sign their three names cannot write well. But Dorothy would have none of this. Typical of her poems was one called "Song." It described a girl named Chloë who was plain-looking, untrustworthy, illiterate, slovenly, and unable to cook or sew. Chloë had only one accomplishment, but it was the only one that mattered—she got the men.

The flippancy of Dorothy's verse surely brightened the *Post*'s page, but the prose that she was contributing was more than bright. It was important. The pieces were quite short, as they had to be for the purposes of the magazine. They were no longer than eleven brief paragraphs each, and like her poems, they were sardonic comments on popularly held beliefs. For example, it was popularly supposed that going to summer hotels and dining out were splended and fashionable things to do, but Dorothy Parker chose to state that these activities were surely among life's most crashing bores.

In her piece "On Any Hotel Porch," guests natter about the weather, the food, the husbands working in the hot city, the servant problem ("I'm thinking of changing my laundress"). There is not one word of description of the speakers or of the porch on which they are sitting. There need not be, for the banality of the conversation tells the reader everything he needs to know: All the ladies are exactly alike, and none of them has anything to say. Cut from exactly this same cloth was her piece "The Restaurant Revelers," another curt little statement of the boring truth.

Those prose squibs were not great literature, but they were important exercises for her to have done. Because she had a perfect ear for the language people use, and because she had an enormous talent for selection, she was able in a tiny space, and solely through dialogue, to re-create people who were only too believable, embedded in scenes of excruciating reality. It was a marvelously effective kind of writing, and of all her brilliant contemporaries, only Ernest Hemingway would ever do this sort of thing as well as or better than she. Her work was not yet art, but it was moving past craft, and as Gilbert Seldes said, "It was so good it touched the higher form."

There was something else remarkable about the prose that Dorothy was sending to the *Post*: her work might be funny, but its message was sour. If the reader laughed, he also shared the author's scorn for the contemptible people who infested summer hotel porches and fashionable restaurants. Hers was the laughter of disdain.

To this extent, what Dorothy Parker was writing in 1922 reflected one view of the contemporary American scene that she and her friends shared, for while she and Charley drank Jack Roses at Tony's together with the rest, played word games at Neysa McMein's studio, and otherwise loved and laughed and worked, they were all of them well aware of the state of the Union, and eager to say what they thought of it.

Reflect for a moment on the three Presidents of the United States during the twenties: Harding, Coolidge, and Hoover. The first was a small-bore Ohio politician whose idea of Presidential responsibility allowed him to play poker and practice adultery while his cronies systematically looted the United States Treasury. The second was the very caricature of the prating Yankee Puritan, a skinny little cheese-parer who took four-hour naps every day on the job and who was the only man in modern times ever to save money on his White House salary. The third was a man who quite seriously believed the rich should be encouraged to become richer, so that they would spend more money, some of which would then trickle down to the poor, thus making everyone happier.

The nineteen-twenties have been called many things, such as the Roaring Twenties, the Crazy Years, and the Dollar Decade. Of all these appellations, the last is the most apt. During the twenties, American universities added graduate schools of business to their campuses. It was a time when humble citizens went about, saying with Coué, "Day by day, in every way, I am getting better and better," trusting that self-improvement in all things was taking place because they told themselves that it was, and trusting, too, that this would shortly be reflected in their bank balances. The dollar became one with God, as the success of a book, *The Man Nobody Knows*, made clear. It was written by Bruce Barton, a salesman of advertising and the son of a clergyman. It was a biography of Jesus, written to prove that the Savior was a great personnel director, an advertising man of genius, the hottest salesman of his age, a real go-getting boss, and, withal, a fine outdoorsman and regular guy who would be a swell hit at any Rotary meeting. The general public did not think this was blasphemy. Instead, clergymen praised the book. It became a national best seller, and young men read it for inspiration, along with the other inspiring books and manuals they were reading on how to get ahead in business.

The prevalent American mood was a thoroughgoing knownothingism. Its principal products included a series of witch hunts for Bolsheviks, popularly confused with anarchists, who were always depicted in newspaper cartoons as being hairy foreign men carrying fizzing bombs. What apparently made them so difficult to discover was the fact that so few of them went about the streets with fizzing bombs in their hands, wherefore the catchpolls of the day had to rely upon the secondary characteristics in the description—hauling in for inquisition the unshorn foreign-born. It was a time of general xenophobia, of high tariffs, of isolationism, of anti-Catholicism, anti-Semitism; a time of great increase in the membership of the Ku Klux Klan, and of a recrudescence of revival meetings conducted by improbable evangelists from Southern and Western backwaters who banged the drum, pranced about, and shouted for that old-time religion.

The twenties were also a time of tremendous concern for trivia—a concern enhanced by the press of the day, which gave an inordinate amount of space to murders in New Jersey, love nests in Hollywood, the prevalence of petting among the young, college football games, professional baseball, and prizefights. A nadir of sensational journalism was reached in New York, where one newspaper, *The Daily Graphic*, earned the sobriquet "The Daily Pornographic."

During these years, a French delegation asked President Coolidge whether the United States wished to be represented in an international art exhibition to take place in Paris. President Coolidge said "No," explaining that there were no painters in the United States.

Not precisely by chance, therefore, it occurred to an editor, Harold Stearns, to ask some thirty artists and intellectuals to contribute to a book, *Civilization in the United States*. Upon reading the galley proofs, Mr. Stearns immediately sailed for France, convinced that the United States had no civilization.

The thought had occurred to others. H. L. Mencken laid about with his literary bladder, joyously whacking the Bible Belt, lambasting the booboisie, the Yahoos, and others of his fellow citizens whom he routinely dismissed as "gaping primates." Sinclair Lewis proved Mencken's point by the simple process of quoting his Midwestern neighbors accurately. In Paris, an expatriate group, including Ernest Hemingway, was creating a literature of disillusionment, predicated on the theory that life was without objective meaning. Much deserved attention has been paid Hemingway and his friends, but perhaps not enough attention has been paid the fact that virtually all of the significant American writing of the twenties was the literature of debunking, disillusionment, and dissent.

There were exceptions, but the literary mainstream did not include them. It certainly did include Dorothy Parker and the Algonquin group, who took as dim a view of the American cultural scene of the twenties as any Mencken or Stearns and, in their several ways, they laughed at it.

Donald Ogden Stewart addressed himself to the American concern for getting ahead in business. He sent a story, "The Secret of Success," to *The Smart Set* magazine. Mr. Stewart's young hero read all the manuals on how to succeed. He worked hard, made cogent suggestions, arrived early in the office and was the last to leave each day, studied his manuals at night, and got nowhere at all—until he discovered that the president of his firm had an ugly, unmarried daughter. So he married the girl and succeeded to the presidency.

Mr. Stewart's satire was typical of the Algonquin group's mood, but Dorothy Parker's was not. She, too, wrote about

American success, and her piece "Such a Pretty Little Picture" appeared in *The Smart Set*'s December 1922 issue:

A man is seen clipping his suburban hedge while his wife and child watch from the porch of their house. The man is bored by his pointless city job, bored by his vapid suburb, bored by the hedge he is clipping, and more than bored by his nagging and domineering wife and their dull blob of a daughter. He would like to say, suddenly, "To hell with it," and vanish. But he has no one to whom he can say this—that is, no one who would understand him if he did say it, for he has no friends. In the kind of life he leads between office and suburb, he has only business and social acquaintances. There is no possibility of his forming friendships in his style of life, of sharing anything important with anyone else. Still, he footlessly dreams, as he clips his hedge, that perhaps a few years from now he might find an opportunity to say "to hell with it" to someone, and to walk away from his empty life and embark upon a new one. Two neighbors, seeing him at work, and seeing his wife and child watching him from the porch, regard the tableau to be such a pretty little picture of suburban success.

In this short story, Dorothy Parker did something more than reach that higher form Mr. Seldes mentioned. And she did something quite different from the kind of thing Mr. Stewart had done. Mr. Stewart's writing was clever and funny. He stated a problem and solved it. His narrative had a beginning, a middle, and an end. Along the way, Mr. Stewart made his point that what counted in the business world was not brains and hard work, as the public believed, but pull. In several hilarious passages he also ridiculed the idea that the work the business world did was either complicated or worthwhile. Mr. Stewart's story had bite to it, but it was all good fun, whereas Dorothy Parker's piece was not funny at all, save in a savage, sardonic way.

She had not written anything that could be called a story, although what she set forth was something more than an anecdote, and it told far more of a story than Mr. Stewart's piece had, for all that his was a well-plotted narrative. She had written an early example of what, for want of a better name, would be called "slice of life" writing. The term conjures up the image of a writer seizing upon reality at random, cutting a cross section out of it, and handing this to the reader without comment. In the nineteen-thirties, this kind of writing would become a predominant style. So as early as 1922, she was moving past and beyond the writing of Mr. Stewart and their friends, but then she was unique among them in a crucially important way. As Mr. Seldes said, "She had a perceptive intelligence that was really something—something the others did not have."

If she had been accused at the time of being a perceptive artist, Dorothy Parker would have rather shortly denied it, for it was a point of honor among the Algonquin group not to take themselves seriously as creative artists. Their refusal to do so was rather like knocking on wood to prevent the ruin of good luck; in any case a bantering self-disparagement was a part of their style, for if they were to take a satirical view of others, simple equity demanded their willingness to take a satirical view of themselves.

In 1922, they were all taking a comic view of life, and Dorothy Parker contributed not only verse and prose squibs to the *Saturday Evening Post*'s comic page, but longer articles for its regular pages, as well as writing more ambitious short stories in the style of "Such a Pretty Little Picture." She also for the first time became the author of a book. It was called *Women I'm Not Married To; Men I'm Not Married To*, and it was nothing more than a reprint of an article she and FPA had written for the *Post* that appeared on facing pages 12 and 13 of the June 17 issue. In the article, FPA had written wittily about the kind of women he loathed, while she had described the kind of men she detested. Among her lines were these: "Lloyd wears washable neckties," and "Mortimer had his photograph taken in his dress suit." This was reprinted in hard covers. FPA's photograph was on one cover, and hers was on the other, upside down from his. The reader could hold either photograph upright, open the book, and begin reading. Halfway through the volume, he would find the type upside down; he would then have to turn the book over and begin reading from the other cover. The book was a very slender joke, but its publication did indicate one mood of the publishing houses of the twenties and the relationship between publishers and the Algonquin set. The high summer of what Corey Ford called The Years of Laughter was at hand.

In August of that year, they all had another place to play, for Jane Grant and her husband, Harold Ross, then editor of *The American Legion Weekly*, had bought a share of a house at 412 West Forty-seventh Street. For the housewarming, Charley MacArthur printed up invitations—and handed them out to passersby on the street. But Jane Grant said he made amends for this by renting a street carrousel together with Dorothy Parker and Harpo Marx and treating the neighborhood children to rides while the party was in progress.

The amusements at 412 West Forty-seventh were, like those at Neysa McMein's studio, word games, conversation, and bootlegged liquor. It seemed important to find a name for the place. Someone suggested "Chinaman's Chance" after Jane Grant and Harold Ross successively, without success, employed a string of Oriental servants. Mr. Woollcott wanted to call it "The Gash House," a name that the squeamish Mr. Ross could not possibly have understood. Dorothy suggested "Wit's End," which Mr. Woollcott liked so much that he later appropriated it for his own apartment.

Comedy was indeed the mood of New York City in 1922, and as the comedian Jimmy Durante was to say, "Everybody wants ta get inta da act." One of those who thought everybody should get into it was Mr. Woollcott. Earlier that year, he had thought it would be a lark for the Algonquin group to put on a Broadway revue of their own: they would do a take-off on a hit European revue of the day, *Chauve Souris*. Everyone had fallen to: Press agent Murdock Pemberton contributed a punning title, *No, Siree!* Dorothy Parker wrote a wry and witty little song, "The Everlastin' Ingenue Blues," sung by Mr. Sherwood. The members of the Algonquin set cast themselves in a series of skits, among them Mr. Benchley giving his subsequently famous "Treasurer's Report." Offstage music was furnished by another Round Tabler, Jascha Heifetz. Harold Ross, for whom no appropriate role could be imagined, was listed in the playbill as a cabdriver who never appeared on stage. They obtained the free use of the Forty-ninth Street Theater for a Sunday night, that of April 30, to stage their revue for the free entertainment of themselves and their friends. Since the latter included actors and actresses, and since several of the Algonquin writers were theater critics, it was felt only fair that criticism of the show should be written by professional actors in the audience. Accordingly, Laurette Taylor filled Mr. Woollcott's regular space in *The New York Times* next day, while Wilton Lackaye took over Heywood Broun's column in *The New York World*—and there with merciless glee they had their revenge upon the critics. All this had been a merry clowning about, but now, in November, Mr. Woollcott had second thoughts about *No, Siree!* He persuaded his friends that their performance had been more professional than it was. This led them to engage the Punch and Judy Theater that month on a commercial basis. They changed the name of their revue to *The Forty Niners*, but kept the format and many of the same skits, and imagined that it would enjoy a long run before paying customers. Mr. Woollcott was hurt that it closed after a month, but it had been fun to do, and the fact that their revue lasted as long as it did was at least a tribute to the group's gathering notoriety.

Taken together, Dorothy Parker's and FPA's little non-book, and the revue *No, Siree!* being reviewed in the *Times* and the *World* and then becoming a serious Broadway venture, added up to something more than fun. These activities indicated that Dorothy Parker and her Algonquin friends evidently believed, like so many Renaissance men, or graduates of Eton, that any of them could do anything easily—write books, write satires, write plays and act in them, sing, dance, make music, found magazines and publishing houses, act as editors, write columns of opinion, serve as critics, be poets. The amazing thing is that so many of them did several of these things so well. Their mutual friendships reinforced one another's talents, and they were, many of them, becoming important to New York and to the nation.

They were becoming important because there they were, on the ground floor, at the very time New York City was becoming the capital of the nation's emergent mass-media communications industry. Within New York, the Algonquin people were steadily becoming a much-talked-about in-group, and a reason why the *Times* and the *World* had permitted Mr. Woollcott and Mr. Broun to treat *No, Siree!* as news (however satirically) was that the Algonquin people were becoming public figures whose activity *was* news. Mr. Woollcott was very much a personage in the town, for what he wrote about plays was listened to (often with rage and despair) by Broadway producers, and Mr. Broun was already something of a national figure. Mr. Broun's column, "It Seems to Me," was written for the *World*, but it was syndicated from New York and sent to several scores of papers in the provinces.

The popularity of Mr. Broun's column nicely demonstrated the effect that the Algonquin people were beginning to have— for Mr. Broun was a member of the Round Table. He had his whole life and being in New York City, principally on the West Side of midtown Manhattan, and his interests were those of his Round Table friends. This is not to say his friends wrote his column for him (although this literally happened on more than one occasion when Mr. Broun had been up too late a night before), but it is to suggest that what his friends thought colored Mr. Broun's own thinking. When he therefore spoke to his several million readers, Mr. Broun was not giving them just an Eastern seaboard point of view, but a specifically Round Table point of view. Much as they might take a satirical view of their own accomplishments, the Algonquinites were, by virtue of their employment as theater critics, newspaper columnists, playwrights, newspaper and magazine editors and writers, in a posi tion to help set taste in the nation's leading intellectual center. The Algonquinites could cause to be published, and could comment on, such new writing as, for example, that of the Paris group, and thereby help to create a climate in which it would find acceptance.

It would be pleasant to believe that Dorothy Parker's life was full and happy during this productive year, replete as it was with burgeoning success, love, and festive occasions with the best of companions who were becoming tastemakers to a nation, but she did not always find it so.

"What are you having?" a bartender at Tony's asked her.

"Not much fun," she said.

The people standing at the bar with her laughed, but she had a great respect for the truth.

When two of her friends who had been living together were eventually married, she wired her congratulations: WHAT'S NEW?

Mr. Sherwood's wife became pregnant, and Dorothy thought Mrs. Sherwood nattered far too much about it. Therefore, when Mrs. Sherwood was delivered, there was a wire from Dorothy Parker: DEAR MARY, WE ALL KNEW YOU HAD IT IN YOU.

Once when playing Twenty Questions with her friends, she guessed they were trying to identify a man they all knew. "Would he be the kind of man who would put the wings back on flies?" she sweetly asked.

She went to the Wyncote, Pennsylvania, estate of George Horace Lorimer, editor of *The Saturday Evening Post*, to be the Lorimers' weekend guest of honor. When she returned to New York her remarks, about what Philadelphia shirts were stuffed with, were amusing—and possibly accurate. But they got back to Mr. Lorimer, who was not a New York wit, and he issued a ukase: Never again would a contribution by Dorothy Parker be accepted by the *Post*.

As always bitterly true, or deserved, as her remarks about anyone may have been, they fell into a pattern: What Dorothy Parker saw in herself and in others was usually the worst and almost never the best. Even her most famous poem, "Men seldom make passes/At girls who wear glasses," was not the lighthearted jape it might superficially seem to be. As a young woman on *Vogue* and *Vanity Fair*, she wore glasses at work because she was badly nearsighted. But she always took them off when anyone stopped at her desk, and she never wore them on social occasions. Her outward reasons were expressed in the couplet. But behind these reasons there were others. The couplet expressed contempt for men and despair over woman's lot. So it was a report on the immemorial human condition, and therefore the poem's title, "News Item," was appropriately sardonic. She would have been bitterly amused to think of a reader, coming across lines like these embedded in FPA's "Conning Tower," grinning to himself and turning the page to go on more cheerfully to accounts of the day's disasters—entirely oblivious of the fact that he had just read a cry from the feminine soul and, of course, completely unaware that he had read a cry from the feminine soul of the basically insecure young girl who had been Dorothy Rothschild. She was constantly denigrating herself, as well as denigrating others, but however amusingly she did this, bitterness was always there.

Few of her acquaintances realized that contempt for herself and others, and a quality of despair, lay behind almost all of her actions and ran through virtually every line she wrote and beneath practically every witty thing she ever said. Most of her acquaintances found her to be irreverent and gay instead, but then they did not know her well, because the occasions of the Algonquin group were seldom ones of stress or intimate sharing. They all knew one another, but they did not all know each other well.

At this time in her life, Dorothy Parker had not one female confidante. She had never had one. She was quite popular among men, who enjoyed what they believed to be the sharp and masculine play of her wit, but her relationship with virtually all of the men she knew was a superficial one. Most of the women she knew were suspicious of her. The one person who served as her faithful counselor, comforter, and spiritual adviser was Mr. Benchley. She could depend on him to gently say, "Dottie, don't be a damned fool."

At length he gave her a warning. "Now here's a thing. Eventually people become the thing they despise the most."

She found this observation to be absolutely hateful. She said it was not true. She said she would not hear of it. It is likely that she would have been equally deaf if Mr. Benchley had tried to get at the matter in another way, such as by suggesting that she seemed to be acting out, in her life, Oscar Wilde's belief that each of us kills the thing he loves.

But she would hear nothing of this sort. In 1922, when all the world seemed full of laughter, her laughter was sardonic. She seemed determined to pursue unhappiness. Her closest friends, Mr. Benchley and Mr. Stewart, sensed this; so had Mr. Seldes. Perhaps some part of her bitterness could be put to the fact that her affair with Charles MacArthur was going badly.

It was going badly as Mr. Stewart had suspected it would, and for the reason he had supposed it would. Charley was not being faithful to Dorothy.

"I was sorry for her about Charley because she did love him

terribly," Mr. Stewart said. "Goddamn it, she was suffering. She was having a hell of a time."

Well, others said, that was the way she was. If a man chased her, she wouldn't look at him. But if he stopped chasing her to chase some other woman, then she was all teeth and claws and tears. Dottie was really all right, they thought. They said a lot of that so-called suffering was just put on. Since self-disparagement was a part of their style, they could not take her self-denigration seriously. Instead, they applauded her for being, as one of them said, "the greatest little runner-downer there ever was." Besides, if all of that suffering was not put on, she would get over it. She had before. Anyway, they said, no one who could say the tough and funny things that she could say could be suffering all that much.

3

She used to sit until a late hour at Jack and Charlie's, or in the funky smoke of Tony's, tapping out yet another cigarette into the full ashtray, and say that what she really wanted was to get out of the city, to live in the country in a little white cottage with green shutters and fill her life with flowers, puppies, and babies.

Everyone laughed, because they had great fun talking about the country. "Where did you get that tie? Back home in Saugerties?" Alexander Woollcott liked to ask. Bumpkins lived in the country. The west began in New Jersey. Goodness only knew what there was out there. It was particularly hilarious to imagine Dottie living in the country. Who would she talk to? The cows? She would go crazy with boredom. And there was no woman in this world less likely to be able to cope with house, flowers, dogs, and children than Dorothy Parker. One of the things they chiefly liked about her was that she was so different from all other women.

"She can't even boil water!" someone reported. They thought it was screamingly funny when once, as a houseguest, she rose early and being hungry went to the kitchen and ate raw bacon rather than try to cook something for herself.

"That's our Dottie!" they said.

There was also Dottie's dog. The dog came down with mange.

"I suppose he got it from a lamppost," she rather helplessly said.

Because of the way she regarded their laughter with a contented little smile, it was impossible for them to take seriously her concern for her dog. It was a bit puzzling about the dog. She did not clean up after it or try to train it. When someone said the presence of the dog added a note of squalor to what otherwise was merely a dull apartment, she said yes, the place *did* seem a bit Hogarthian.

"But, oh, the poor thing," she would say. "Why, he can't help it."

There was no doubt about it; Dottie was different.

So they all hooted when she told how much she longed for the simple life of a country housewife, knowing perfectly well how absolutely wedded she was to the indoor life of midtown Manhattan. But she went on talking about her little white house to the extent that it became boring, and when tears came, they found it all too tiresome for words, and presumed her tears to be alcoholic ones.

What they failed to realize was that Dorothy Parker was like all other women in one terrifyingly simple respect.

When she became pregnant, there was never a question in her mind as to what to do. There was no place in her life for a child. New York sophisticate that she was, she knew very well that abortion was not always a furtive business gone about in dark tenement rooms by unlicensed physicians using septic instruments. The operation could be performed in the best of hospitals. All one needed was money, and the signed statements of three physicians that the operation was necessary to the physical and mental health of the patient. She went to a hospital.

Of course, there was gossip. Midtown Manhattan is not without the aspect of a small village. One wit quoted Dorothy Parker as having said, "It serves me right for putting all my eggs in one bastard." Another said the man responsible for her pregnancy had sent her thirty dollars toward the cost of the operation, and that she thought of him as Judas making a refund.

Whether Dorothy Parker suffered a trauma as the result of her abortion is something no one can ever know. Many doctors believe that no woman has such an operation without psychic shock. Perhaps Dorothy's friends were right to presume she had the mind of a man imprisoned in a woman's body. If so, then the doctors' caveat might not wholly apply to her. Still, she may have felt trapped. Her experience could have deepened her mood of loneliness and affirmed her suspicion that life was without meaning. She may have felt as lost as Gertrude Stein said her entire generation was.

She returned to the apartment she shared with her canary and her dog.

Then one night she was to go to the theater with an Algonquin friend, but she did not show up. It was late at night before her friend learned why.

That night she had telephoned for food to be sent up to her room. She put the telephone receiver back on the cradle. The waiter found her in the bathroom. She had slashed her wrists with a razor that had belonged to Edwin Parker.

Once again there was gossip, and this time, debate. Some of her friends argued that she must have known she would have been saved by the waiter bringing up supper. Other friends suggested it would have been unlike her to have thought so far ahead. One of them pointed out that she was ever a creature of the moment, and one of the most disorganized women who ever lived. It was his opinion that one moment, she was hungry, and therefore ordered food. The next moment, she was in a mood of darkest despair, and therefore cut her wrists. No relationship existed between act one and act two, and while engaged in act two, act one was completely forgotten.

Much was said for both points of view, but the important fact, upon which all were agreed, was that anyone who even thinks of suicide is in need of help. She was back in hospital again, and her friends went there to be of what cheer they might —such as by suggesting that anyone might well slash her wrists if the alternative was going to that particular show. It was important in the twenties to be amusing.

Dorothy Parker received them sitting up in bed. She had put gay blue ribbons over the bandages on her wrists, and she fluttered them at her friends. She had been a fool, but that was over now; she was prepared to resume her role as jester. Falling in with her mood, and in the tradition of the twenties, Mr.

Benchley suggested she cut deeper next time. Well, she tried, Mrs. Parker said, but the trouble was that Eddie hadn't even been able to sharpen his own razors.

It was as if they all wished to reach out to her, and she to them, but that the protocol of their generation prevented this.

Returned from hospital, she resumed the pattern of her days. Outwardly, she seemed the well-loved Dottie, although it was presently observed that in addition to chain smoking, she was now beginning to drink. She did not drink much in public, but there was often a reason why: she sometimes arrived at parties in such condition that another drink would have been too many. Everyone thought well of her for this, because the ability to hold one's liquor was also a criterion of the twenties. No one was willing then to state that excessive smoking and drinking are slow ways of committing suicide.

Perhaps none of her friends except Mr. Benchley would have understood her perfume. She ordered soaps and perfumes from Cyclax of London, and her favorite scent was tuberose. Mrs. Parker's and Mr. Benchley's researches into the world of the undertaker would have at once disclosed that undertakers use the heavy scent of tuberose to mask the reek of the corpse.

A portrait of Dorothy Parker, painted in October of her thirtieth year by Neysa McMein, showed a tense and wary woman.

4

In 1924, a new kind of society was emerging in New York City. It was a compound of the wealthy, the fashionable, the notorious, and the talented, and it could best be seen at Jack and Charlie's. Its diverse elements included the younger members of wealthy and socially prominent New York families; visiting actors and actresses from the London stage; motion picture people in from the Coast, as Hollywood was called; celebrated gangsters and their equally celebrated molls; champion athletes; people in the headlines of the moment; and a good many Algonquinites—including Dorothy Parker.

All of these people may originally have been drawn together by the excellent foods and liquors that Jack Kriendler and Charles Berns provided, but food and drink equally good could have been found elsewhere in New York for less money. So there was something else: a kind of glitter. It all followed Jack and Charlie when they moved their establishment three blocks uptown to 21 West Fifty-second Street and called it The Iron Gate or, more simply, "21."

To a certain extent, the glitter was provided by the presence of High Society's princelings, because Society was then believed to be important. High Society's comings and goings were minutely reported in the press. Urchins, shopgirls, tradesmen, mechanics, clerks, and what used to be the servant class would gather on the street on opening night at the Metropolitan Opera House to see Society arrive in its limousines and ermine-trimmed velvet cloaks. They did not come to laugh, but to gape wistfully and wonderingly at the rich. True, the comic strip "Bringing Up Father" satirized Society and the efforts of the humble to climb into it, but the strip would have had no meaning if the public gaze had not been fixed upon Society.

But "in those days," Dorothy Parker's friend Donald Ogden Stewart said, "the borders were merging together in the interests of having a good time. I think it was partly the breaking down of the barriers after the war, but certainly that stuffy Belmont-Newport thing was dead, and young Al Vanderbilt and Sonny Whitney didn't draw any particular lines. The speakeasy was a kind of club where what counted was not social position, but whether the people one met there were fun to be with."

Mr. Stewart was fun to be with, and so, of course, was his friend Mrs. Parker. She could turn to a table companion who had called her attention to a woman wearing a cape trimmed with monkey fur, and murmur, "Really? I thought they were beards," or assure a hostess proud of her crystal wine glasses, "Oh yes, paper cups really wouldn't do."

The young socialites found this sort of wit as enchanting as it was unexpected, but neither Dorothy Parker nor anyone else was taken up by them simply on the basis of being amusing. As one of the Algonquin group said, "the Whitney set would not go for cheap guys. I like to think that the set was more exclusive than the group that was later called Café Society, and now the Beautiful People."

Indeed it was: the two groups should never be confused, although what became known as Café Society was even then present among Jack and Charlie's clientele. For purposes of distinction, Café Society could be said to include all of the well-publicized, whereas the socialites to whom Mr. Stewart introduced his friend Mrs. Parker were, like himself, well-bred and well-educated people who demanded of others a genuine intelligence, a discriminating tolerance, and good manners.

So within the emergent new society that included the simply notorious, there was a kind of inner but open-ended aristocracy. Entrance to this inner group did not depend on wealth, birth, or social position, but upon performance. Yet some members of this inner group were enormously wealthy, and so out of a speak-easy acquaintance, a somewhat symbiotic relationship developed between the literary and theatrical group (to which Mr. Stewart belonged) and the wealthy young people (in whose company Mr. Stewart, as an Exeter, Yale, and Skull and Bones man himself, also belonged). The Algonquinites provided the young socialites with entertainment, and in turn the socialites provided them with an audience, free food, free drink, house parties on Long Island estates, and invitations to visit at Paris and at Cap d'Antibes. The rich would also occasionally back plays, buy paintings, sponsor magazines, and otherwise engage in the stuff of Bohemia.

Dorothy Parker's reactions to this were very mixed. Mr. Stewart often escorted her to the Manhattan town houses and to the Long Island estates of his wealthy friends, but she said the rich made her feel nervous and uncomfortable. She told him she hated the rich. She may have told him this as a way of assuring him that she would rather be in his company than that of anyone else, but the fact of the matter is that she did form close friendships with the Robert Lovetts, the Averill Harrimans, and Jock Whitney and his sister Joan, among others of the Long Island–Manhattan High Society. Perhaps she hated rich people in general, while liking some wealthy people in particular. In any case, she accepted their invitations.

One person who nicely appreciated the implications of the emergent new society was Harold Ross. What he saw helped him to work out in his mind a format for a new magazine. It was to be a magazine of the city, to be called *The New Yorker*. The magazine would be smart, and as his wife Jane Grant said, snobbish. It would not be written for the little old lady in Dubuque. It would be written, Mr. Ross said, for the man who knew his way around town "or wanted to." Such a man was Mr. Ross himself.

He dreamed his dreams, and in the summer of 1924 they began to come true for him. *The New Yorker*'s eventual appearance on the newsstands was precisely due to the marriage of wit and wealth that was taking place in the city, and to the use Mr. Ross made of it. Briefly, he found an angel within the circumference of the Algonquin group's expanding circle—a New Yorker named Raoul Fleischmann, heir to a baking fortune. Mr. Ross told him that the new magazine's board of editors would include fascinating people Mr. Fleischmann had met or known about through Mr. Ross or whose names were already public property, such well-publicized Algonquin figures as FPA, Mr. Woollcott, Mr. Broun, Edna Ferber, Marc Connelly, Laurence Stallings, George Kaufman, Alice Duer Miller, and Dorothy Parker. Telling Mr. Fleischmann this was, Mr. Ross admitted, the only dishonest thing he ever did, inasmuch as none of these people had been asked to serve on an editorial board at the time Mr. Ross told Mr. Fleischmann they all belonged to it, and inasmuch as some of them could not legally have served on such a board anyway, because they were under contract to other publishers. Dorothy Parker not only did not serve as a member of that board, but did not contribute a single line to the magazine during its first year of publication, nor, to Mr. Ross' despair, did many of the others. Yet she and they were all a part of Mr. Ross' magazine in that their companionship helped to shape his thought. And Dorothy Parker's irreverence, her impudence, her hedonism, her flippancy, and her contempt for stupid, stuffy and boring people and dull convention, all marched exactly with the attitude of the Algonquin group and with that of the magazine in its first days.

Dorothy Parker's acceptance at Jack and Charlie's; her acceptance there by the innermost group, the New Yorkers of gracious wealth; Harold Ross' thinking of her as a staff member of a new, sophisticated magazine of the city; her wide acquaintance in New York's publishing, journalistic, and theatrical worlds—all this testified to her central position in what *The New Yorker* magazine would call "goings on about town." She and her friends lived in a pouring stream of thought; they floated, as it were, just ahead of the rushing flood crest of such a stream, aware of what was new before it came to the attention of most others. By the time the flood crest reached any particular point, they would have marked and buoyed the channel. Thus it was that an occasional Algonquinite, the cartoonist John Held, Jr., satirized the sheiks and shebas of the twenties before Betty Co-Ed and Joe College had appeared in any great numbers in their bobbed hair and coonskin coats, drinking gin out of hip flasks in the rumble seats of parked coupés. By the time Flaming Youth did appear in full blaze, Mr. Held, Dorothy Parker, and various of the Algonquin group had already gone on record as being disgusted by its empty-headedness and bad manners.

They were equally sensitive to the appearance of what promised to be truly valuable, and they were as quick to pay respect to it. Donald Ogden Stewart had been spending summers abroad; last year he had met Ernest Hemingway and become his friend. More important, he had read Hemingway's *Three Stories and Ten Poems*, recently published in Paris, and knew how good they were. F. Scott Fitzgerald had read Hemingway's work, too. Both men advised New York publishers that Hemingway should be encouraged and be published in America.

Now, in 1924, Mr. Stewart returned to New York from a summer visit, filled with more news of the Paris group. Paris was exciting; Paris was the city for the artist, for the writer. In America if a young man sat around painting or writing, his parents were apt to rebuke him for not getting out of the house and looking for a job (Hemingway's parents had done this), whereas in Paris the creative artist was respected, even honored. The French did not take the view that a man was not successful if he was not making money: near-poverty was a normal European condition. Europeans valued the life of the mind. A dollar in Paris went a long, long way farther than a dollar in New York. Life was civilized. It was not, as Hemingway said, the kind of YMCA show that life was in the United States. There was no such nonsense as Prohibition, and good wine could be had for very little money. Mr. Stewart had gone with Hemingway to the Fiesta of San Fermín at Pamplona, and they had taken part in the amateur bullfighting in the mornings. Mr. Stewart said he had a couple of cracked ribs as a souvenir, but that the local wine had had great therapeutic values. He returned from Europe more convinced of Hemingway's writing, and helped to persuade the publisher Horace Liveright to sign Hemingway to a contract.

Listening to stories of the American expatriate group in Paris, and reading Hemingway's early work, had an effect on Dorothy Parker. Hemingway's basic attitude toward life and his way of writing were remarkably similar to hers. The attitude was that love can have no good end, and that the end of life is death. Just as she was doing, so Hemingway was going straight to reality for his material, in apparent belief that the facts, if carefully selected and arranged, would speak to the reader. The humor and irony in Hemingway's work were as sardonic as her own. She sensed an artistic affinity, and thought of Paris.

She also thought long upon the kind of life she was leading. Her life was an amusing one in many ways, but she thought it was an irresponsible one that went nowhere in particular, and that she was just passing time. Even though she lived in the center of a group of people who were abnormally talented and sensitive to the slightest shifts of thought and taste, it seemed to her that life was just a business in which one day was very like every other. She wished life made more sense, and she said as much to Mr. Benchley in a poem called "For R.C.B.," in which she chided him (and herself) for his apparent refusal to take life seriously. She would not permit this poem to appear in her collected works, but she returned to the same theme in her sarcastic little poem "Comment":

> Oh, life is a glorious cycle of song,
> A medley of extemporanea;
> And love is a thing that can never go wrong,
> And I am Marie of Roumania.

Nor was this all, for at this time, when for most of her friends the sun seemed to stand still at a moment of glorious summer, and while she herself was so often the gayest of those gamboling about in the sunlight, she continually entertained thoughts of death, as in the poem "Coda":

> There's little in taking or giving,
>   There's little in water or wine;
> This living, this living, this living,
>   Was never a project of mine.
> Oh, hard is the struggle, and sparse is
>   The gain of the one at the top.
> For art is a form of catharsis,
>   And love is a permanent flop,

> And work is the province of cattle,
>   And rest's for a clam in a shell,
> So I'm thinking of throwing the battle—
>   Would you kindly direct me to hell?

However lightly she might write of it, self-doubt was always there, and a suspicion that she and her friends ought to examine their lives more closely.

If age thirty is a difficult time for many women, it was particularly difficult for her. She was at the height of her beauty, but she was also neither married nor divorced nor celibate. Her marriage had been one disaster, and her affair with Charles MacArthur turned out to be another. Other people came from families of a certain position, but she had entered life as an anomaly and there was nothing in her background to make her feel that she had come from anywhere or belonged to anything. Other people had houses, and she had a stupid room in a cheap apartment house. The closest thing she had to a family was the company of her friends, but her relationship with most of them was an abstract, city kind of thing. She was uneasy and silent whenever she found herself in a household that contained children. She had had an abortion. She lived in a city whose one constant was change. Change was exciting, but after a while it was *plus la même chose.* New York was also one of the most expensive cities on earth, and as a free-lance writer she had no more economic security than a prospector. Except for occasional verse, she was not writing much.

The one thing to which she could cling with any certainty was her talent, but she knew it to be different from the talents of her friends. She also knew that something separated her from all other people, and she stated it in her poem "Interior":

> Her mind lives tidily, apart
> From cold and noise and pain,
> And bolts the door against her heart,
> Out wailing in the rain.

This was more than a statement of loneliness; it was also an attitude that could breed internal violence. If she thought of herself as being lonely and unique, she nevertheless thought of herself as being a superior person, for in her poem "For a Sad Lady" she said:

> And let her loves, when she is dead,
>   Write this above her bones:
> "No more she lives to give us bread
>   Who asked her only stones."

There were those of the Round Table group who found this latter attitude to be insufferable. One of them frankly disliked her, and said he "could not get excited about a sour little girl who was always going around slashing her wrists." But most of her acquaintances were bemused, rather than bothered, by Dorothy Parker's darker moods.

"Oh, darling," she could say to a woman, "how good it is to see you again! I've been thinking of you all week—of how good and kind and generous you are. Why is it that we never see each other?"

Then, as the woman moved away, she could mutter, as if to herself, "Do you suppose she came out of the woodwork?"

Not everyone found evidence of the most contemptuous social insincerity in this sort of behavior. That was too easy an explanation for the complicated minds in Dorothy Parker's circle. One theory was that she could really believe that a person *was* good, kind and generous, and that she really *did* wish to see more of that person, but that she was afraid of commitment, that she felt it necessary to say something nasty about someone she liked, in order to preserve a wary distance.

Donald Ogden Stewart supposed that her problems stemmed from her basic inability to love.

Striking an equally Freudian note—for Freud's theories were percolating through New York in the twenties—her friend George Oppenheimer, a publisher and playwright, said he considered her to be "a masochist whose passion for unhappiness knew no bounds."

Another theory was offered by Vincent Sheean, foreign correspondent and author of *Personal History*, who was not a member of the Algonquin group, but who had met Dorothy Parker in New York and who had been intrigued by her. Mr. Sheean agreed with Gilbert Seldes that she was essentially an artist, whereas no one else in her circle was. People like Mr. Benchley, Mr. Stewart, FPA, Mr. Woollcott, Mr. Ross, Mr. Broun, and Mr. Berlin were not so much artists as they were highly competent craftsmen and popular entertainers. Mr. Sheean supposed that she knew this, and that her knowledge made her unhappy. Certainly she said as much in several poems, and, much later in life, in conversation as well.

As much of an artist as she may have been, she gave very little outward evidence of it. Throughout 1924, except for occasional verse, she made scant use of her typewriter. She wrote one short story for the *American Mercury*, an unrelievedly bitter piece called "Mr. Durant." It described a man who impregnated his secretary, gave her twenty-five dollars toward the expense of an abortion, and forgot about her. It is a depressing story to read, and perhaps after writing it she was too depressed herself to write much else. Instead of working, she spent many afternoons in *Life*'s offices, talking and joking with Mr. Benchley and Mr. Sherwood. She went to Jack and Charlie's in the evening to do what was done there: eat and drink and talk with people who were fun to be with. She went to parties on Long Island, and if she seemed in a blue mood one day, she was as wry and tart and bright as ever the next. She went to the theater, and, late in the year, she embarked upon a quite ambitious literary project: she wrote a play together with Elmer Rice.

Mr. Rice was already an established playwright. He had written two earlier Broadway hits, *The Adding Machine* and *On Trial*. This was astonishing, for if the chances of writing a Broadway hit today are 97 to 1, the odds were even greater in the early twenties when a great many more plays would open each season. Mr. Rice was therefore regarded as something of a phenomenon, and New York's inner circle thought that nothing but good things would happen as a result of any collaboration between the trenchant Mr. Rice and funny, clever little Mrs. Parker. The name of their play, *Close Harmony*, seemed most appropriate.

The play opened on December 1, 1924, and the critics applauded it. Unfortunately, very few other people did. A problem might have been that there were four other openings that night, including two smash hits: Irving Berlin's *Music Box Revue* and *Lady Be Good*, starring the dancing Astaires. In any case, *Close Harmony* began to die at the box office almost at once. It lasted four weeks in a state of declining health, and toward the end Dorothy Parker sent one of her telegrams. This one was addressed to the Round Table, and it said CLOSE HARMONY DID A COOL NINETY DOLLARS AT THE MATINEE. ASK THE BOYS IN THE BACK ROOM WHAT THEY WILL HAVE.

Her private reaction was not all that brave and gay, however, for when pressed about the play, all she would say was, "It was dull. You have my apologies." It was not a farce, it was not a comment on the war between the sexes, it was nothing at all. She would not discuss it. She did say that Mr. Rice was a difficult man. It was the nearest thing she said to an admission that her venture into the theater had been a personal disaster. The theater, so much a concern of the Algonquin group, and seemingly so near at hand to almost any of them, had proved to be beyond her artistic grasp.

Throughout the ensuing year, she seemed to be drifting. Her only magazine assignments were to help *Life* publish two parody issues, one taking off on the lurid New York tabloid newspapers of the day; the other a parody of the "true confessions" magazines. The second issue, promising readers "Thrills, Sensations, Confessions and Other Popular Forms of Bunk," carried a photograph showing Marc Connelly explaining to Dorothy Parker and her dog that two men seated at a table (Harpo Marx and Robert Sherwood) had been encouraged by him to read good books. Behind the table was a bookshelf. Mr. Marx and Mr. Sherwood were reading a scandal sheet. Dorothy appeared wearing a huge black straw hat, beads, and a baggy dress with a pleated skirt and a waistline around the hips. Apparently her dress was not intended to be a part of the satire—it was a fashionable dress of the time, but the fashion of 1925 would have done nothing for her, even if she had been able to wear her clothes well.

Nor could the issue of *Life* have done much for her, either. The humor throughout was as heavy as the example above. Her contribution, apart from having her picture taken, was a parody on the kind of sex confession article then appearing in *True Story* magazine. She might well have wondered if *True Story* was worth derision. Perhaps it all seemed funny at the time. It is difficult to say, because topical satire of ephemeral trivia has as much trouble crossing a space of time as a joke has in crossing a language barrier. In any case, the humor is not vividly obvious today, whereas genuine humor is timeless, and inasmuch as Dorothy Parker said and wrote a great many imperishable lines, and was well aware of the difference between a gag and real wit, she could only have found the parody issues of *Life* to be tiresome. Her real reward no doubt lay in the idle fun of gossiping with Mr. Sherwood, Mr. Benchley, Mr. Connelly, and Mr. Marx as they planned the two issues.

Throughout 1925 she was, however, writing those poems that, with others, would presently be published by Boni and Liveright under the title *Enough Rope*. Taken together, all of her poems amounted to a kind of diary of shifting moods, most of them ranging from black to blue, some of them sweet and poignant, others ironic and flippant, and all of them written out of experience. Here, and in her subsequent books of verse, she thought a great deal about love, and passed her considered judgment on it in the nineteen-twenties. In "Unfortunate Coincidence," she remarked:

> By the time you swear you're his,
>   Shivering and sighing,
> And he vows his passion is
>   Infinite, undying—
> Lady, make a note of this:
>   One of you is lying.

In "Two Volume Novel," she added:

> The sun's gone dim, and
>   The moon's turned black;
> For I loved him, and
>   He didn't love back.

In "Rhyme Against Living," she decided:

> If wild my breast and sore my pride,
> I bask in dreams of suicide;
> If cool my heart and high my head,
> I think, "How lucky are the dead!"

Yet, in "Theory," she entertained this suspicion about herself:

> Into love and out again,
>   Thus I went, and thus I go.
> Spare your voice, and hold your pen—
>   Well and bitterly I know
> All the songs were ever sung
> All the words were ever said;
> Could it be, when I was young,
>   Someone dropped me on my head?

There were many more such poems, written in that allegedly golden Era of Wonderful Nonsense, when everyone was believed to be Making Whoopee. Some of her friends regarded Dorothy Parker as personifying the spirit of the twenties—laughing, playing games, drinking along with some of the stoutest drinkers during a time of heavy drinking and representing all that is meant in the best sense of the word "sophistication." It was therefore difficult for them to believe that she actually meant everything she said and wrote.

But one night, when the moon again turned black, she took an overdose of sleeping pills.

This time, her friends were seriously alarmed. Mr. Benchley was not as amused as he might have been by her poking her head out of the oxygen tent and brightly asking the doctor, "May I have a flag for my tent?" In the tradition of the twenties, Mr. Benchley said, "Dottie, if you don't stop this sort of thing, you'll make yourself sick," but he went on to read her the riot act.

He described how he and others had found her comatose in her apartment.

"If you realized how repulsive you looked, you'd never try this again," he said. "You were a mess. You were lying there drooling, and if you had any consideration for your friends, you'd shoot yourself—but don't be this messy."

Mr. Benchley went on to describe a scene as wretched as it was disgusting and sordid, and she paid close attention. She would one day use what Mr. Benchley said about her, but it is unlikely that she was consciously taking notes when she listened to him in the hospital, because she was not then thinking in terms of a future—at least, not one that made sense. This living was no pr ct of hers. For all that it might consist of the companionship of witty, talented, wealthy, and charming people, life was not clearly preferable to death. In the end, everyone died anyway, so there was no point to anything. It did not matter if people wrote plays or started magazines or had Long Island estates or said funny things at Jack and Charlie's, for the plays would close and no one would remember them and the magazines would run their moment in the sun and then fold someday, and the Long Island estates would eventually become ruins, and wit was just doing calisthenics with words. Love was supposed to be wonderful, but love could hurt, and in the end love died, too. Love was a permanent flop. Nothing really mattered.

But her mood could change so quickly. It could change within a few lines of a single poem.

She decided to give life another chance. "Into love and out again/Thus I went and thus I go," she said, and so it was with her. She would give love another chance, too, but this time on her own terms.

"I require only three things of a man," she said. "He must be handsome, ruthless, and stupid."

She looked about New York, and her choice settled on a member of that innermost circle of the emergent new society. His name was Seward Collins, and he failed to meet her three requirements in every single particular. Mr. Collins was very rich: he was the heir to a national chain of tobacco shops. He paid her debts and gave her money. More than this, he gave her his complete respect, for in addition to being wealthy, Mr. Collins was a discriminating patron of the arts. He was editor of *The Bookman*, a national literary magazine that printed the ranking writers of the day. It seemed to some that Dorothy Parker had at last struck upon an alliance that, if not yet a marriage, was nonetheless made in heaven, for Mr. Collins, in addition to all else, plainly adored her.

Perhaps they might have thought differently if they had heard what she told Mr. Stewart about the rich. Then, they might have wondered why, if she felt that way, she accepted their invitations.

5

They all came out of the dim coolness of the restaurant into the white hot light of Cap d'Antibes, and there on the stone sidewalk, against the building line, was a man with a tray full of nuts. He had worked them into intricate designs according to their kinds and colors and sizes. It must have taken him hours to arrange them on his tray. Perhaps his wife and children had helped. He regarded the six Americans with the tentative, not too hopeful smile of the French merchant.

"Mesdames? M'sieurs?"

One of the Americans lurched into him, and the tray upset, and the nuts went sliding, spilling, bouncing, and rolling over the sidewalk and into the street.

F. Scott Fitzgerald thought it was marvelously funny. The vendor looked so horrified, so amazed, so uncomprehending, and so angry all at once. A torrent of French ensued, subsiding into a mutter and then into a grudging acceptance as Mr. Fitzgerald pressed a banknote into the vendor's hand.

"Wasn't that funny?" Mr. Fitzgerald asked his friends.

No one else was laughing, not Mr. Fitzgerald's wife, Zelda, nor Dorothy Parker, nor Seward Collins, nor their hosts, Sara and Gerald Murphy.

"Wasn't that funny?" Mr. Fitzgerald pleaded. "It was funny, wasn't it?"

The vendor was on his hands and knees, scrabbling around after his wares.

"But I gave him a hundred francs," Mr. Fitzgerald explained.

Dorothy Parker was disgusted. Scott could be attractive and sweet and she knew he wanted to be nice, but the trouble with Scott was that he was boring. He wanted to be funny, but he didn't know how; he couldn't understand what was funny and what was not. He could be funny in his books, but here, in real life, he had thought it was funny to upset that tray of nuts and he thought that giving the man money made up for it.

They all went back to the Murphys' elegant Villa Amèrica. Dorothy wondered what the Murphys saw in the Fitzgeralds. She thought Zelda was working overtime trying to be a *femme fatale*, but of course Zelda was insane. Zelda and Scott seemed so young and talented and beautiful; surely that was what the Murphys and everyone else saw in them; but Scott was boring and his wife was, well, a tragedy. And Scott sometimes acted as if he were deliberately trying to embarrass the Murphys.

Dorothy rather liked the Murphys, even though they were very rich. Gerald had inherited the Mark Cross leather goods company, but he was not a businessman. He was a tall, kindly young man, handsome, but with a certain weakness in his features. He had gone to Yale and studied architecture, but he wanted to be a painter. This was why he and Sara had come to France. They had wanted to get away from New York Society and had come to France to paint. Sara detested Society and said so: Dorothy appreciated a forthright woman. Gerald did not look like a painter. He was always neatly shaved and combed and fashionably dressed, like a guest at a summer hotel. Sara and the Murphy children called him Dow-Dow, which seemed unfortunately apt. But he was very pleasant, and generous to a fault. The Murphys had their villa on the Riviera and a marvelous establishment on the Quai des Grands-Augustins in Paris, and in each place they presided over a kind of perpetual house party for all the American crowd in France. They served caviar and champagne, and everyone centered on the Murphys. They were great friends with John Dos Passos, Ada and Archibald MacLeish, Donald Ogden Stewart, Ernest and Hadley Hemingway, and the Fitzgeralds. Very little painting seemed to get done. Instead, as Hemingway put it, the Murphys had the quality of making every day a fiesta. Like Dorothy, Hemingway seemed suspicious and uneasy in the company of the rich, but like her, he certainly accepted their invitations.

It seemed to Dorothy Parker as if everyone was in France in that summer of 1926. Don Stewart was there with his blonde and beautiful bride, Beatrice Ames. Dorothy and Seward Collins had been sitting in the Cotton Bar at Cannes, and in came Don and Bea, and it was somehow no more surprising than if they were all meeting at Jack and Charlie's. Gilbert Seldes and his wife turned up: they, too, were visiting the Murphys. As Gertrude Stein might have put it, they were all in New York and then they were all in France, and whenever they were anywhere, there they were.

They had all been in New York in February, when Hemingway came bounding into town to break a contract with Boni and Liveright in order to make a new contract with Scribner's, and Dorothy and Mr. Benchley had met him at a party. Hemingway met all her requirements of a man, for he was more than six feet tall, young, strong, handsome as a movie star, ruthless and, with respect to women, quite stupid. She was tremendously impressed: she had been curious to meet the man Don Stewart had talked so much about, and whose subject matter, style, and philosophy were so similar in many ways to her own. The bulk of his work was superior to the bulk of hers; it was the kind of work she would like to be able to do all the time, if only she could. She wanted to go to Paris and write. Hemingway was nearly three weeks in New York, and when he sailed back to France on the *Roosevelt*, the passenger list included Seward Collins and Dorothy Parker, and Mr. Benchley, who professed surprise upon finding himself out at sea aboard a ship.

So then they were in Paris and Dorothy met the Murphys, and now they were all visiting the Murphys on the Riviera: the Stewarts, the MacLeishes, the Seldeses, the Fitzgeralds, and Seward Collins and Dorothy Parker. Hemingway was in Spain, watching the bullfights, and it seemed to be a good idea to go there, too.

In the free and easy way that one thing could lead into something else, with nothing being planned because in the company of the rich there is never a need for planning when there is always enough money to do whatever anyone wants to do whenever anyone wants to do it, Dorothy found herself and Mr. Collins saying good-bye to the Murphys and leaving Cap d'Antibes together with the Seldeses, bound for Spain to see a *corrida* at Barcelona. Mr. Collins had invited the Seldeses to go with them. Since Mr. Collins was the only one of the four who spoke French, and since he was paying for first-class accommodations for everyone, they let him make the arrangements.

Dorothy did not resent the Seldeses coming along; rather, she was glad of their company, for she and Seward had been quarreling. They had quarreled all the way across the ocean, and again in Paris. She was finding him tiresome. The Seldeses' company would reduce, or at least distribute, the tension. Her fears were for what she knew she would see in the bullring. She could not see a stray dog without saying she wanted to take it home; she could not pass a horse without going up to it and talking to it. And now she was sitting in a first-class carriage with a man she really did not care for, who was taking her to see and hear animals being killed.

In those days, before the Spanish government concerned itself about tourists' sensibilities, the horses did not wear protective padding. The horses used in the bullfights were antique and rickety ones, and in Hemingway's opinion, the function they served was a comic one. Unfortunately, the comedy of the horses was lost upon Dorothy. She saw the first bull explode from the dark gate, pause, and then with an incredible gathering speed burst into the first horse. She saw the horns go into the belly and lift, and things coming out of the horse, and she heard the noises that the horse and the crowd made, and she became completely hysterical.

"Out she went, and Seward with her," as Mr. Seldes said, while the Seldeses remained in the excellent seats Mr. Collins had provided, to watch what would eventually happen to the bull.

"The next day, on to Madrid," Mr. Seldes said. "My wife was pregnant at the time and she was lying on one side of the compartment, the rest of us on the other. It was quite hot. I rose and kissed her on the forehead, and at that moment a guard walked by and pulled open the door and said, 'If you are going to commit indecencies, please pull down the shade.' "

Mr. Seldes, of course, did not know at the time what the guard was saying, but Mr. Collins did, and perhaps it was just one thing too many for him. Dorothy had insisted on separate rooms; she had said she wanted to go to Spain and see a bullfight, and he had taken her and she had gone into hysterics, and somehow everything seemed to be all his fault and never hers, and now, when in the privacy of their own compartment a man wanted to comfort his wife on a hot, uncomfortable day on a jolting train, a guard objected to that. Mr. Collins angrily asked the guard for his badge number. Arrived at the Madrid station, the guard glared at them and went loping off, and they all thought the guard was afraid of being reported. But not at all—he had merely gone in search of another guard to help him with Mr. Collins, whom they hauled off the train and frog-marched between them down the platform, holding him by the collar and the seat of his pants and bouncing him along. Dorothy and the Seldeses trailed along in the wake to a police station, where it was explained that the four of them would be expected to get out of Spain the following day or appear in court. They all went angrily off to the American consulate, where they were told they were lucky to have been given the option.

"Now get the hell out of here," the consul said. He spoke with the tired accents of a consul whose patience was sorely tried each summer by Spanish officialdom and by his touring countrymen.

"Seward and Dottie had separate rooms at the hotel," Mr. Seldes said, "but that night Dottie said, 'I'm going to sleep with him no matter if the police come'—she was so angry at the whole thing."

Whereupon, Mr. Collins' chivalry having been duly rewarded, the four of them the following morning left a land where animals were tortured and stabbed to death, and where pregnant wives cannot be kissed on the forehead by their husbands while riding in private compartments, arriving in due course in Paris, where Dorothy sent Mr. Collins home.

No one remembers the cause of the quarrel—merely that there

was one. In the midst of it, Dorothy took off a wristwatch that Mr. Collins had given her, and threw it out their fifth-story hotel window. Mr. Collins had the poor judgment to rush out of the room, down the stairs, into the street, find the watch, and bring it back to her. And that was probably the real end of whatever chances he ever had of marrying her. When Mr. Collins brought the watch back, Mr. Seldes said, "Oh, what contempt she had for him."

Mr. Collins was not universally missed by the Americans in Paris. Beatrice Ames Stewart liked him, and everyone admitted that he was in many ways quite bright, but he impressed some members of the group as being a mama's boy, and not at all the right man for Dorothy.

"Oh, Sewie," Beatrice said. "I've never seen anyone love anybody so much as Sewie loved Dorothy. He was so good to her. He loved her so, oh, how he loved her, and he was just a little dust mop that she used to wipe up the floor with."

Dorothy Parker did not want to talk about it. Late in life, all she would say about Mr. Collins was that after Edwin Parker had been committed to a hospital to be treated for morphine addiction, "I ran off to the Riviera with a Trotskyite." But it would seem that Mr. Parker had not been addicted to morphine, and that Mr. Collins was not then a Trotskyite, although he did later become friends with Leon Trotsky's secretary in Mexico, and still later would pass through a Trotskyite phase and on into the most distant of political right wings—a common enough progression.

Mr. Collins' obedient departure would seem to have raised the question of how Dorothy would support herself in France for the rest of that summer. In part, the answer could have been provided by her publisher, Boni and Liveright, for *Enough Rope* appeared late in the year and promised to be an enormous success. But the rest of the answer, if not all of it, could lie in that word "group." She joined the Stewarts' honeymoon, and they all went back to the Riviera to stay with the Murphys, and in the fall they were all in Paris again.

In October there was a party at Ada and Archibald MacLeish's apartment in Paris, where the Stewarts and the Fitzgeralds were present, but Dorothy Parker was not, and Hemingway raised his glass and proposed a toast.

"Here's to Dorothy Parker," he said. "Life will never become her so much as her almost leaving it."

Then, plunging insensately ahead into an embarrassed silence, Hemingway read a poem he had written. It was about Dorothy's not having returned his portable typewriter (which she had), and having worn down the keys, and Hemingway thought his poem was quite funny. Everyone else thought it was scatological and scurrilous.

"Really," Mr. Stewart said, "she didn't deserve it. It was mean. It was terribly mean, right in front of all those people, and Dottie not there. Ernest's humor, you know, had its gaps, and as you know, Ernest was not one not to get angry at his friends. But I called him on it, and that was the end of our beautiful friendship."

At the time, Hemingway had been putting that friendship to the test. Some weeks earlier, at a birthday party the Murphys had given for Mr. Stewart's bride, Hemingway had the boorishness to break the news to the honeymooners that he and Hadley were going to be divorced, and this news quite satisfactorily ruined Beatrice's evening.

Of course, the story of Hemingway's toast and his poem got back to Dorothy Parker, for anything said about any one of them became known to all of them: their great interest was themselves. Dorothy was hurt. She had offered Hemingway friendship and deep respect, and he had stabbed her in the back. For once she had nothing to say. Not, that is, until at last she and the Stewarts took ship back to the United States.

There was a party at Cherbourg, where Dorothy and the Stewarts boarded the *Rotterdam*. For whatever reasons of his own, Hemingway was there, too. At the end of it, the Paris group clustered on the dock, waving to the people at the ship's rail, and Hemingway, still implacably pursuing his joke, shouted up to Dorothy:

"What am I going to do? I have no typewriter!"

Dorothy leaned over the rail and threw down the new portable typewriter she had bought.

She turned coolly back to the astonished Stewarts, and said, "Good God, I have just thrown away my only means of livelihood."

And that was very much the way it was when they were all in New York and then they were all in Paris and on the Riviera and in Spain that year, when, in the company of the rich, every day had the quality of a fiesta so that not much painting or writing got done. When they were all together, wherever they were, they traveled and looked at things and drank a good deal and ate very well, and the rich paid for everything, and during the perpetual fiesta a marriage ended in divorce and a friendship was broken and a one-sided love affair collapsed. It was not until much later, when they were all older, and apart, that some of them began to write about the others.

Two of them wrote about the Murphys. Scott Fitzgerald made the Murphys the pathetic protagonists of his novel *Tender Is the Night*. In his book *A Moveable Feast*, Hemingway called them "the rich" and held them partly responsible for the ruin of his marriage to Hadley. He also said how much he loathed John Dos Passos for having introduced him to the generous and kindly Murphys. He wrote with bullying condescension about drunken Scott Fitzgerald and with bitter contempt about poor, crazy Zelda.

Dorothy Parker never wrote about the Murphys, whom she liked. She had gone to Paris to see the literary life that everyone had talked about in New York, thinking that she might want to live there herself and write, but she did not stay in Paris and she never wrote about Europe—possibly because she had not really been there. Europe had been hotels and trains and apartments and a villa by the sea, and Europeans were waiters and officials and janitors and servants; Europe had been another backdrop for the continual having of fun. She had not, during this time, seen much of Ernest Hemingway, whom she greatly admired. She had instead seen a good deal of the oafish side of him that he liked to call Old Dr. Hemingstein. When she threw her typewriter over the ship's rail, she could well have been telling Old Dr. Hemingstein to shut up, so that Ernest Hemingway could use the typewriter.

6

When she returned from France in the fall of 1926, her first volume of poetry, *Enough Rope,* was on its way to its huge success. In America, poets are usually published at their publishers' expense, but *Enough Rope* became a national best seller and ran to eight printings, which many well-regarded novels never do. The book made Dorothy Parker something of a national institution; it made her and her publisher a good deal of money, and it also helped to make her more than ever the prisoner of her notoriety.

"Dorothy Parker runs her little show as if it were a circus," Genevieve Taggard assured her readers in *The New York Herald-Tribune.* "She cracks her whip and the big elephant joke pounds his four legs in glee and the pink ladies of fantastic behavior begin to float in the air like lozenges. . . . Mrs. Parker had begun in the thoroughly familiar Millay manner and worked into something quite her own. . . . Miss Millay remains lyrically, of course, far superior to Mrs. Parker. . . . But there are moods when Dorothy Parker is more acceptable, whisky straight, not champagne."

Writing in *Poetry* magazine, Marie Luhrs said that "in its lightness, its cynicism, its pose, she has done the right thing; she is in a class with the Prince of Wales, the Theater Guild, Gramercy Park, and H. L. Mencken. . . . It is high time that a poet with a monocle looked at the populace, instead of the populace looking at the poet through a *lorgnette.*"

The two ladies' views reflected that of the majority of critics: Dorothy Parker's verse was "of course" inferior to Edna St. Vincent Millay's in a lyrical sense; it was light, flippant, cynical, and really just a joke. Hers was a "little" show. This majority opinion exasperated Alexander Woollcott, who took a proprietary and protective view of his friends, and who was exceedingly fond of little Mrs. Parker. He complained that one did not weigh a poem to determine its value. He thought much of her work was witty, while some of it was "thrilling poetry of a piercing and rueful beauty," but in any case he felt it wrong to call her verse "light" and by implication, to dismiss it as being inconsequential.

Unfortunately for her, Mr. Woollcott's position was a relatively lonely one at the time. Miss Luhrs, Miss Taggard, and the majority of critics were not wrong, but their judgment was only partially right. Many of the poems *were* light, cynical, and joking. Others were variously bitter, truthful, unfair, self-deceptive, beautiful, and passionate. All the critics were right, Mr. Woollcott included. It was perfectly possible for anyone to find whatever he was looking for in *Enough Rope.* The sales record indicated that the general public could find much, in her easily quotable lines, with which to identify itself. This was because Dorothy Parker had, in a volume of poetry, written a kind of autobiography of her life and times, frequently using a monocle to be sure, for the fashion of those times called for a lens that distorted. In the poem "Résumé," she said:

> Razors pain you;
> Rivers are damp;
> Acids stain you;
> And drugs cause cramp.
> Guns aren't lawful;
> Nooses give;
> Gas smells awful;
> You might as well live.

In "They Part," she wrote:

And if, my friends you'd have it end,
   There's naught to hear or tell.
But need you try to black my eye
   In wishing me farewell?

Though I admit an edged wit
   In woe is warranted,
May I be frank? . . . Such words as ". . . ."
   Are better left unsaid.

There's rosemary for you and me;
   But is it usual, dear,
To hire a man, and fill a van
   By way of *souvenir?*

Such flippant lines, funny in a macabre way, were perfectly appropriate to the mood of the twenties, when it was important to appear to be sophisticated and to be able to make jokes about anything. Yet these poems, and the many more that were cool, light and funny, together with such sober poems as "For a Sad Lady" and "The Dark Girl's Rhyme," all alluded to episodes that were not at all funny to Dorothy Parker at the times they occurred. Taken together, her poems demonstrated her ability to look back upon emotional storms and disasters, and then to pass judgments on herself. Many of these judgments were wry and mocking, but when all the poems were read together, they portrayed a woman who said she was suspicious of joy, disillusioned as to love, contemptuous of and sorry for herself, and given to thoughts of death.

In her review, Miss Luhrs had used the words "cynicism" and "pose." Yet what strikes one person as being cynical might seem to be nothing but God's honest truth to someone else; and insofar as pose is concerned, it is always difficult to know whether what one sees is the mask, and not the face—for if pose is a successful disguise, there is reason to suspect it could not have been successful had it been only a pose. Miss Taggard saw fantasy and moods that seemed to her to be as astringent as straight whisky. Mr. Woollcott found beauty, and the public found a voice that expressed what was in, or behind, the public mind. A portrait of Dorothy Parker, painted by G. T. Hartmann in 1927, this year of her first great literary success, showed a moody and sour woman. Clippings in the nation's newspaper and magazine files identified her as a wit, and the author of light verse. The information stored in such files is apt to be as incomplete and as inaccurate, but as permanent, as an epitaph on a tombstone. The newspapers and magazines gave Dorothy Parker a reputation as a comedienne, and she was never able to escape this public reputation, just as she was never wholly able to live down to it. Her poems were not one thing or another, and neither was she. She was cynical, fantastic, sour, comic, witty, and lonely. In passing judgments on herself, she saw quite clearly the comical aspects of every tragedy, and the tragical aspects of every jape. She helped the public of the twenties to see this, too. "The wits of the town," as the philosopher Irwin Edman later wrote, were "delighted to see a Sappho who could combine a heart-break with a wisecrack."

Perhaps the wits of the town paid insufficient attention to the same Sappho who had written:

> All her hours were yellow sands,
> Blown in foolish whorls and tassels;
> Slipping warmly through her hands;
> Patted into little castles.
>
> Shiny day on shiny day
> Tumbled in a rainbow clutter,
> As she flipped them all away,
> Sent them spinning down the gutter.
>
> Leave for her a red young rose,
> Go your way, and save your pity;
> She is happy, for she knows
> That her dust is very pretty.

She called that poem, "Epitaph for a Darling Lady." It could as easily have been an epitaph for an era.

7

As one of the Round Table said, "You can't spend your whole life having lunch at the Algonquin." So some drifted away to other restaurants and other friends; some went to Hollywood to write for the motion pictures; some of them married and moved out of town; others arrived to take their places. The original camaraderie of the Round Table lasted a very few years, perhaps only between the years 1920 and 1923. A masculine inner circle, whose original members were FPA, Alexander Woollcott, and Harold Ross, continued to play night-long poker in an Algonquin hotel room provided them free of charge by the Algonquin's owner, Frank Case. They called their group the Thanatopsis Pleasure and Literary Club at first, then changed its name to the Thanatopsis Poker and Inside Straight Club, and as they all made more money, the stakes mounted. But Thanatopsis changed in membership, too, and by 1927 the poker games had become less funny and more serious, while downstairs in the diningroom, what once had been a congenial group was now a competitive institution that some of its members called the Vicious Circle.

Mr. Sherwood stopped going to the Algonquin; so did Mr. Benchley; Mr. Stewart followed suit. Of the original quartet, only Dorothy Parker remained.

"It wasn't much fun to go there, with everybody on stage,"

Mr. Stewart said. "Everybody was waiting his chance to say the bright remark so that it would be in FPA's column the next day, and there was a kind of—well, it wasn't friendly. There was a kind of strain about it—at least there was for me—and I don't think Dottie ever enjoyed going there. But what the hell else was there to do? Who else was there? They weren't friends, and yet they were much more than acquaintances. Woollcott, for instance, did some awfully nice things for me. There was a terrible sentimental streak in Alec, but at the same time, there was a streak of hate that was malicious."

Over the years, good humor had given way to banter, and now banter had given way to insult. If any one person could be considered instrumental in having brought this change about, that would have been Alexander Woollcott, whose sense of humor was undependable. On one occasion it led him to advise a young lady that her brains were made of popcorn soaked in urine. His customary greeting to a friend was, "Hello, repulsive." His affectionate name for Dorothy Parker was "Sheeny," once he discovered her maiden name was Rothschild. Mr. Woollcott was a perplexing man, given to many kindnesses and generosities, but at the same time he seemed to feel a need to find the minutest chinks in his friends' armor, wherein to insert a poisoned needle. Some gave him back full value for insults received; the novelist Edna Ferber ticked him off as a New Jersey Nero who mistook his pinafore for a toga. But trading insults was not everyone's idea of a good time.

When Mr. Stewart complained that everybody was on stage, he was on target. FPA and Mr. Woollcott incessantly wrote about members of the group in their newspaper columns, detailing their activities and repeating their remarks, and people began to come to the Algonquin solely to sit near the celebrated Round Table to overhear its sparkling witticisms. In this, the public was not always disappointed, for those seated at the table would rather loudly declaim prerehearsed jests for the benefit of the eavesdroppers.

An outsider's view of the group was provided by Anita Loos, author of *Gentlemen Prefer Blondes*. In 1927, she published a sequel, *But Gentlemen Marry Brunettes*, in which she had her heroine say:

"Well, I soon found out that the most literary enviroment in New York is the Algonquin Hotel, where all the literary geniuses eat their luncheon. . . . The first genius who came in was Joel Crabtree, the great writer who writes a long collum every day on the subjeck of everything. I mean, providing it happened to some friend of his. Because it makes Mr. Crabtree feel very very good to have everybody think that *his* friends are greater geniuses than anybody elses friends. So the day never goes by, that every one of his friends are not mentioned in his literary collum, and all of the public that is interested in literature enough to read it, can find out what they have been doing every hour of the day or night. So naturally they are always trying to do something readable on purpose, like a match game of amuseing tideldywinks, or sharades at one anothers parties, or some laughable croquay championship in Central Park where you can draw quite a crowd with almost anything. . . ."

Anyone familiar with the group would have had no trouble identifying Miss Loos' Crabtree as FPA, nor linking up Mr. Woollcott with charades and croquet. Miss Loos had her heroine conclude:

"So then they all started to tell about a famous trip they took to Europe. And they had a marvelous time, because everywhere they went, they would sit in the hotel, and play cute games and tell reminiscences about the Algonquin. And I think it is wonderful to have so many internal resources that you never have to bother to go outside yourself to see anything. . . . And I really do not know why the geniuses at the Algonquin should bother to learn about Europe any more than Europe bothers to learn about them. So they came back, because they like the Algonquin best after all. And I think it is remarkable, because the old Proverb tells about the Profit who was without honor in his own home. But with them, it is just the reverse."

The usual defense offered by members of the Algonquin group is that the people who disliked them were the chewers of sour grapes. Whatever else they might have been, they were, after all, now at stage center in New York's literary and theatrical world, helping to create a climate of taste at a time when, as Miss Loos herself said, "America was very uncultured."

The disparaging banter and insult at the Algonquin were

actually a part of the taste-creating process. It was as if Mr. Woollcott and his friends realized that they needed to destroy pretense, and it is in this context that the often-cruel wit of the Vicious Circle must be judged. If they were often guilty of posturing themselves, their neglect of motes was not more important than their concern for beams, and they took pride in being just as rough on each other as they were rough in their judgments of anyone else. Mr. Woollcott used to greet *Vanity Fair*'s young humorist Corey Ford, thus: "How's everything at the frat, Corey? How are the boys at the dorm?" It was Mr. Woollcott's way of advising Mr. Ford, then newly hatched from Columbia University, to put undergraduate ways of thinking and writing aside, now that he was out in the great world. The way Mr. Woollcott put it may have been cruel, but the advice was sound.

Dorothy Parker remained at the center of this somewhat uncomfortable circle even though some of her closest friends left the Round Table to merge with that allied and overlapping group of mutual acquaintances who were to be more specifically identified with *The New Yorker* magazine than with the Algonquin Hotel. Her friendship was not exclusive: she was also a part of *The New Yorker* set, and so, for a long while, was Mr. Woollcott. There was, however, something about her that made people wish that her friendship was exclusive—i.e., exclusively their own. She not only inspired a kind of jealousy, but cultivated it by her habit of complimenting the person with whom she was talking, while simultaneously being derisive of absent friends. Beatrice Ames, who since her marriage to Donald Ogden Stewart had become Dorothy's confidante (the first Dorothy Parker ever had, and a woman who would be her friend for more than forty years), was no admirer of the Woollcott group. She called them "Broadway people, Forty-second Streeters," and said that Dorothy had assured her that she did not like them, either, and in fact looked down on them.

But if Mr. Woollcott and his friends ever bored Dorothy Parker, she seems to have been entirely successful in never letting them know it. She was as often at parties in Mr. Woollcott's apartment as she was at the Algonquin or at the theater with Mr. Woollcott, and she was among those who visited at Neshobe Island, in Lake Bomoseen, Vermont, which Mr. Woollcott regarded as his own principality, and where everyone played Botticelli, The Game, and croquet at Mr. Woollcott's command. Mr. Woollcott always held her in great esteem, although what she really thought of him, or of anyone else, is difficult to say because she said so many different things to so many different people.

Since 1925, when Mr. Woollcott discovered it, the island in the lake had served for a few weeks each summer as the playground of Mr. Woollcott's Thanatopsis and Broadway friends. They were later to buy it and operate it as a club; still later Mr. Woollcott would absorb it. At any time, when they were there, it was a kind of outdoor extension of midtown Manhattan, and Dorothy Parker was surprised to see Vincent Sheean there one day, because she knew that he detested New York City in general, its glitter and its wit in particular, and specifically had no use for Mr. Woollcott and all his works.

Mr. Sheean reported that Dorothy Parker disliked the island and Mr. Woollcott as much as he did. "She couldn't stand Alec and his goddamned games," he said. "We both drank, which Alec couldn't stand. We sat in a corner and drank whisky and talked about balls. Alec was simply furious. We were in disgrace. We were anathema. We weren't paying any attention to his witticisms and his goddamned games."

He said that Dorothy Parker hated croquet and never played it. He said this with the authority of one whose relationship with her was more than superficial. But it is possible that Mr. Sheean had been completely misled. Perhaps, sensing Mr. Sheean's distaste for the Woollcottian world of Lake Bomoseen, she sat in the corner and drank with him in order to make Mr. Sheean feel he had at least one understanding friend there. It is also likely that, knowing Mr. Sheean, she monopolized him only to irritate Mr. Woollcott—looking forward to enjoying Mr. Woollcott's sulphurous reactions and to teasing him about them later, when they played croquet. She would tell one man that her true friends called her Dorothy, not Dottie. She would assure another that her real friends called her Dottie, never Dorothy. She once told an interviewer she seldom went to the Algonquin because it cost too much to eat there. She might have said this only because the interviewer looked young, hungry, and poor.

Like many another woman, she could convince the man with whom she was talking that he, alone of all men, really understood her. As many women know, this is easily done: all a woman has to do is let the man talk about himself. Her contribution to this antique ploy was to add slighting remarks about other men, thereby confirming her companion in his good opinion of himself and leading him to believe that he was at last in the presence of an understanding woman. The measure of her success in this regard is that, while all her friends were uneasily aware that she would probably say as derisive things about them as she said about others, each continued to believe that his relationship with her was nevertheless something separate and special.

Each of her friends thought he knew that Dorothy Parker was not the woman that other people saw, and each one of them was right. At the same time, each was aware that she was a highly complicated woman, and Corey Ford (who knew her well enough to share a few kisses in a taxicab) said, "I'd hate to be the alienist who had Dorothy Parker stretched out on his couch." But rushing in where alienists might fear to tread, her friends tried to explain who she really was.

To Vincent Sheean (who knew her well enough to wonder if they once might not have been on the edge of love), she was a terrified soul. "When it came time to leave the apartment to get a taxi, you could see this look of resolution come on her face," he said. "Her chin would go up and her shoulders would go back; she would almost be fighting back fear and tears, as if to say to the world, 'Do your worst; I'll make it home all right.' If the doorbell rang in her apartment, she would say, 'What fresh hell can this be?'—and it wasn't funny; she meant it.

"There was also a great element of suppressed fury in Dottie," he said. "She was a terrified woman and a terrified artist. She was a true artist. Among contemporary artists, I would put her next to Hemingway and Bill Faulkner. She wasn't Shakespeare, but what she was, was true. If every word has to be true, this is terrifying. That's what Dottie had; every word had to be true."

To George Oppenheimer (who knew her well enough to write

a play about her, *Here Today*), she often seemed to be putting on an act. "With any discipline," he said, "she would have been a marvelous actress."

Everyone who saw a different Dorothy Parker saw one that was just as real as any Dorothy Parker seen by anyone else. It does no good to ask, "Will the real Dorothy Parker stand up?" because it is only the minor characters in bad novels who are uncomplicated. All the various Dorothy Parkers added up to an endless and puzzling variety—and this was a reason why her friends found her to be so intriguing.

When Vincent Sheean brought his English bride, Diana Forbes-Robertson, to New York, Diana at once found Dorothy Parker to be wonderful company. On one occasion the two ladies enjoyed a long and somewhat too-alcoholic dinner together in a restaurant where a Viennese orchestra played, and as every remark seemed to be funnier than the last, they fell into a fit of giggling. The following day, in her more proper British senses, Mrs. Sheean telephoned Mrs. Parker, wondering what that restaurant full of people must have thought of them.

"I think we were rather quaint and Old World," Dorothy said. "Don't you?"

The gaiety was one thing, but there was another.

"She gave off an aura of troubledness," Mrs. Sheean said. "I think she drank because of her perception. She wanted to dull her perceptions. Her vision of life was almost more than she could bear.

"She was terrific about drawing you out, as if to ask 'Who are you?' to keep from having to say who she was. Everybody was grist for Dottie's mill. She could dissect everyone she ever met. Did she suffer from the most overpowering ego? Did she wonder if everybody was stupid? Was she suffering from being so damned clever? I do believe that Dottie was infinitely superior to her surroundings—she had some inner ear that the others didn't have; she wasn't 'smart.' I wonder if that extremely apologetic way of hers wasn't a supreme effort to hide the contempt she may have felt. The politer her language, the more lethal was what was going to come out next. I am sure there was a core in Dottie that was tough as nails. She would do what she wanted regardless of anyone else. Possibly, she was a very unamiable character. But what she was, was sheer charm that made you forget everything else."

Moss Hart's actress wife, Kitty Carlisle, had bitter reason to know what Mrs. Sheean had to say about Dorothy Parker's ability to draw people out.

"Tell me all about yourself," Dorothy said, and Miss Carlisle did, eventually reaching the point of saying, "And there I was, at the Capitol Theater at ten thirty in the morning, walking out on a stage for the first time in my life to face thirty-six hundred people"—only to hear Dorothy murmur in tones of such great understanding, "How could they do that to you?"

And the actress Helen Hayes, who had married Dorothy Parker's early lover, Charles MacArthur, realized after a party that Dorothy had got her to tell the story of her life. "I feel like such a fool—I told her everything," Miss Hayes later told friends. She wondered what Dorothy would say about her now.

Dorothy Parker's ability to get people to talk about themselves suggests something more than curiosity on her part. The fact that she could seem to be all things to all people suggests a kind of human vacuum into which people rushed, obeying a natural law. Certainly an aura hovered about her, which her New York friends called helplessness, and which the essentially European Diana Sheean called troubledness. This aura, contrasting with her spritelike physical charm and the quick, wild play of her mind, was one of the things that drew people to her. But this aura could have been a sign, "This way to the vacuum," and people would rush into Dorothy Parker mistakenly thinking they had found her, when what they had actually discovered was, chiefly, themselves. Many a literary critic said that she gave a unique voice to her generation, but perhaps her wit was not merely fashionable. It could also have stemmed from her lonely belief that, for all her cleverness, she really had nothing constructive to contribute, but could only lash out against what she found to be stupid about people, conventions, and circumstances. At the same time she wanted to please, to be admired, to be thought clever and amusing. Therefore, as Mr. Oppenheimer and others noticed, she often did put on an act, and because, as Mr. Stewart said, she hated sham and pretense, she particularly hated herself whenever she was guilty of pretending, whenever she said something that was not true, but which might bring applause.

Her indictments of herself were plentiful in the poems of *Enough Rope*. The careful reader could find good reason to believe that she hated herself and, if he had only known, even more reason to believe this in view of the fact that she had tried to kill herself on at least two occasions (and, according to one of her friends, on five). So that singular, puzzling, and intriguing aura could have represented her wretchedness upon thinking herself to be so brilliant, but so empty and full of sham.

"When she feels admiration," Mr. Woollcott said, "she can find no words for it." Nor was he alone in noticing that in her wit, her poetry, and her prose, Dorothy Parker was a far more effective counterpuncher than she was an advocate. This was apparent in the book reviews she began to write in 1927 for *The New Yorker* magazine, in the column "Constant Reader." Her taste was most uneven, but her writing was consistent. It was consistently awkward whenever she sought to praise a book, and consistently vivid and crisp when she did not, as was more often the case.

The reviews for which she was best known were cut, as it were, from the Round Table's cloth. She said of one book that it was written without fear and without research; of another that it must be a gift book because no one would take it on any other terms; of a third that it was not something to be tossed aside lightly, but thrown away with great force. Equally in the Round Table's mood were the personal vendettas she conducted against authors whose pretense she detested. Of the four-volume autobiography of the English countess, Margot Asquith, she said, "The affair between Margot Asquith and Margot Asquith will live as one of the prettiest love stories in all literature." And when she came eventually to A. A. Milne's *The House at Pooh Corner*, she was less merciful. Mr. Milne had romantically and sentimentally portrayed a cute little boy and his dear, fuzzy stuffed animals that talked, and after saying what she thought of this sticky-sweet concoction, Dorothy Parker reported, simply, "tonstant weader fwowed up."

Her *New Yorker* reviews added another dimension to her public reputation because in 1927, and much to the honest puzzlement of its editor, the magazine was becoming important. Harold Ross might like to refer to it as an "adult comic book" and "a fifteen-cent magazine," but a brilliant and discriminating staff was being assembled, and the magazine was becoming less smart and more wise, as was Mr. Ross, himself. In the magazine's first days, Mr. Ross, thinking to capitalize on snob appeal, had hired many young socialites to be staff members, but it had shortly become apparent that something more than social position was required of the staff, and only those of the socialites who had it remained. Janet Flanner was writing from Paris; Katherine Angell was selecting short stories; E. B. White (who later married Miss Angell) was perfecting his paragraphs; James Thurber and Wolcott Gibbs, together with Rea Irwin and Lois Long, were all of them helping to convert what had begun as a kind of city version of a college humor magazine into a publication whose humor was becoming increasingly subtle, and the bulk of its content quite serious.

As the magazine gained prestige, Dorothy Parker became increasingly identified as a *New Yorker* writer, even though she worked only two years for the magazine as a regular contributor of book reviews. This was more of a tribute to *The New Yorker*'s position than it was to her contributions. This is not to say that hers were minor ones, but rather that the magazine's stature began to confer a kind of literary nobility upon its contributors, and in Dorothy Parker's case this obscured the fact that some of her best poems and short stories were published elsewhere, notably in Seward Collins' *The Bookman*.

But what she was writing for *The New Yorker* was all of a piece with her poems and her bright remarks. Her lines were fastidious enough, but there was a quality of desperation about them; her mood was wary, grimly gay, sweetly sour. She blithely and bitterly reported that her worst suspicions were invariably confirmed.

At the same time she was also a great success by New York's standards. As a best-selling poet and as a contributor to *The New Yorker*, she was making money; she was a much-talked-about and well-publicized figure in both the city's literary and sophisticated societies. Still, she was obviously troubled, and what Ernest Hemingway had to say might provide an explanation of her malaise. Hemingway put what he thought of the New York literary life into a passage in his *Green Hills of Africa*:

"Writers should work alone. They should see each other only after their work is done, and not too often then. Otherwise they become like writers in New York. All angleworms in a bottle, trying to derive knowledge and nourishment from their own contact and from the bottle. Sometimes the bottle is shaped art, sometimes economics, sometimes economic-religion. But once they are in the bottle they stay there. They are lonesome outside of the bottle. They do not want to be lonesome. They are afraid to be alone in their beliefs and no woman would love any of them enough so that they could kill their lonesomeness in that woman, or pool it with hers, or make something with her that makes the rest unimportant."

Perhaps Dorothy Parker knew this as well as Hemingway did. Perhaps this knowledge lay behind what her friends thought to be her maudlin nattering about wanting that house in the country. Perhaps if her entire literary generation was satirically searching for sound values in the random nonsense of the twenties, she was bitterly wishing she could find some holdfast, too— and was suspiciously aware that neither she nor anyone else would ever find it in the New York bottle that was shaped fun. But it was such a cozy bottle, filled with such amusing people. Maybe Dorothy Parker feared to be alone outside the bottle. Yet she was terribly alone inside it, for all the contact she had with all the others there. She quite successfully made this clear in her poems, and in what she said—and more successfully yet in the short stories she was now beginning to write.

8

In 1928–29, the newspapers were reporting that Japan's population explosion was ominous—that there would be a hundred million Japanese by 1956; that migration was the only answer for Japan, but that since no nation in the Pacific basin wanted Japanese immigrants, an Asian war was more likely. Picking up a phrase from the deposed German Kaiser, the Hearst press warned that the United States was faced with a Yellow Peril. The papers also reported that American businessmen and bankers greatly favored Mussolini, whereas the American academic community was concerned that the Duce was murdering, jailing and exiling his opponents; suppressing free speech, press, and parliament. The businessmen retorted that Italy had no strikes and no unemployment, that the lira was sound, and that Mussolini had made the trains run on time. True liberty is impossible without order, the bankers said—to which the editorial writers said that Fascism invited violence, and since either a revolution in Italy or an imperialistic war might involve the United States, we may be forgiven for viewing the situation with foreboding. The papers also reported, without comment, the existence of a belligerent Nazi party in Germany. The financial pages reported economic chaos in Germany; they also said that Britain had exported twenty-eight millions of sterling worth of goods, but had imported thirty millions worth.

The papers said that if this situation continued, it would not only wreck the economy of the Empire, but the economy of the world as well.

As for the state of the Union, the papers in 1929 were reporting that Prohibition was making everyone disrespectful of all law. They said that consumer credit was dangerously overextended and that the stock market was perilously inflated. The press was also concerned about youth—not about those who resembled the John Held, Jr., caricature of the simpleton in the coonskin coat, but those who, in their thousands, were arguing against militarism, capitalism, religious denominationalism, and war, and were arguing for an end to the death penalty, for positive education for peace, for the application of Christian principles to race relations, for sex education, for America's entrance into the League of Nations, for the ecumenical movement, and for disarmament. They were written off by some of their own professors as being "irresponsible, superficial, and radical."

With respect to urban life, social critics were remarking upon the disappearance of moral standards among the middle classes. There was, to a degree hitherto unknown, promiscuity both homosexual and heterosexual, unrestrained hard drinking, and a rather casual taking of drugs. "What the parents of the time seldom grasped at all," Vincent Sheean recalled in *Personal History*, "was that such wickednesses were not restricted to abandoned Bohemians, creatures of the underworld . . . but were common among their children and their friends' children, however outwardly 'respectable.'" Never, he said, had there been such an immense gulf between the generations. "All had progressed so far," he wrote, "that frank conversations with . . . parents had become an impossibility." He was not referring so much to college youth as to his own contemporaries of the twenties who "had to hide the liquor, conceal some of the books, and exercise a stern control over their conversation when mother came to call." He said the root problem was that his middle-class contemporaries had abdicated their moral responsibilities as they became members of a leisured class during the years of Coolidge Prosperity—and that taste, fashion, suggestion, and whim had come whirling in to fill the vacuum.

Of course, when Dorothy Parker met her friends at Jack and

Charlie's, neither she nor anyone else bled at the social heart, or otherwise breathed heavily over this sad state of the world. They met there to have fun.

But with the possible exception of hermits, no one can remain entirely unresponsive to the moods and events of his time, writers least of all, and particularly not writers so perceptive as Dorothy Parker. She was concerned for causes, especially for lost ones. As a child, she had been aware of the plight of the unemployed and of the immigrants; as a schoolgirl, she had taken the part of the feminists and read the reports of the muck-rakers. Her social conscience was mobilized in June 1921 when two immigrant anarchists, Nicola Sacco and Bartolomeo Vanzetti, were charged with murder in the course of a payroll robbery in South Braintree, Massachusetts. The political climate was then one of witch hunts for radicals, and in all fairness it must be said there was at least cause for concern: anarchists *had* been responsible for setting off bombs in public places. In the case of Sacco and Vanzetti, however, there was reason to believe they were innocent of the charges, that they had not been at the scene at the time, that their anarchism went no further than advocacy. This was certainly the view of the nation's intellectual community, which almost to a man protested that the two men were being railroaded, that they were innocent victims of American xenophobia and of a frightened public reaction. So there was a picket line outside the courtroom, and Dorothy Parker and Mr. Benchley were in the line. She was there out of conviction and out of friendship for Mr. Benchley. He was there because his honor required it, for he had become personally involved in the case.

Mr. Benchley's problem was this: One of his friends had told him that he had overheard Judge Webster Thayer, coming out of the Worcester Golf Club's locker room, say that "radicals" were trying to influence him, but that he "would show them and get those guys hanged," referring to the two immigrants as "those bastards down there," and promising "to get them good and proper." Mr. Benchley felt the Judge seemed not without prejudice in making these remarks while the trial was still in progress before him.

Sacco and Vanzetti were convicted and sentenced to death.

They remained in their jail's Death Row for six years while an extraordinary series of appeals were fought out. Mr. Benchley filed an affidavit as to what his friend had told him of Judge Thayer's locker room remarks—only to have the friend deny having told Mr. Benchley any such things. In the end, Sacco and Vanzetti were executed, and demonstrations against Massachusetts justice were held not only in the United States but also in cities abroad. The two anarchists were put to death on Dorothy Parker's thirty-fourth birthday. Inasmuch as she had made an emotional commitment to their cause, protesting for their lives, the occasion of their deaths upon the anniversary of her life may have had more impact on her than if they had been executed at any other time.

In any case, her commitment to Sacco and Vanzetti, and to any and all other humanitarian causes, was unquestionably genuine, and in the closing years of the twenties, it depressed her to realize that the world was full of fears and horrors, and that the public's reaction to virtually anything, no matter how horrible, was so nicely expressed in a catchword of the day: "It's a lot of applesauce!"

She was discouraged to think that so many of the people she knew were wasting their time and their intelligence upon trivia. Mr. Benchley, sometime walker of picket lines, was concentrating on such topics as "Glorifying the American Flea," and she reproved him for doing this. It was all very well to be gay and amusing, she said, but not to the exclusion of being anything else, not when there was something else that ought to be said.

She thought there was something wrong with the fun they were all supposed to be having, although she went right along with it, and she was oppressed by the thought that life lacked meaning. But art, as both Freud and she said, is a form of catharsis, and she was growing as an artist—and growing apart from her friends in this regard. In 1928, she published her second collection of poems, *Sunset Gun*. The title, and one of the poems, "Pour Prendre Congé," suggested her decision to pursue a literary objective other than poetry. The poem said:

> I'm sick of embarking in dories
> Upon an emotional sea.

I'm wearied of playing Dolores
(A role never written for me).

I'll never again like a cub lick
My wounds while I squeal at the hurt.
No more I'll go walking in public,
My heart hanging out of my shirt.

I'm tired of entwining me garlands
Of weather-worn hemlock and bay.
I'm over my longing for far lands—
I wouldn't give that for Cathay.

I'm through with performing the ballet
Of love unrequited and told.
Euterpe, I tender you *vale*;
Goodby, and take care of that cold.

I'm done with this burning and giving
And reeling the rhymes of my woes.
And how I'll be making my living,
The Lord in His mystery knows.

But the Lord's answer was already known: she was beginning to write those short stories on which her true claim to literary stature would be based. She was by no means through with poetry—some of her best poems were in her future—but she was moving past verse, and it is in her stories that the value, to her, of her lovers, her friends, and her dogs becomes apparent. They were valuable to her in exactly the sense that experience, paint, and canvas are valuable to a painter. She used her materials with the iciest detachment.

She had drifted into an affair with a businessman, John Garrett, who somehow reminded everyone of Edwin Parker. No one made any moral judgments about this; everyone presumed that everyone had a sexual life and ought to have a sexual partner. It was just her choice that they all deplored. Her friends seemed to think that anyone who had seen one tall, handsome, dull businessman had certainly seen them all, and that she ought to have been bright enough to know this herself.

"We were all rather embarrassed about it," Donald Ogden

Stewart said. "But we thought, 'All right, he was Dorothy's current beau, and he was crazy about her.' You took a protective view about Dottie. She was so open to love. She was your Dottie, and you wanted to keep her from getting hurt."

If Mr. Stewart entertained rather conflicting opinions about her, saying in one case that she was incapable of loving and, in the second case, always open to love, her friends were also puzzled that she could so clearly distinguish between love and desire in her poetry, but not in her personal life. Several of her friends thought she feared the responsibility of having to return someone's love, and that in choosing Mr. Garrett, she had selected someone who didn't matter. They felt she was in love with love, rather like the humanitarian who professes a love for mankind, but who detests his neighbors. She meanwhile had recorded one view of herself in her poem "Ballade at Thirty-Five":

> This, no song of an ingénue,
>   This, no ballad of innocence;
> This, the rhyme of a lady who
>   Followed ever her natural bents.
>   This, a solo of sapience,
> This, a chantey of sophistry,
>   This, the sum of experiments—
> I loved them until they loved me.

She went on to say:

> Pictures pass me in long review—
>   Marching columns of dead events.
> I was tender, and often, true;
>   Ever a prey to coincidence,
>   Always I knew the consequence;
> Always saw what the end would be.
>   We're as Nature has made us—hence
> I loved them until they loved me.

For whatever reasons, she seemed always to hold something back in her relationships, and the same thing could be said of her friendships. Her friends knew that she wanted to be warm and generous, but something made her fearful and vulnerable—and therefore just a bit remote.

"God knows," the *New Yorker* humorist Frank Sullivan said, "she would have liked to have helped someone in need."

On at least one occasion, she helped him. She sent him two poems at a time when he was floundering around in his attempts to conduct the column "The Conning Tower" while FPA was away on a honeymoon.

"Maybe someone in her hearing had said my stuff was lousy, or maybe she just felt sorry for me that I couldn't fill Frank Adams' shoes, but that was enough to arouse her interest, and she sent me these poems," Mr. Sullivan said. "God knows she could have sold them. I have never forgotten that. I've always felt a great sense of gratitude to her. It was the kind of thing she did."

Still, there was something in the gift that at least barely hinted at a reproach, and there was also the kind of help that Dorothy Parker offered to Mr. Benchley's wife, Gertrude. At a party, Mrs. Benchley needed to powder her nose, but had mislaid her compact. Dorothy offered hers. When Mrs. Benchley reached the powder room, she found that Dorothy had given her rouge.

On another occasion, one of her friends was nervous and fearful. He confessed that he was that night going to begin an affair with Neysa McMein. She told him there was nothing to worry about.

"But isn't there something I have to do?" he asked.

Dorothy, who told this story to people who knew and liked the man, explained that there was.

"But I'd be too embarrassed to go to a drugstore and ask for something like that," the man said.

She said she would go to the drugstore for him. But still he had the gravest doubts. He said it was the first time that he would be unfaithful to his wife.

"Oh, don't worry," she comforted him. "I'm sure it won't be the last."

While it is certainly possible that nothing of the sort ever happened, and that she had made it all up for the sake of the last line, the story does say something of the nature of her friendships. There was also the sort of help she gave Donald Ogden Stewart.

"Dottie had one wonderful habit," he said. "If you had a hangover, she always had a worse one. She had always made more of a fool of herself than you had. She was terribly sympathetic to anybody on the day after. She was the best person in the world because she would not tell you if you had been terrible. She just made you feel all right again."

So far, so good—until one reads her short story, "You Were Perfectly Fine." In it, a young woman assures a young man he had been perfectly fine the night before, that everyone thought he had been terribly funny when he poured the clam juice down a woman's back. When the young man groaned, saying he had no memory of this, the young woman told him not to worry—everybody had thought it was a scream, just as he had been when he started singing those dirty songs in the restaurant. On she went, through a catalogue of horrors, once she was sure he remembered nothing of the evening.

In the light of this story, the comfort she gave Mr. Stewart on bad mornings might be reviewed. In all this, one hears in mind's ear a warning chanted by a kind of Greek chorus of Dorothy Parker's friends: "You were never sure where you stood with Dottie." There was always something incomplete and rather puzzling, and something that was sometimes more than a bit theatrical. That same remote quality also characterized her attitude toward animals.

As all the world knew, Dorothy Parker doted on dogs. She talked about them, she talked to them, and she wrote about them, as in her poem "Verse for a Certain Dog," which begins:

> Such glorious faith as fills your limpid eyes,
> Dear little friend of mine, I never knew.
> All-innocent you are, and yet all-wise.
> (For Heaven's sake, stop worrying that shoe!)
> You look about, and all you see is fair;
> This mighty globe was made for you alone.
> Of all the thunderous ages, you're the heir.
> (Get off the pillow with that dirty bone!)

These lines may at once remind the reader of Thomas Hood's "A Parental Ode to My Son, Aged Three Years and Five Months," which begins:

> Thou happy, happy elf!
> (But stop—first let me kiss away that tear.)
> Thou tiny image of myself!
> (My love, he's poking peas into his ear!)
> Thou merry, laughing sprite!
> With spirits feather-light,
> Untouched by sorrow and unsoiled by sin—
> (Good Heavens! the child is swallowing a pin!)

The nineteenth-century poet was an enthusiasm of Dorothy Parker's, and she would borrow his title "The Song of the Shirt" for a short story of her own, but the point is that she liked to play with her dogs. She would cuddle them close to her and murmur into their ears; she would gush over them in a way that might have made Christopher Robin and Winnie-ther-Pooh blush, but she would leave it to someone else to clean up their messes. She never seemed to know that discipline is a form of kindness. But she said she loved dogs. One of her friends had a child who struck her as being particularly obnoxious, but she forgave the child everything, she said, because he was the doggiest looking boy she'd ever seen.

On one occasion, George Oppenheimer, Dorothy, and a mutual friend drove to a dog show. In the car with them was a boxer that claimed her entire attention on the way uptown. Arrived at the showplace, she expressed amazement when she learned that the boxer could not be admitted as a guest, like any other.

"You mean he can't see other dogs?" she demanded.

The door warden explained that the only dogs allowed inside were those being shown. Since the boxer was not to be shown, it would have to remain outside. In scornful outrage, she returned to the car, and gently spoke to the boxer through the partly open window.

"We are going to a fish show," she told the dog, for the benefit of her audience—and comically disparaging her own sentimentality as well.

On other occasions, she would talk to other animals. Emerging from Tony's at an early hour of the morning, and seeing along the darkened streets the horse-drawn wagons with the horses nuzzling into their feedbags, she would leave her friends to wander up and down the street, talking to the horses.

"I won't say they could speak English," Vincent Sheean said, "but they paid attention to her."

As, of course, did her friends, some of whom thought her great love of animals was somewhat misdirected when it was not overflowingly sentimental.

"That poor Robinson," Frank Sullivan said of Dorothy Parker's dachshund. "That poor little dog spent more time in Tony's, in that smoky atmosphere, under the table, at two in the morning. I thought that for all her vaunted affection for animals, she could have been a little more considerate."

So did Beatrice Ames Stewart, who adored dogs herself. Stories about Dorothy the friend and champion of dogs would fill libraries, but Beatrice told a rather chilling one. She said that Dorothy Parker actually disliked some of the many dogs she had during her life, and that she was so bored by one of them that she fed it only a single slice of tongue a day, as if hoping it would die, but not wishing to be charged with having starved it to death.

If she seemed incapable of complete commitment to a lover, a friend or a dog, her attitude toward children was one that most women would never imagine. Perhaps children made her uncomfortable because, during her own childhood, she had no childhood friend; perhaps because she was single and barren at thirty-five while her friends were raising families; perhaps her abortion was a shadow in her mind. Such thoughts could have added to the distaste she had for the sentimentality of A. A. Milne.

But Dorothy Parker yearned for children, and when she became godmother to the Stewarts' son, Ames Stewart, she wrote him a little note saying he never need fear his future so long as one poorhouse remained in the land. She watched the Sheeans' daughter toddle down the steps to go to a park to play alone, and said, "Isn't it a pity she never married?" As these remarks indicate, she badly wanted to care. She seemed to fear that an expression of her true feelings would be taken for sentimentality. More important, her heart went out to a child because she was convinced that life was a tragedy, and she had expressed this most poignantly in two poems, published in the 1927 and 1928 Christmas issues of *The Bookman*. The first was "The Maid-Servant at the Inn":

> "It's queer," she said; "I see the light
>   As plain as I beheld it then,
> All silver-like and calm and bright—
>   We've not had stars like that again!
>
> "And she was such a gentle thing
>   To birth a baby in the cold.
> The barn was dark and frightening—
>   This new one's better than the old.
>
> "I mind my eyes were full of tears,
>   For I was young, and quick distressed,
> But she was less than me in years
>   That held a son against her breast.
>
> "I never saw a sweeter child—
>   The little one, the darling one!—
> I mind I told her, when he smiled
>   You'd know he was his mother's son.
>
> "It's queer that I should see them so—
>   The time they came to Bethlehem
> Was more than thirty years ago;
>   I've prayed that all is well with them."

The same foreboding was expressed in "Prayer for a New Mother":

> The things she knew, let her forget again—
>   The voices in the sky, the fear, the cold,
> The gaping shepherds, and the queer old men
>   Piling their clumsy gifts of foreign gold.
>
> Let her have laughter with her little one;
>   Teach her the endless, tuneless songs to sing,

Grant her her right to whisper to her son
  The foolish names one dare not call a king.

Keep from her dreams the rumble of a crowd,
  The smell of rough-cut wood, the trail of red,
The thick and chilly whiteness of the shroud
  That wrapped the strange new body of the dead.

Ah, let her go, kind Lord, where mothers go
  And boast his pretty words and ways, and plan
The proud and happy years that they shall know
  Together, when her son is grown a man.

She wrote again about Mary and the Christ in her poem "The Gentlest Lady," which ends:

They say she'd kiss the boy awake,
  And hail Him gay and clear,
But oh, her heart was like to break
  To count another year.

She was haunted by this sense of foreboding, by the dread of being Mary. She yearned toward children, but she said she did not want to be responsible for bringing a child into the world, for it could only grow up to know horror, and tragedy, and die. Her attitude toward other people's children was one of compassion—but with her hands held behind her back, not stretched forth.

Her sense of foreboding, her reluctance to accept responsibilities, and her quality of forever holding something back from her relationship with friends, animals, and children could be explained by the memory of her own childhood and, perhaps, by the context of the time and place into which she did not want to introduce a child. Her poems make it clear enough that she thought the world was a terrible place; the headlines of the day confirmed her in this belief. She thought life lacked meaning, and her actions indicated her willingness to leave it. But her mind still lived tidily apart, and however much she may have held something of herself back from any lover, friend, dog, or child, she held nothing back from her typewriter. She looked steadily and coldly upon the life she saw about her in the last years of the twenties; and in her short story "Just a Little One," she had something to say about a woman who drank too much, talked too much, and went on and on about animals.

It was the story of a woman in a speakeasy, pleading for a man's friendship, meanwhile growing more and more drunk. It is probably no accident that she called the man Fred in the story, which ends:

". . . Do you realize, Fred, what a rare thing a friend is, when you think of all the terrible people there are in this world? Animals are much better than people. God, I love animals. That's what I like about you, Fred. You're so fond of animals.

"Look, I'll tell you what let's do, after we've had just a little highball. Let's go out and pick up a lot of stray dogs. I never had enough dogs in my life, did you? We ought to have more dogs. And maybe there'd be some cats around, if we looked. And a horse, I've never had one single horse, Fred. Isn't that rotten? Not a single horse. Ah, I'd like a nice old cab-horse, Fred. Wouldn't you? I'd like to take care of it and comb its hair and everything. Ah, don't be stuffy about it, Fred, please don't. I need a horse, honestly I do. Wouldn't you like one? It would be so sweet and kind. Let's have a drink and then let's you and I go out and get a horsie, Freddie—just a little one, darling, just a little one."

Alexander Woollcott said the woman in the story was Dorothy Parker to the life, that she had created a fictional character who exactly demonstrated something that she knew to be true about herself. Oh, just a little one, Fred, not too much. We're being gay and amusing and having a good time, aren't we. Just a little one, just another little drink, and then just a little horsie. Neither a drink nor a horse so big as to present a problem. Let's pretend that another little drink won't be a problem, and that we really love animals that are small enough not to present problems, and let's pretend we really would take care of it and comb its hair if we had a little horsie that would be sweet and kind.

Hemingway said a writer can write only what he knows and that a writer must, as nearly as possible, know everything. Dorothy Parker's stories were enormously informed. As was the case with her poems, her stories also demonstrated her ability to look pitilessly upon herself; but they did not, as her poems so often did, turn the heartbreak into a wisecrack. One of them, "Big Blonde," seemed to have been written from some clear, cold realm far beyond judgment.

It was published in *The Bookman*, and it told of a woman in her middle thirties who lived alone in a New York apartment. She had been married, but not divorced. She had no child. She had never thought of having a child, not even at the moment of her marriage. Except for a hazy image of a dead mother, she had no family that she could, or wanted to, remember. The woman, Hazel Morse, believed it to be fundamentally important to be popular among men. "Popularity seemed to be worth all the work that had to be put into its achievement," the author commented, and had Mrs. Morse reflect, "Men liked you because you were fun, and when they liked you, they took you out, and there you were."

Mrs. Morse seemed to be fun to a great many men. The fun consisted of drinking in apartments and in speakeasies, and after the drinking, Mrs. Morse would be a good sport about going to bed with the men. It is not recorded that she enjoyed the going to bed, just that she wanted to be a good sport about it, and that men gave her money and presents for being such a good sport.

In the beginning, all seemed to go well enough. Mrs. Morse was delighted to be living in New York: "There was always something immensely comic to her in the thought of living elsewhere." She was sentimental to a fault, particularly about horses. She also cried easily over almost anything else as well, and her friends thought her tears were funny. Friends, by the way, meant nothing much to her. Mrs. Morse would forget old friends and make new ones.

There was nothing separate about her days. "Like drops upon a windowpane, they ran together and trickled away," the author said—as the author also said in her poem "The New Love."

Eventually, although Mrs. Morse was not an introspective woman, it was borne in upon her that there was a certain emptiness about her life. She was lonely, and began to drink to offset the feeling of loneliness. She now lived in a haze of alcohol; life took on a dreamlike quality for her; nothing was astonishing. She ate less and less. She drank coffee during the day, along with the nips of whisky, and her one meal was supper. "She was never noticeably drunk and seldom nearly sober. It required a larger daily allowance to keep her misty-minded."

She began to run to alcoholic fat, and this threatened whatever security she had, predicated as that was upon her being attractive to men. She took to going to Jimmy's speakeasy alone, in the daytime. She trusted that some man would always come along to pay her bills when funds ran low. But her loneliness was always there, and so was a feeling of deep depression. "She had never been troubled by religious belief and no vision of an after-life intimidated her," the author said, preparing the way for Mrs. Morse to contemplate suicide.

Mrs. Morse ran through the catalogue of various means, hitting at last upon Veronal. She took a massive overdose of it, thinking it rather funny to be killing herself. She turned out the bathroom light and went into her bedroom and laid herself down on the bed, chuckling softly all the time, the author said. She talked to herself: "Gee, I'm nearly dead. That's a hot one!"

But Mrs. Morse was saved by her part-time maid, Nettie, who discovered her next day and summoned a physician. Revived from her deep coma, disappointed to be alive, and disgusted to think she had to go on living, Mrs. Morse asked Nettie to get her a drink.

"Maybe," Mrs. Morse thought, "when you had been knocked cold for a few days, your very first drink would give you a lift. Maybe whisky would be her friend again. She prayed without addressing a God, without knowing a God. Oh, please, please, let her be able to get drunk, please keep her always drunk."

The maid giggled, and said, "You cheer up now."

"Yeah," said Mrs. Morse. "Sure."

And that is the way the story ends. It had begun at a relatively high point in the life of Hazel Morse, and followed her steadily downhill from there. There is not the slightest suggestion in the story that anything good could ever happen to Mrs. Morse. There was every guarantee that things would just grow worse and worse until, one day, there would be an old drunk dead in a cheap room and someone would have to call the city.

"Big Blonde" won the national O. Henry Prize for the best short story published during 1929, and it established Dorothy's reputation as a serious prose artist. Winning the O. Henry Prize was in a way ironic, for the essence of an O. Henry story is that it leads the reader up the garden path to a wow at the end. But by 1929, literary fashions were changing. The new writers, particularly Dorothy Parker and Hemingway, were convinced that life lacked wows. Instead of contriving some surprise or some meaning to fit reality, they searched for meaning in experience. They did not, however, write into their stories the meanings they found. They believed it was the artist's job to select from the chaos of reality only those facts that added up to a meaning. They believed that if they did this well enough, the meaning would emerge from the facts and enter the reader's mind, just as it had emerged from the facts to enter theirs. "Big Blonde" was a first-rate example of the new writing.

The story's great strength was its verisimilitude. Jimmy's place existed in fact; Dorothy Parker had made nothing up. More important, she had put on paper exactly the way perfectly recognizable people spoke and thought. She had perfectly described someone that everyone knew. The party girl, not exactly a whore and not exactly anything else, has always been with us; but in a special way, Hazel Morse was very much the party girl of the twenties. It was the great fiction of the twenties that women could and should be the great pals of men. They did their hair in boyish bobs; they bandaged their breasts tight and flat; they wore mannish clothes when their dresses were not otherwise designed to be as sexless as possible; they tried to look and act like pals. It was not always necessary for the woman of the twenties to be a bed pal, but it was necessary for her to be ready to share boyish fun with the boys. Dorothy Parker had plainly said how little fun there was for a woman in that sort of fun—particularly when the woman was in her middle thirties and her "boys" were in their late forties and middle fifties, and when the fun chiefly amounted to drinking too much in speakeasies. Her story showed all this, and clearly forecast the only possible end of it.

More people than the O. Henry Prize judges found the story to be compelling. The story was a tremendous popular success, which at least implies that the public agreed that what Dorothy had said was true, for they could scarcely have thought it to be funny, or romantic, or light entertainment.

In writing about Hazel Morse, Dorothy Parker had written about herself, but of course the Hazel Morse in the story was not Dorothy Parker. The fictional Mrs. Morse could not possibly have seen in herself what Dorothy could see in *herself*. Mrs. Morse was a big, blowsy, dumb blonde of the lower classes who associated with traveling salesmen in cheap bars. Mrs. Parker was an intelligent little brunette of the upper classes who associated with fascinating men in expensive bars. But Dorothy Parker knew enough about Mrs. Morse's class to be able to describe her and her friends, and enough about herself to perceive the truth of Kipling's observation about Judy O'Grady and the Colonel's lady.

Mrs. Morse nipped at whisky all day long. So did Mrs. Parker, who now had whisky sours at breakfast. Mrs. Morse considered the various means of suicide. So did Dorothy Parker, whose poem "Résumé" was not just a joke. Mrs. Morse hit at last upon Veronal, and so had Mrs. Parker. In all, the fictional woman and the author had no less than twenty-eight specific attributes in common, including running to alcoholic fat in the middle thirties. Perhaps the only part of the story that was not written out of Dorothy Parker's direct personal experience was the description of Mrs. Morse when her maid, Nettie, found her:

> Mrs. Morse lay on her back, one flabby, white arm flung up, the wrist against her forehead. Her stiff hair hung untenderly along her face. The bed covers were pushed down, exposing a deep square of soft neck and a pink nightgown, its fabric worn uneven by many launderings; her great breasts, freed from their tight confiner, sagged beneath her arm-pits. Now and then she made knotted, snoring sounds, and from the corner of her opened mouth to the blurred turn of her jaw ran a lane of crusted spittle.

But Mrs. Parker had learned enough from an eyewitness, Mr. Benchley, to be able to write such a scene.

Of course she knew what she was doing when she invested Mrs. Morse with those twenty-eight characteristics specific of herself; of course she understood the meaning of what she had written. To a greater extent than in her poems, she spoke the truth in her prose. As contemporary critics said, her poems reflected an attitude of the twenties. But her stories, particularly "Big Blonde," went beneath the attitudes, and in them she said exactly what she found to be true of an era, of New York, of herself, and of the nature of the fun.

Perhaps she could never have done this had she been able to commit herself wholly to her lovers or her friends, if her mind had not lived to some extent tidily apart. Hemingway said that a writer must be an outlier, like a Gypsy. Otherwise he would be unable to be objective. In addition to all else she was, Dorothy Parker was also a writer. Perhaps to the extent that she was a writer, it was difficult for her to be a lover, a friend, a woman—particularly, if what she saw as a writer was the pointlessness of a kind of living that, as she said, was no project of hers.

9

On the night of October 29, 1929, the usual crowd was wedged thickly into Jack and Charlie's. Dorothy Parker sat with friends in a corner. Nearby sat a clot of those carefully dressed businessmen who seem to have Yale invisibly stamped in blue block letters on their no-longer-youthful foreheads. There was the usual seasoning of New York women who, at any distance farther than two yards away in a dim room, look strange and beautiful, sitting with those escorts who under any light at any range look undependable. A convocation of agents, brokers, and polo players pressed against the bar. Ordinarily, given such a crowd, there would be a hard, high sound of alcoholic voices, and you would have almost to shout what you wanted into the waiter's ear as he bent, frowning, over the table, trying to slide under the noise.

But on this night there was a kind of muttering, and the women were trying to understand what their escorts were talking about. Everyone sought to think through something that even the Yale businessmen could not explain, and a great deal of quite serious drinking was going on.

Then one of those good-time Charlies, the life of every party, made his way through the smoke and the bodies to the bar. No one at Dorothy Parker's table heard what he said—it was a wisecrack of some sort, they were later told—but they did see what happened. One of the Old Blues hit him over the head with a bottle.

"It wasn't a fun night," Donald Ogden Stewart explained. "I mean, everybody that afternoon had lost every shirt he had."

He was scarcely exaggerating. Nearly everyone drinking at Jack and Charlie's that night had every spare penny he owned in the stock market, rather than in a bank, and if the day's ticker tape was to be believed, many of the serious drinkers were now in no position to pay their bar bills.

In the more sober light of the following day, it was possible to joke again, because no one could really believe that what had happened had, in fact, occurred, and a man whose paper fortune had disappeared overnight found his Florida orange juice on his breakfast table as usual, together with *The New York Times*. His clothes were still in his closets, his children were in college, his wife was in bed, and the maid was in the kitchen. President Hoover said the nation's economy was basically sound, and few people could doubt that it was. After all, it was God's country, the land of limitless resources. The factories were running, the streets were busy, and the stores were open. Some, who found themselves now worth less on paper than they had been the day before, said the thing to do was hang on and wait for the market to go up again—and if their brokers called, to say they were out of town. Others, who instead of having a fortune now had an impossible debt, said they would wait and see: somebody would do something. There was even a mood of adventure: one Broadway producer who had lost his invested money supposed he would have to bring in another hit and make some more. Easy come, easy go; easy go, easy come.

But something had occurred. There was a brief rally, but the market lost again. Within a remarkably short time following the day of the crash, more than thirty billion dollars in paper promises simply vanished from the American economy. Yet many months passed before the maid had to be let go and the children had to leave college. The nation did not plunge into the Great Depression. It sank into it, as into quicksand.

So the fun and laughter did not stop at once for everyone, and insofar as Dorothy Parker and many of her friends were concerned, life for a long time went on quite as usual because people continued to buy books, magazines, and newspapers and to go to plays and motion pictures. For some of the writers and actors, matters even improved. Hemingway's A *Farewell to Arms* appeared and became a national best seller. Donald Ogden Stewart accepted what everyone thought to be a fabulous Hollywood contract, and he and several of the Algonquin group drifted out to the Coast. Frank Sullivan, offered a Hollywood contract, wired back DON'T BE SILLY, but he was an exception.

Dorothy Parker was meanwhile riding the crest of a personal wave. Her volumes of poetry were earning royalties; the O. Henry Prize was hers; she was offered a publishing contract for a book that would consist of her collected short stories; she was contributing to *The New Yorker*; she was in full command of her talent; she was invited everywhere; and even though she still never seemed to have money for a taxi, she had fame, fortune, and a degree of power—for her opinions had an effect far beyond the immediate circle of her friends.

One of these opinions passed into the language. In November of 1929, she published a profile of Ernest Hemingway in *The New Yorker*. If she had ever been hurt by Old Dr. Hemingstein's stupid poem, nothing of the hurt surfaced when she wrote about Hemingway. She wrote that he was "far and away the first American artist." She defined the Hemingway hero as one who showed "grace under pressure." Forty years later, Hemingway's biographer, Carlos Baker, wrote that her profile was in many ways adoring, silly, and inaccurate, but he did give her credit for having been the one who first defined the nature of the Hemingway hero in those three words, which have ever since been used by teachers of English who try to explain the essential message in Hemingway's work.

In that profile, she also said that Hemingway "avoids New York, for he has the most valuable asset an artist can possess—the fear of what he knows is bad for him." Nor, she said, was Hemingway's ambition "beckoned toward the North Shore of Long Island. 'Scratch a writer,' once I heard him say, 'and find a social climber.' "

Donald Ogden Stewart read those lines and was deeply hurt, for he suspected that he was the writer Hemingway had been talking about. He had defended his friend Dorothy against his

friend Ernest, and this had cost him Ernest's friendship. Coun-
terattacking, Hemingway had been derisive of Mr. Stewart's
friendship with the Vanderbilts and the Whitneys. And now
here was Dorothy, the woman he had defended, turning on the
man who had defended her and siding with the man who had
written such a nasty poem about her. So, at least, it seemed to
him: she could have reported that Hemingway avoided New
York and Long Island without having added that bit about
social-climbing writers. The remark would have had no particular
meaning to the general reader. The only people who knew to
whom it referred were himself, Dorothy, Ernest, and the people
who had been at the MacLeishes' Paris apartment on the night
he quarreled with Hemingway. He supposed this sort of thing
was the price one had to pay for her friendship.

Another kind of price was increasingly being paid by Dorothy
Parker's editors and publishers. She would accept a magazine
assignment, together with its deadline, and the editor would
begin to worry as the deadline approached and still her copy had
failed to appear. The word around town was that she thoroughly
disliked to write, welcomed distractions, and invented alibis. It
was as if she simply did not understand that there were such
things as publishing schedules, and that these were important.
Her friend George Oppenheimer, who was also her editor and
publisher at The Viking Press, which was to publish her collected
short stories under the title *Laments for the Living*, literally had
to force her to work. She was supposed to have read and corrected
the page proofs he sent her. He discovered she not only had done
neither but wanted to burn them. He took a copy of the page
proofs to her—she was then at the house of a mutual friend—
and, he said, he locked her into a room together with himself and
a bottle of whisky.

"The more she drank, the less she liked what she had written,
but a few drinks more and she mellowed, and put the proofs into
shape," he said.

Mr. Oppenheimer was one who believed she really hated to
write, and perhaps this was so. But as Mr. Seldes said, she was
in the tradition of the artist, and artists seldom operate on Eastern Standard Time. Sometimes the well is full; often it is dry.
An artist can seldom sit down and produce on demand, nor are

the productions of genius always of a uniformly high quality. Michelangelo ruined plenty of marble. No one knows what gives rise to artistic creativity, nor why an artist cannot always be creative. This is just as much an inexplicable mystery to the artist as it is to anyone else. In Dorothy Parker's case, the problems of creativity were complicated by her incessant search for perfection.

She may have hated to write, as Mr. Oppenheimer and other editors believed. But it is just as possible that she may have hated being asked to write, fearing that she might go to the well and find it dry, and knowing that she was nonetheless obliged to turn in something by a certain time, and fearing, too, that whatever she came up with in such a case would fall short of her expectations of herself. Perhaps she really wanted to burn the page proofs of her collected stories because she believed the quality of the stories to be uneven—which it was.

So her alibis and evasions may not have reflected hatred of writing or, as some believed, laziness. She could have been the terrified artist Vincent Sheean thought she was. A reason for her alibis could be that she was unable to explain why she had not got the work done because she herself did not know. Meanwhile, she did not want to disappoint her friends by telling them that she had been unable to begin it or by telling them that her critical sense informed her that what she had written should not be published, no matter what they thought of it. She was, as her reputation and literary position grew, discovering a problem that fame brings to the famous: the necessity of seeming to be the person one is popularly assumed to be. For her, this posed a formidable task. Her reputation demanded that she be gay, witty, and impudently charming, while at the same time her literary position required her to produce serious works of art.

In addition to having to cope with this double burden as 1929 became 1930, she was tiring of Mr. Garrett, and as always near the end of an affair, she was moody and occasionally distraught. The workaday world went gradually slipping into the quicksand, but this did not unduly disturb her, for in the special world that Dorothy Parker inhabited, it was still possible to live without being afflicted by any problems other than one's own—or to live easily and well without particular concern for the future, and to decide like a Hemingway heroine to have fun and not think about anything. Then, as the year turned, the Murphys invited her to be their houseguest in Switzerland, and this must have seemed to her a marvelous solution to many things. Moreover, she liked the Murphys and wanted to help them. Their son Patrick had contracted tuberculosis, and the Murphys could certainly do with a bit of cheering up.

The Murphys bought her tickets, and her wardrobe trunk was packed, but on the day of her departure when friends called to take her to dockside, Dorothy Parker could not be found. It grew close on to sailing hour; the matter was serious. While her luggage went aboard ship, Mr. Oppenheimer frantically tried to locate her by telephone. He was one of a number of people who were beginning to discover that a certain part of their lives would have to be devoted to helping her through her own. Eventually, he located her: she was drinking with Mr. Garrett at Jack and Charlie's—apparently in a mood of indecision or of farewell.

To Mr. Oppenheimer and the others, the pressing matter was not to speculate as to her motivations, but to pry her out of that bar and put her on the ship. Mr. Oppenheimer thoughtfully procured a bottle of Scotch, hailed a taxi, and planned out an attack as the cab made its peristaltic way across Manhattan. Arrived at Jack and Charlie's, he told the cabbie to wait, engine running.

Inasmuch as Mr. Oppenheimer feared causing a scene, he resorted to guile. He knew that Dorothy had very little to do with her siblings, that she almost never saw them. But he knew she was curious and sentimental to a fault, and that her heart went impulsively out to any man or beast in trouble. So he sent a waiter into the bar with a message: Dorothy's brother and sister needed to see her at once and were waiting in the lobby.

Mr. Oppenheimer caught her by the arm as she hurried out of the bar, and he guided her at a kind of trot out the door and down the steps, into the waiting cab. He slammed the door in the face of an angry Mr. Garrett who came running out after them, as the driver pulled away from the curb.

He informed Mrs. Parker that she was catching a ship for Europe. She did not seem to think she ought to be. Mr. Oppenheimer handed her the bottle of Scotch he had opened. By the time the taxi reached dockside in Brooklyn, there was less whisky in the bottle, and both Mr. Oppenheimer and she were in better frames of mind. She went obediently up the gangplank and onto the ship.

Shortly thereafter, she appeared at the rail to wave good-bye to Mr. Oppenheimer and the friends who had seen to her baggage for her.

"Guess who's on the boat," she called. "Marlene Dietrich. And guess who's not on the boat—my trunk!"

Her friends waved as the water widened between ship and pier. In time, someone would bring her baggage to her cabin. She was a woman, they thought, who needed a good deal of looking after.

She did not return until early in 1931, and she told one group of her friends that she would prefer to be with them in a New York street in a driving rainstorm than to be alone in Switzerland in the bright sunshine of high summer.

She had stayed with the Murphys through a summer, fall and winter at a sanitarium at Montana Vermala, where all the patients were slowly dying of their incurable disease. This latter fact was sufficiently depressing to drive almost anyone out of his mind, but as if to make a basically tragic and hopeless situation entirely repellent, she had been utterly and madly bored. She told her friends she had been so bored that she had even been glad to see F. Scott Fitzgerald when he came to visit the Murphys. She complained, comically, about what a sad, dull time she had, but she had nothing but good things to say about her hosts. The Murphys had gone to great expense to convert a room at the sanitarium into a bar, simply to give the poor devils in the sanitarium a place where they could enjoy themselves to some extent before they died—glad to spend their money to bring what happiness they could to others. And, as she told her friends about her Helvetian experience, it was perfectly clear to them that Dorothy had made a willing sacrifice of her own. For, all joking and complaining aside, Dorothy Parker had been willing to forego her beloved New York and its gossip to help the Murphys, as best she could, to look past their personal tragedy.

When she did return to the city, she brought nothing of Europe back with her.

Just as she wrote nothing out of her first European experience in the golden summer of 1926, so she wrote nothing out of her nearly year-long sojourn in Europe in 1930. Nowhere in her poems or in her stories is there a cobbled street, a tile-roofed pastel villa by the sea, a look of olive trees and vineyards. She wrote nothing of Alpine meadows, of the opulence and smells of the Grand Canal, of the little tables in cafés and the pile of saucers and the dingy look of Paris in the rain. Her prose was always much more concerned with dramatizing human motivation by means of dialogue than it was with anything else, but just as she was silent as to the European scene, so she was silent as to the Europeans. Perhaps, because her French was sketchy, she did not want to try to write about places and people she did not wholly understand, but it would seem that she had managed to spend the greater part of a year abroad without having really been there and without having met anyone other than the Murphys and occasional visitors from New York. For so interested and perceptive a writer as she, her silence on a unique and prolonged experience seems wholly remarkable. But her life and her writing had their center and being with New Yorkers— and preferably in New York. Then too, when she returned to America, it could very well have seemed to her that the special kind of Europe she had known was completely divorced from contemporary reality and was therefore unusable as literary material.

She returned to a country now well mired in the Depression. The wealthy had retrenched by means that almost always included letting the servants go. The factory owners battened down by what they called cutting their labor costs. There were lines of unemployed men in tattered clothes, newspapers stuffed into their broken shoes, waiting hopelessly outside locked factory gates. President Hoover still insisted the nation's economy was basically sound, but very few people now believed him. Veterans of the first World War were living in shanties on the edges of cities; they called their encampments Hoovervilles. All this would grow steadily worse. Yet, there was still a degree of fun and glitter. The number of Broadway openings had shrunk, and so had the number of legitimate theaters, but otherwise the dramatic and communicative arts were flourishing like the green bay tree. The haggard multitudes were willing to spend what little they had on amusements and dreams. They went to the Follies and to the Scandals. The bleak years for the nation were golden ones for Hollywood, for the big bands, for the radio entertainers, for the syndicated columnists, and, as matters eventually turned out, for Dorothy Parker.

She moved into the Algonquin Hotel, back into the gossip and the glitter, and, because "thus I am and thus I go," into another affair.

She first met John McClain at Tony's one night, and saw a big, good-looking young fellow in his early twenties. He was fresh from college football fields and was a clerk in a Wall Street brokerage house, sharing an apartment with two other young men on Morton Street in Greenwich Village. In the beginning, she was enormously set up; it must have been reassuring to her to know that, at age thirty-eight, she was attractive to handsome boys in their twenties. It might have been better for her had she only known, then and there, what he really thought of her and of himself.

Mr. McClain, to use his own words, considered himself to be a hell of a swordsman, a he-whore, and he told his roommates that he intended to roll up a score with well-known women in Society, on the stage, and in the literary world. He was quite frank about this. He was also witty and charming, drank wonderfully well, and was so completely natural in anyone's presence that he was as welcome in Society as he was at Jack and Charlie's and Polly Adler's. He was immediately drawn to Dorothy but, as one of his friends said, "If Dottie had not been a renowned writer, I am sure John would never have touched her."

Shortly after that first meeting at Tony's, Mr. McClain announced the good news to his roommates. Dottie, he said, was marvelous. He said he bedded her in her Algonquin hotel room, and that she gave him "the treatment. It was excellent. She knew all the tricks."

He told everyone he knew about his great success, and how much Dorothy Parker appreciated him. Beatrice Ames Stewart could not stand him. In Dorothy's circle, there were those who muttered about cradle robbery, and others who wondered why she could not see that Mr. McClain was just using her. But she was more than pleased with her new young man. She dreamed dreams for him. She got him a job more closely aligned with her interests than Wall Street was: she persuaded a friend at *The New York Sun* to take Mr. McClain on as a reporter. He was assigned to cover the shipping news.

It was not long, however, before Mr. McClain began to complain that she would not leave him alone. It was not that he minded the bed-work, he said, but he did not want to be always on call. He said she would keep calling him on the telephone, wanting to know where he'd been and when and why he had not kept their date last night, and would he see her that night—and he was tired of such nonsense.

He began to make excuses for not seeing her. He belonged to a health club, and he would say he was sorry that he could not take her to cocktails that afternoon because he had to work out in the gymnasium. In the evening, she would telephone again, and he would explain that his workout had been so strenuous that he simply could not move, much less see her that night— and then he would go out with another woman. The way Mr. McClain presented the case, Dorothy Parker appeared in the ridiculous role of the older woman of fading charms, hopelessly infatuated with a virile young man and pathetically grateful for whatever ardent moments he condescended to allot her, and senselessly jealous every time he looked at a younger woman.

They began to quarrel whenever they were together. The last one ended, she said, with Mr. McClain jumping up, dressing, shouting at her, "You're a lousy lay!" slamming the door, and pounding away down the Algonquin corridor.

"That sounds like him," one of Dorothy's friends said, seeking to console her.

"Yes, his body went to his head," she explained.

She tried to regard him with a cold contempt, but she was outraged to hear that he had left her bed for that of a wealthy woman.

"Well," she rather grimly said, "he'll come back. He'll come back to me when he's finished licking all the gilt off her bottom."

But Mr. McClain did not come back, and however much contempt and scorn Dorothy Parker may have claimed to have had for him, she was despondent. Friends told Mr. McClain that she was actually heartbroken to the point of being suicidal. He said he thought she was just being dramatic. He said she had already tried that ploy—that she had staged one phony suicide in the Algonquin in the hope of binding him to her. He said she had taken a fistful of barbiturates, and then had telephoned the Algonquin desk, and everybody else in town, to say she had done this, in order to be sure that somebody would come to take her to a hospital and have her pumped out. As for her tears, well, Mr. McClain said, repeating a then-current gag line, "She cries at card tricks."

Some of her friends thought there was a bit of truth in what Mr. McClain had to say about her tears, because she so often said and did things that were difficult to explain in any rational way. She moved out of the Algonquin to the quiet Lowell apartment-hotel on East Sixty-third Street, and then, she disappeared. A few days later, however, she telephoned Frank Sullivan from wherever she was.

"She was all woe over the phone," Mr. Sullivan said. "She told me she had had a row with John McClain, and she said, 'I've had to get away from it all.

" 'I'm seeing nobody,' she said. 'Nobody knows I'm here. Now, you're the one person I'd like to see. You come up. Say nothing to anyone. Come to the Plaza this afternoon and have a drink with me.'

"So of course I sprang to the call," Mr. Sullivan said. "You always sprang to the call when Dottie needed you, and I went to the Plaza that afternoon about five o'clock, and there must have been at least ten people in that room. You know, they were all the only people she wanted to see—and she'd moved from a quiet hotel to one of the busiest hotels in New York to get away from it all—five blocks away!"

Everyone thought this was funny, and so like her. It was also like her to have moved from a relatively inexpensive hotel into one of the city's most expensive ones when it was well known that she never had money. Her books were earning money, but she spent it faster than it arrived, as if she were afraid of having money.

She was chronically bankrupt, but as Mr. Sullivan said, people always sprang to the call. Shortly after the Plaza episode, the call went out from her bedside in the Harkness Pavilion of New York's Presbyterian Hospital, where Dorothy Parker had undergone an appendectomy. There was something about hospitals that struck her as being lugubrious. She was always funny about hospitals. She called this one Bedpan Alley. When Alexander Woollcott came to call, she immediately rang for the nurse—in order, she told Mr. Woollcott, to assure them forty-five minutes of absolute privacy. But the funniest thing of all was that she did not have enough money to pay her bill, and she asked Beatrice Ames Stewart to see what could be done.

"Just remember," she said, "I don't take money from people I disapprove of. No rich people."

Beatrice thought about this, and hit upon John Gilbert, who was then the nation's leading film star. Mrs. Parker, Mr. Benchley, and their particular friends had met Mr. Gilbert in New York, and never called him John, or Jack, but always Great Lover of the Silver Screen. So if a waiter should come to the table at Jack and Charlie's, no one would say, "What's yours, Jack?" but "What's yours, Great Lover of the Silver Screen?" Mr. Gilbert had fallen in with this fun, and therefore, Beatrice decided, Dorothy would not think of him as a rich man, but rather as a friend who had money.

Beatrice sent a telegram to Hollywood, and Mr. Gilbert promptly wired back twenty-five hundred dollars, which Beatrice persuaded the telegraph office to give her in the form of one-dollar bills, which she crammed into a paper bag.

"I went to the room where Dorothy was sitting up in bed with a blue ribbon in her hair," she said, "and I opened the bag and all the money flew all over the room like leaves from a tree.

" 'Is this insanity?' the nurse said, and I said, 'It's a form of it.' "

The nurse seemed horrified and stunned. At a time when able-bodied men, willing to work, were reduced to standing in lines waiting for free soup on street corners, two giggling ladies were playing with dollar bills as if they were confetti. They laughed at the nurse's consternation, and gathered up the fallen leaves, and Dorothy rose and dressed and paid her way out of the hospital.

She returned to the world of fun in the same merry mood, but her life took on a pattern that was funny in quite another sense of the word. She chose handsome young actors to escort her around town, and the odd thing here was not her worship of male beauty, but rather that these particular beauties were not precisely male. Her explanation was simple: she said she needed good fairies to take care of her. The more dubious of her friends, however, supposed that since Mr. McClain had turned out such a disaster for her, she wished to avoid the dangers of another affair. That seemed to them to be the only explanation that made sense, even as they laughed at the one she offered. They also thought it was funny when, looking in on a homosexuals' costume ball, she called down from the balcony, "Come on up, anybody—I'm a man!"

No small part of her life seemed to be a madcap one; a friend said that the free, wild play of her mind was as zany and carefree as a Marx Brothers movie. No one could predict what she would do or say, and once, at predawn hours, she dashed off with a mad crowd to visit the Bowery, a derelict area of ten-cent restaurants and flophouses and human wreckage asleep in nests of empty bottles and old newspapers in doorways. It seemed like great fun for everyone to go there, and once there, she thought it would be great fun to be tattooed. One of her friends remembered the occasion well. He said that she and a young actor, Alan Campbell, had the resident artist of a tattoo parlor inscribe small, dark blue stars on the insides of their upper left arms. "It had been a mad, mad night," he explained, but next day she came more into her senses, and ever afterward wore long-sleeved dresses to conceal her mistake.

Not at all, said another of Dorothy Parker's friends. He remembered the tattoo perfectly well; in fact, he would never forget it. "It was a dark blue or black star on her right thigh," he said, "and she showed it to everybody."

Not so, said Beatrice Ames Stewart. She said that Dorothy and two other women had gone down to Greenwich Village late one night, and there Dorothy was tattooed with a small blue star on her left shoulder, "just below the shoulder joint."

None of these three memories was at fault. Rather, each of her friends placed that small blue star where he thought it belonged on the Dorothy Parker he thought he knew. It was as if she had *three* tattoos, acquired at three different times in different company, and she decided which of them to disclose to which of her friends.

As she pursued such antic gaiety, she began to drink more heavily, and her friends talked about this—usually with an admiration for her capacity. "For a small woman, she does well," one of them said, but there were those who said they thought that beginning the day with whisky sours for breakfast might be overdoing it just a bit. Mr. Benchley was concerned enough to suggest that she ought to have a chat with Alcoholics Anonymous. This she did, and brought back word to the drinkers at Tony's that she thought the organization was perfectly wonderful.

"Are you going to join?" Mr. Benchley asked hopefully.

"Certainly not," she said. "They want me to stop *now*."

That gay remark was, however, for the benefit of the drinkers at Tony's. She had something else to say about her drinking to her confidante, Beatrice.

"Her talent was the most precious thing in the world to her," Beatrice said. "She respected her talent even more than her attraction for beautiful men. She had an absolute, solid gratitude for her talent. She said to me, 'I'm betraying it, I'm drinking, I'm not working. I have the most horrendous guilt.'"

She did enough work, however, to further consolidate her literary reputation. She filled in at *The New Yorker* when Mr. Benchley, that magazine's theater critic, departed on vacation, and her reviews of the plays were as frequently acerbic as "Constant Reader's" reviews of books. Of one play, she wrote, "In the last act [the heroine] is strangled by one of her admirers. For me, the murder came too late." Of another, a play by Mr. Milne, entitled *Give Me Yesterday*, she said, "It's hero is caused, by a novel device, to fall asleep and a-dream; and thus he is given yesterday. Me, I should have given him twenty years to life." The play *The House Beautiful* was, she said, "the play lousy." Increasingly depressed by the plays she had to suffer through as the theatrical season wore on, she took to ending her columns, "Mr. Benchley, please come home. Nothing is forgiven," and "Mr. Benchley, please come home. A joke's a joke."

She also in 1931 was one of many contributors of lyrics to Heywood Broun's revue *Shoot the Works*, which had a run of eighty-seven performances before collapsing—and while a two months' run was not spectacular, it was by no means a complete failure, and being associated with this revue was, if not a feather in her cap, at least an additional touch of color. But more important, her third collection of poems, *Death and Taxes*, appeared that year, and the reviews no longer talked about jokes and lorgnettes.

"In verse of a Horatian lightness, with an exquisite certainty of technique, which, like the lustre on a Persian bowl, is proof that civilization is itself a philosophy, Dorothy Parker is writing poetry deserving of high praise," Henry Seidel Canby wrote in *The Saturday Review*. "I suspect that one should quote Latin rather than English to parallel the edged fineness of Dorothy Parker's verse. This belle dame sans merci has the ruthlessness of the great tragic lyricists whose work was allegorized in the fable of the nightingale singing with her breast against a thorn. It is disillusion recollected in tranquility where the imagination has at last controlled the emotions. It comes out clear, and with the authentic sparkle of a great vintage."

"More certain than either death or taxes is the high and shining art of Dorothy Parker," her friend FPA wrote in *The New York Herald-Tribune*. "Bitterness, humor, wit, yearning for beauty and love, and a foreknowledge of their futility—with rue her heart is laden, but her lads are gold-plated—these, you might say, are the elements of the Parkerian formula; these, and the divine talent to find the right word and reject the wrong one. The result is a simplicity that almost startles."

The burden of Dorothy Parker's message was what it had always been: a steadfast belief that the best of things will end badly. But in the thirties, this message was apparently less of a joke than it had seemed in the twenties. Perhaps the worsening turn of events made her appear to the reviewers to be more of a poet than she had seemed to be heretofore; perhaps her increased reputation had something to do with the much more laudatory reviews. Something had changed the reviewers' minds, and it could not have been the new poems, which were no more and no less succinct, precise, and bittersweet than those in her earlier collections.

She was, in the first years of the thirties, nearing a kind of apogee. Criticism of her work was assuming the tone of a paean; her public was a vast one, and the college youth of the nation regarded her as their principal literary goddess who told them the actual facts of life. Within New York's inner circle of wit and fashion, people hung close to hear her famous mutterings and to enjoy her prejudices; the story went around that she could not stand Southerners, and in the presence of a Southern gentlewoman had said, "You know, the sublimest thoughts in the English language can be reduced to utter idiocy by pronouncing them with a Southern accent"—and then going on to illustrate, in her best Southern drawl, "Ah stray-ut lion is tha shoat-ess distance between two pints, d'ya heah?"

She was a darling of the Vicious Circle; she was an author, a poet, and a molder of opinion, she was gay and funny and talked about, and more than this, she seemed to have hit upon the secret of perpetual youth. Few women who have walked this world have aged more slowly than she. In 1932, at age thirty-nine, she had her looks and her figure—a lovely clear complexion and a figure that, if pleasingly plump, was still pleasing—and she looked out from beneath girlish bangs through great dark eyes. A charming picture of her in 1932 was created that year by George Oppenheimer in his play *Here Today*, in which she is portrayed as "Mary Hilliard," lady playwright and one of America's quickest wits.

The stage directions say Mary Hilliard is in her early thirties. "She is petite, auburn hair, very pert looking, dressed in a simple tailored suit. . . . In the beach scene she wears beach pajamas, gloves and a hat, so that she is completely protected from the sun. Inclined to be a bit eccentric in her clothes."

Mary comes bouncing on stage, a bundle of roses in her arms. She has just picked them from her hostess's garden, and thrusts them at this startled woman, saying, "How do you do? I brought you a few roses. It isn't much, but I had so little room in my trunk."

A moment later, she has looked and dashed about the room, and calls gaily to the man who has brought her to the house, "Look Stanley! They have *White Rock*," and turning to her hostess, who is a very proper dowager, she says, "How do you like yours, Mrs. Windrew? Out of the bottle?"

During the course of this farce, Mr. Oppenheimer provides his heroine with such lines as these:

"I was engaged to three men when I married you. [*Suddenly recalling*] Say, I never broke one of those engagements. Oh, that's terrible! He may still be waiting."

"An egg! It was right out in the middle of the table, without a stitch on . . ."

"There's no use putting cracked glass in her food. She thrives on it."

"She speaks five languages and doesn't know a civil word in any one of them."

"And that sofa she gave us. Made out of her own hair."

"Washington slept there. Not while I was there, of course."

The real Dorothy Parker, coming down a theater aisle and finding the actress Ruth Gordon on stage, playing the role of Marty Hilliard, stared at Miss Gordon's clothes and manner, and listened to what Miss Gordon was saying. She had read the play before production, but she turned to her escort and, pretending surprise at what Mr. Oppenheimer had written, said of him, "Why, the son of a bitch!"

Only too often the theatrical world believes that one successful play should be followed by another like it. This thought, plus the fact that Dorothy Parker was so well known in New York, and so vivid and quotable a person, gave rise to another play, *Over 21*, which Ruth Gordon wrote, and in which she was once again cast as a Dorothy-like madcap, saying and doing the most outrageous but Dorothy-like things. All of which left Dorothy Parker muttering darkly that she wanted to write her autobiography, but was afraid that if she did, "George Oppenheimer and Ruth Gordon would sue me for plagiarism."

The plays did not portray those aspects of her that were strange and moody, but then, the plays were comedies. No more did her friends concern themselves, beyond a guess that Dottie was really all right, and more than a little given to self-dramatization. Her friends did not see as deeply into her as she saw into herself, perhaps because they could not, or did not wish to, but perhaps because, as Diana Sheean said, she could be so charming that everyone forgot or forgave everything else. In feeling protective of her, it was her charm they wished to protect, no matter if they themselves were sometimes her victims, as Joseph Bryan, III, a young Southern aristocrat, once innocently was.

Mr. Bryan had come recently to the city in 1932; he had just contributed an article to *The New Yorker,* a profile of Rosa Lewis of the Cavendish Hotel in London. He found himself one evening among more than a hundred guests invited to a dance in the home of a wealthy New Yorker. He also found himself very much alone until he was astonished to see a most familiar face, that of a boyhood friend from Richmond, Alan Campbell.

"I hadn't seen him for several years," Mr. Bryan said, "so we had a warm reunion. Presently he told me, 'Dorothy Parker is here, and she's crazy to meet you.' Crazy to meet me? Golly! I followed him over to where she was sitting, in a gilt chair on the edge of the floor, and he introduced me. Dottie said, 'Joe Bryan? Oh, no! Oh, no! It's somebody else, but it's certainly not Joe Bryan.'

"I was trying to say, 'Yes, it is,' or maybe 'Yes, I am,' but she went right on: 'Oh, no! Not little me. Not with my luck! I'm never going to meet the man who wrote that Rosa Lewis piece. That's saved for rich, attractive women, not for little Mrs. Parker. She doesn't meet those men.'

"I stood there like a great gawk, still mumbling that inane 'Yes, I am' and 'Indeed it is,' until she finally said, 'You swear you are?' Then, to the room at large, she said, 'All you dreadful people go away and leave this wonderful man with me! Go away, all of you!'

"'Sit down,' she ordered. I sat. "You're going to think this very strange,' she said. 'I've just met you, and here I am about to ask you a favor. It's not will you collaborate with me on a play, but how soon can you start?'

"In the years ahead, I often heard Dottie describe herself as 'dimpling and blushing, twisting my handkerchief, and digging my toe in the sand.' That's what I did then," Mr. Bryan said. "Imagine it: the famous Dorothy Parker, the brilliant writer, the wittiest woman in New York, was asking me to collaborate with her! Asking me? Ordering me! We agreed to meet at her apartment at eleven the next morning, and I went home wrapped in a pink mist.

"She was then living at the extreme end of East Forty-ninth

Street. She'd said eleven, but I couldn't possibly get there until ten thirty, and I remember walking up and down the block, trying to kill time—poor, innocent young idiot that I was. Finally it was eleven, and I told the doorman, 'Mr. Bryan to see Mrs. Parker, please.'

"He rang her up on the house phone. 'Mr. Bryan, madam . . . Mr. Bryan.' He turned to me. 'Would you spell it, sir?' I spelled it, and he repeated it: 'B,r,y,a,n, madam . . . Yes, madam.' He turned to me again: 'Mrs. Parker wants to know what you want to see her about?'

"Right then and there my heart cracked. When I was finally shown up to her apartment, it became quite apparent that she had no recollection—none whatsoever—of our glittering plans from the evening before, or even of our having met. I saw Dottie many, many times afterward, but never once was that first evening mentioned."

Mr. Bryan laughed at the memory. Everyone said that was just like Dottie, it was all there: she saw a handsome young man and wanted to meet him, and then did not want to see him again when he showed interest in her; she had been bored and uncomfortable in the presence of great wealth; she had amused herself by playing a part; she remembered nothing the following day because she had been drunk at the party. Of course, Mr. Bryan had not known she was drunk, because she held her liquor so very well. No one thought she might have played a joke on Mr. Bryan, because no one thought she could have been that cruel.

Everyone thought it perfectly natural that Dorothy should not have remembered the night before, and they saw no harm in this. That, they knew, was what often happened when one got drunk. What no one mentioned, probably because no one knew it, was that momentary amnesia could be one early symptom of alcoholism. The people of the twenties and the early thirties thought that drinking was fun. However, as *The Merck Manual of Diagnosis and Therapy* says: "Modern studies indicate that, with few exceptions, only individuals with serious personality maladjustments become chronic alcoholics. They are emotionally dependent, insecure, oversensitive, and anxious. Without alcohol they are unable to meet and enjoy people socially, and suffer from marked feelings of inferiority." Given alcohol, such persons become "more impulsive, untruthful and unreliable, and display a growing tendency to gloss over discreditable behavior. Money may be squandered, responsibility evaded, and feelings of affection lost; the patient is touchy, irritable, critical." The *Merck Manual* goes on to say that symptoms of incipient alcoholism include loss of appetite and scant interest in food, and the taking on of puffy, unhealthful fat; that alcoholics typically go through periods of "unwarranted euphoria" that "readily give way to . . . tears"; that they swing back and forth between melancholia and merriment.

The quotations come from a modern handbook for physicians, but to the fun-loving heavy drinkers of the twenties and thirties, an alcoholic would have been a derelict on the Bowery—not an utterly charming, witty little woman who was such great fun to be with. Going to the Bowery to be tattooed was not silliness to them—it was just a madly merry thing to do. If next day Dottie was down in the dumps, well, that was the price of staying up late and having a hell of a good time.

There were, however, minority opinions. One of Dorothy Parker's friends guessed that she really hated parties and "had to get tanked up enough to go to them," while Diana Sheean believed she drank to blot out the horror of her vision of reality. Perhaps those who scoffed at these suggestions never read Dorothy Parker's stories closely enough, or else did not entirely understand that the woman who wrote them was just as real as the one who scampered off to the Bowery. The stories reflected a good deal that was shoddy about that special little world she inhabited—the New York bottle, as Hemingway would say—and they also had something to say about the steadily darkening world outside it. Her subject matter was abortion, the distance between rich and poor, social pretense, the stupidity of parties and gossip, the ridiculousness of an older woman yearning after a callous young man, the tawdriness of an actress when seen off stage, the cavalier way in which the rich treated servants, the banalities of a suburban marriage, the emptiness of love affairs, the stupidity of drinking too much, the luckless lot of being a woman. One of the stories was called "From the Diary of a New York Lady," subtitled "During Days of Horror, Despair, and World Change." It begins:

"Monday. Breakfast tray about eleven; didn't want it. The champagne at the Amorys' last night was *too* revolting, but what *can* you do? You can't stay until five o'clock on just *nothing*. They had those *divine* Hungarian musicians in the green coats, and Stewie Hunter took off one of his shoes and led them with it, and it *couldn't* have been funnier. He is *the* wittiest number in the entire world; he *couldn't* be more perfect. Ollie Martin brought me home and we both fell asleep in the car—*too* screaming. Miss Rose came about noon to do my nails, simply *covered* with *the* most divine gossip. The Morrises are going to separate *any minute*, and Freddie Warren *definitely* has ulcers, and Gertie Leonard simply *won't* let Bill Crawford out of her sight even with Jack Leonard *right there in the room*, and it's all *true* about Sheila Phillips and Babs Deering. It *couldn't* have been more thrilling. Miss Rose is *too* marvelous; I really think that a lot of times people like that are a lot more intelligent than a lot of people. Didn't notice until after she had gone that the damn fool had put that *revolting* tangerine-colored polish on my nails; *couldn't* have been more furious. Started to read a book, but too nervous. Called up and found I could get two tickets for the opening of *Run Like a Rabbit* tonight for forty-eight dollars. Told them they had *the* nerve of the world, but what *can* you do? Think Joe said he was dining out, so telephoned some *divine* numbers to get someone to go to the theater with me, but they were all tied up. Finally got Ollie Martin. He *couldn't* have more poise, and what do *I* care if he *is* one? *Can't* decide whether to wear the green crepe or the red wool. Every time I look at my fingernails, I could *spit*. *Damn* Miss Rose."

The diary runs from Monday through Friday, and all of the days are the same, filled with the same people.

Perhaps in that special little New York world, there were those who thought the story was funny. That little world laughed and glittered while in the larger world outside, men stopped passersby to ask, "Brother, can you spare a dime?" and President Hoover claimed that prosperity was just around the corner, and the banks failed. The land itself began to blow away in clouds of dust in the American Midwest, and Franklin Roosevelt spoke of the danger of fear. The Japanese marched into China and Hitler came to power, borne on the frustrations of the Germans, and for a long while the conversations in the little New York world that Dorothy Parker knew so well turned on gossip, on Broadway comedies, on plays and motion pictures, and on such civic matters as whether Jack and Charlie's "21" would be quite as much fun after the repeal of Prohibition, which would make its operations legal. The people in the little world talked about the grim external events, too, but in a theoretical way, because these events had not yet impinged upon them. The tone of *The New Yorker*'s paragraphs was urbane, wry, and a bit condescending; the time for passionate concern and for taking sides had not quite yet arrived. But Dorothy Parker in her stories indicated that she had already taken sides, and that one side of her intensely disliked the other. She was acutely depressed by horror, despair and world change; she loathed the insensate featherhead of the diary; at the same time she could not leave the New York world of fun and glitter; she loved the gossip. In "The Dark Girl's Rhyme," she had asked:

> How shall I be mating
>   Who have looked above—
> Living for a hating,
>   Dying of a love?

The question was still unanswered. She drank a great deal and she swung between silliness and melancholy; she was creative and despondent, famous, sought-after, and lonely. Between the years 1930 and 1933 she dismissed one lover and was dismissed by another, established through her stories the basis for her claim to a serious literary reputation, went abroad and was lonely for New York, returned to New York to attend parties that bored her, delighted in the life she was leading and was sickened by it, made money and spent it as if repelled by it, looked steadily out upon the beggars on the streets, and was contemptuous of the young men she gathered around her. At length she came upon an answer to the question she had asked herself. To no one's particular surprise, she took up with another lover in 1932, but to everyone's absolute astonishment in 1933, she married him.

She married Alan Campbell, Mr. Bryan's boyhood friend from Richmond, a graduate of Virginia Military Institute, now a Broadway actor.

PART
THREE

"I am a Communist," Dorothy Parker said.
"Define your terms," Vincent Sheean demanded.

1

When they were married in 1933, Alan Camp-
bell was twenty-nine years old, and Dorothy was forty. Wholly
apart from her other attributes, she was still a desirable woman,
and, as one of her friends said, "My God! Those eyes! When
she turned them on you, I don't see how any creature of the
opposite sex could have resisted them."

For his part, Alan was a beautifully built, handsome, and clever
young man. As people said, "Alan was a very sweet guy," and
he strongly reminded some of Dorothy's older friends of Edwin
Parker.

Still, like those fathers who view dimly the boys their daughters bring home, Dorothy's friends wondered what the devil
Dorothy thought she was doing when she married Alan, and like
those mothers who suspect the worst of the girls their sons
marry, Alan's friends wondered what he saw in that woman.
Most of the gossip centered on the disparity in age.

"Oh, he's so young," Dorothy's friends would say, to which
she would murmur:

"Yes. I'm thinking of sending him to military school when
he's old enough."

In fact, Dorothy Parker was only twelve years younger than
Alan's mother, a matter that his mother, Hortense, did not
conceal. Worse luck, Hortense looked as young as Dorothy, and

she would introduce herself at parties by saying, "I'm Mrs. Campbell—the mother, not the wife."

Dorothy loathed Hortense with all her heart. "She exudes that particular odor of Djer Kiss face powder and dried perspiration that characterizes the Southern gentlewoman," Dorothy explained. "She is the only woman I know who pronounces the word 'egg' with three syllables."

Hortense retaliated, after her fashion. She would too-sweetly refer to Dorothy Parker as "my little daughter" who had "snatched that boy out of the cradle."

"I'm not her little anything!" Dorothy would rage—and with serene indifference to the facts, she would say that she was only a year and a half older than Alan and therefore Hortense had no right to talk about cradle robbery. To listen to her, Dorothy said, you'd think Hortense was the only mother who had ever lived.

There was a lively gossip about the warfare between the two Mrs. Campbells, and gossip too about Dorothy's and Alan's motivations—more about his than hers—for while it was plain enough that she liked beautiful young men, there was a strong suspicion that Alan was something of an opportunist marrying to further his career. Even the courtly Joseph Bryan, III, who was a friend to both Alan and Dorothy, said, "Alan was not the kind to marry for advantage, exclusively."

So the marriage left a good many New Yorkers all atingle with dubiety, and some marveled that Dorothy Parker, whose dislike of Southerners was well known, should have married one. But Alan, for all that his father may have been what the newspapers called "a Virginia tobacco man," felt no allegiance to the gallant South. In fact, he had been made to feel in Richmond that the South had no place for him, because his mother, far from being a Southern gentlewoman in the sense that such a person is the proud descendant of landed cavaliers, was the daughter of a kosher butcher.

So Alan, like Dorothy, was half a Scot and half a Jew. From earliest childhood he, like her, had been made to feel a stranger within the gates, and their shared feeling of anomaly lay at the very base of what was in every way a complementary marriage.

They had arrived in each other's lives at the very moment each most needed the other. Alan was at a turning point. He was an unsung actor of minor roles in unimportant plays, and at the time of his marriage, he had faced up to the fact that his talents as an actor were meager and that there was no real point in his continuing in a career in which he would never do particularly well. On the other hand, he had definite abilities as a script-writer, and he felt sure he could write successfully for the motion pictures. Moreover, he knew he could find work in Hollywood if he were to offer himself and Dorothy Parker to a studio as a writing team, for Hollywood was raiding New York's writing talent. He knew she would be offered work there, because she had been working on the Coast a year earlier. Metro-Goldwyn-Mayer had given her a three-month contract, and Alan also knew what had come of that, for as she had told a newspaper interviewer, "after some weeks, I ran away. I could not stand it more. I just sat in a cell-like office and did nothing. The life was expensive and the thousands of people I met were impossible. They never seemed to behave naturally, as if all their money gave them a wonderful background they could never stop to marvel over. I would imagine the Klondike like that—a place where people rush for gold." So Alan knew all this well enough. But he needed work. He thought things would be different for her if he was with her in Hollywood. He also guessed that, despite her having run away once, any studio would still be glad to sign the famous Dorothy Parker to a contract. The studio need not know how much of their scripts would be his work.

Dorothy Parker's need of Alan Campbell was of a different order. She badly needed someone to take her in charge and give some point to her days. Alan's beauty may not have been quite as masculine as Apollo's, and he may not have been so masterful as Lochinvar, but he made a wonderful major-domo. When they were living together in New York before their marriage, Alan had bought the food, done the cooking, done all of the interior decorating in their apartment, painted all the insides of the bureau drawers, cleaned up after the dogs, washed and dried the dishes, made the beds, told Dorothy to wear her coat on cold days, shaken the cocktails, paid the bills, amused her, adored her, made love to her, got her to cut down on her drinking, otherwise created space and time in her life for her to write, and taken her to parties.

"He took her and probably kept her living," Donald Ogden Stewart said. "He was important insofar as taking care of her was concerned, and she was well worth taking care of. Alan was an actor, and he may have been playing a part which little by little took over, but he wasn't a villain. He kept her living and working."

He also swept her off into the sunset—specifically, into the sun which sets over Hollywood's Garden of Allah—after a honeymoon at George Oppenheimer's California house. The Garden of Allah was a commercial enterprise that included a bar, a restaurant, and a number of cottages each different from the other and all of them architectural implausibilities. Here several screenwriters lived, Mr. Benchley among them. Mr. Benchley was endlessly fascinated by what, to him, were the Garden of Allah's hideous incongruities. And here it was that Dorothy and Alan played as dollar bills sifted gently down on them, for Alan had been quite right to think that Dorothy's reputation would find them employment. It certainly did—and at $5,200 a week, which, during the Depression, was equivalent in purchasing power to a salary of $15,000 a week today.

So it would seem that Dorothy Parker's days of footless drifting were at an end, and what a happy ending it was! Now she was not only famous but rich as well; she had an ardent young husband who brought order and a sense of security to her life at long last, and who respected her talent and sought to give her the time to do the work she was capable of doing. What more could any woman want?

"Presents!" Dorothy Parker cried.

2

Metro-Goldwyn-Mayer producer Hunt Stromberg waded back and forth through his office rug. So far the film had two stars, Nelson Eddy and Jeanette MacDonald, and a title, *Sweethearts*. The remaining problem was to think up some sort of story. To that end, a buzz session, or story conference, had been called, and Mr. Stromberg waded around in his rug, wondering aloud what the film ought to say and do, and asking the assembled writers whether it should. From time to time Alan Campbell would spring to his feet and buzz, "adding," as one of the writers said, "to this compost heap we were piling up." Dorothy Parker sat in a corner, knitting.

From time to time Mr. Stromberg would halt in midstride and look at the little woman in the corner. He had a great opinion of her opinions, possibly because he shared Hollywood's view that the more something cost, the more it must be worth.

"What do you think about this, Dottie?" Mr. Stromberg would ask. "Does this satisfy you?"

"Oh, yes," she would breathe. "I think so, don't you?"

Then she would lower her great, soulful eyes, and go on with her knitting.

Actually, her opinion of the stars and of the film could not have been sent through the mail. Her opinion of Mr. Stromberg was that if a physician should tap one of his knees, probing for a reflex, both of Mr. Stromberg's feet would fly into the air at once, kicking off his shoes.

Alan Campbell, however, amused himself with no such flights of fancy. To him, this was quite serious.

"He was always up there, buzzing," one of the writers said. "He was very faithful and articulate, and he did everything that a screenwriter was supposed to do. He made sense in terms of what this nonsense was about—it was really revolting—and he knew how to dish it out and he wrote it down and Dottie just sat there and knitted those long, shapeless garments."

Sweethearts was released in 1938, but the film and the story conference the writer described were in every way indicative of Dorothy Parker's and Alan Campbell's contributions to Hollywood and of their attitudes toward their work. Between 1933 and 1938, they received screen credits for fifteen films, including *Sweethearts*. The others were *Here Is My Heart, One Hour Late, The Big Broadcast of 1936, Mary Burns, Fugitive, Hands Across the Table, Paris in the Spring, Three Married Men, Lady Be Careful, The Moon's Our Home, Suzy, A Star Is Born, Crime Takes a Holiday, Trade Winds,* and *Flight into Nowhere.* One of these films, *A Star Is Born,* was nominated for an Academy Award, probably because show business people are sentimental about show business people, and think that everyone else is just as much interested in show business as they are, and this was a film about a girl becoming a star. But it was only less empty and banal than all the other films that Dorothy Parker and Alan Campbell worked on—a fact that was apparent to Dorothy but not to Alan. She believed they were living in Babylonian captivity, "working for cretins," and although she would loyally do what she could to brighten up the dialogue in Alan's scripts, she was oppressed by the feeling that she was giving a real gloss to false pearls.

She was also depressed to think that the scripts she and Alan worked over would carry their names. A Hollywood film would typically be written by not one or two, but by several writers, with the results that the finished script might be an uneven jumble of compromises if not non sequiturs, and no writer in his right mind would want to have his name attached to such a thing. Yet it was important to have his name attached to it.

He would fight with all the resources at his command for a share of the screen credit, because a writer without screen credits would very shortly cease to be a Hollywood writer, and that would be the end of his thousands-of-dollars-a-week salary.

None of this affected Alan, who was quite willing and able to fight for contracts and screen credits, and who was good at the work he was asked to do. His talents as a writer were perfectly matched to Hollywood's standards. His work was a labor of love. He loved being in Hollywood. He was thrilled to meet stars. He was a creature of the theater and the films, and all the people who had to do with stage and screen were at one time or another in Hollywood: he was at the center of his world. Coming out to the Coast had not been just a step up for him—it had been entering the Promised Land. It was not just the money, it was also the glamour and the success that he loved.

Of course, the money helped. He and Dorothy Parker did not stay long at the Garden of Allah. They shortly moved into a big house in Beverly Hills, one with a great white colonnade, a butler and a cook, and Alan could be the proud figure of a Southern gentleman as he stood at the door of his mansion to welcome guests whose names press agents had made familiar to every shopgirl in the nation.

On these occasions, Dorothy Parker would stand beside him, "reaching out my arms in my well-known gesture of welcome," she said, and saying to her guests, "Oh, how marvelous it is to see you again."

Then, in accents so soft as barely to be heard, but full of anxious solicitude, she would ask, "Do you want to meet any of the shits in here?"

"Well," one of her Hollywood friends said, "of course, when you went in, you became one of the shits, too."

That word always bothered Alan. Early in the twenties, Dorothy Parker had often used bawdy words, but only when their shock effect was necessary; and whenever she used them, she brought them out with little invisible quotation marks around them. But Alan saw nothing bright, funny or shocking in the way she used this word now. It was becoming her most usual descriptive noun, and she used it at home, at parties, and on the job. A filmwriter said she and Alan shared a cubicle in an office building reserved for screen writers, "and these rooms had very thin walls, and you could hear the typewriter going very busily, and then the faint drone of Alan's voice as he would read what he had apparently written.

"Suddenly you would hear his voice lifted, very loudly: 'Dottie! If you use that word once more, I'm walking out of this office and I'm never coming back!'

"Well," he said, "you knew what that word was."

It is possible that she was trying to tell Alan something. For her, the Promised Land was bounded by Central Park to the north and Greenwich Village to the south, by the East River and the Hudson, and its most pleasant area was just west of Fifth Avenue in the Forties and Fifties. She agreed with her friends Donald Ogden Stewart and Robert Benchley that Hollywood was an utterly preposterous Graustark where false values bounded about like demented rabbits; but in the beginning of her life there with Alan, her view of the place was that of a visitor to a zoo: she was fascinated by the curiosities she found there. She stared for a long while at a photograph appearing on page one of a Hollywood newspaper. It showed three elephants. One wore a silk hat, another a clerical collar, and the third, a bridal veil.

"I give it six months," she muttered, and turned the page.

She attended the ostentatious cocktail parties, where the conversation almost exclusively concerned salaries, options, agents, and who had to do what to or for whom in order to obtain a contract. She drank in the studio gossip, nearly all of which was salacious. She heard, marveling, that one producer had spent thousands upon thousands of dollars to hire a first-rate choral group, a symphony orchestra, and a world-famous conductor to make a recording of a song the producer had written to music by Bach. The point of all this was to make a phonograph record for private distribution among the producer's friends. The song was scatological, and as sick as it was filthy. As had been the case in New York and in the Europe she had seen, she was once again living in a special world, wherein a small group of people had money enough to do whatever they wanted; but whereas the New York rich and the Murphys in Europe had a dignity and an informed intelligence, the Hollywood rich, some of them, were as infantile and as irresponsible as Caligula.

In her first Hollywood year, 1933, she was still the visitor to the zoo, and did not consider herself to be one of the inmates. She was a New Yorker, and in New York her literary stock was going up. Her second collection of stories, *After Such Pleasures*, appeared, and the critics of her stories no longer deplored her subject matter as being sordid.

"To say that Mrs. Parker writes well is as fatuous, I'm afraid, as proclaiming that Cellini was clever with his hands," Ogden Nash told the readers of *The Saturday Review*. "But it's fun to see the lamented English language rise from the Parisian bone-yard and race out front with the right jockey in the saddle, and I cannot help attempting to communicate to others my pleasure in the performance. . . . The trick about her writing is the trick about Ring Lardner's writing or Ernest Hemingway's writing. It isn't a trick."

"Drunk or sober, angry or affectionate, stupid or inspired, these people of Mrs. Parker's speak with an accent we immediately recognize and relish," Mark Van Doren said in the *English Journal*. "Mrs. Parker has listened to her contemporaries with as sharp a pair of eyes as anyone has had in the present century, unless, to be sure, Lardner is to be considered, as he probably is, without a rival in his field. Mrs. Parker is more limited than Lardner; she is expert only with sophisticates. . . . But she does her lesser job quite perfectly, achieving as she does it a tone half-way between sympathy and satire. . . . Again it is only Ring Lardner who can be compared with her in the matter of hatred for stupidity, cruelty, and weakness."

While it was refreshing to hear that the critics were taking this more generous view, and comparing her prose to Hemingway's, Dorothy Parker nevertheless must have wondered at their equation of her writing and Ring Lardner's. She liked Mr. Lardner and, by her own account, had even for a brief while slept with him, but she must have shared Hemingway's view that Ring Lardner had no ear for the language that people actually used. The colloquialisms used by his characters were Mr. Lardner's idea of the way common people talked, or ought to talk. Still, the critics could hardly be blamed for their failure to distinguish between authentic dialogue and synthetic, for they lived on a plane remote from common speech. So, with the exception of this unfortunate comparison with Mr. Lardner, the reviews were good: she was being taken seriously in the one artistic medium that she now wanted to succeed in; she was being taken seriously in the only city that really mattered.

Hollywood did not matter. She thought the town was as asinine as the motion picture scripts she and Alan Campbell were assigned to write. The Hollywood money was convenient, however, and the money came flooding in. It enabled her to live within marble halls, with servants at her side. She ordered huge pink jersey hats and enormous black lace hats from John Frederics at $35 apiece, and, in the same week, another hat for $86.36 from Bullocks Wilshire. She ordered $628.45 worth of handmade lingerie from Emma Maloof in New York, and $80.03 worth of perfume from Cyclax of London, and she ran up a bill of $176.39 at Lilly Daché, and she gave her purchases no more thought than would a woman buying a roll of flypaper. The modern equivalent of the prices she paid, in terms of the purchasing power of today's dollar, may be obtained by multiplying by three. But the money did not matter; more was always coming in. In view of all the money that came in, one wonders how she succeeded in doing it, but she did: her bank account was frequently overdrawn.

Dorothy Parker's vague economic sense did not, however, prevent her remembering her obligations. No sooner did the money begin to arrive than she repaid the $2,500 that John Gilbert had sent her. She could not have chosen a happier time to return it, for the arrival of sound films—the talkies, people called them—had meanwhile put an abrupt end to the career of the Great Lover of the Silver Screen, whose voice was high and squeaky. Mr. Gilbert sent her a wire: THANK YOU, MISS FINLAND—Finland being the only nation in the world to repay its first World War debts to the United States.

Much as she lived in a golden splendor in a town not without its aspects as a freak show, Dorothy Parker was not always entertained. Alan Campbell would take her to parties and manage to get a game going, because he thought she loved playing word games. He thought this because she was extraordinarily good at them, although she professed to despise them. Like anyone from New York sojourning on the Coast, she felt far away from everything. She noticed that everyone, including native Californians, said "out here," as if they were all living out of suitcases and counting the hours until they could take the next train East. It helped that there were so many New York people in Hollywood. In addition to Mr. Benchley and Mr. Stewart, George Oppenheimer was there, and a mutual friend, Charles Brackett. So was F. Scott Fitzgerald, and Dow-Dow and Sara Murphy came to the Coast. Then too, various members of the international theatrical set came drifting in and out of Hollywood, including the British novelist and playwright Somerset Maugham.

It turned out that Mr. Maugham adored her writing, to the extent that he had not only purchased all her books but had them bound in red leather and made a part of his portable library —the library kept in wooden boxes that accompanied him everywhere. On meeting Dorothy Parker at a Hollywood party, and finding to his great joy that she was to be his table partner, he said, "Why don't you write a poem for me?"

She agreed, and when a servant supplied them with a blunt pencil and a piece of ragged wrapping paper, she wrote:

> Higgledy Piggledy, my white hen;
> She lays eggs for gentlemen.

"Yes," Mr. Maugham said, "I've always liked those lines."

He said she favored him with "a thin, cool smile, and without an instant's hesitation" added:

> You cannot persuade her with gun or lariat
> To come across for the proletariat.

Mr. Maugham was ecstatic. He said that with this brilliant rhyme she had gathered Higgledy Piggledy into the august company of Jove's Eagle, Sinbad the Sailor's Roc, the Capitoline Geese, Boccaccio's Falcon, Shelly's Skylark, and Poe's Raven; in fact, Chaucer's Chanticleer was the fitting mate for Dorothy's hen.

It was perhaps just as well that Willie, as Mr. Maugham's friends called him, did not hear what Dorothy Parker thought of him.

For her taste, a much more pleasant occasion was that of Vincent Sheean's visit. They sat having drinks together in the darkened bar at the Garden of Allah. They had gone there because everything about the place, including its grotesque name, appealed to their sense of humor.

"We sat in the darkest corner," Mr. Sheean said, "and she would go on for forty-five minutes or so about something like this: like what kind of shrouds we would like to be buried in; and it was a hell of a lot of fun. She said, 'I want to be buried in a shroud made of unpaid bills from Valentina.' "

Mr. Sheean was amused by her huge black wool lace hat. He said she was always looking for a place to hide, and with that hat, she had found one. But while he was amused, Mr. Sheean was also intrigued by the Alpine graph of her emotions, for as they chattered and gossiped together, her eyes suddenly filled with tears.

She cried for a moment. Then she looked straight at Mr. Sheean. "I used to be a poet," she said.

So that was a problem. Another problem was that she did not meet her New York friends nearly as often as she wished. Although many of them were working in Hollywood, they did not all work in the same studio, nor did they all live in the same neighborhood. The studios and the neighborhoods were far apart in space. There were no intimate speakeasies that served as clubs. There was no small hotel where she could be with Mr. Benchley and Mr. Stewart at lunch. Nor did she find the Hollywood people to be as congenial to her as Alan Campbell found them to be to him. She was homesick and lonely.

Early in their marriage, Alan managed to get Dorothy to cut down on her drinking but she soon began to drink too much again. So, for that matter, did Alan. There was an important difference in their drinking: She never seemed to be drunk, not in public at any rate, whereas Alan would become maudlin, sometimes violent. He would literally walk into walls; he would go sprawling on the floor when trying to rise from a chair. There were occasions when he could not find his way home unaided.

Following one of these, Dorothy Parker wrote out a check for seventy-two dollars to cover the "reward for cabdriver" and the new shirt and necktie that it had been necessary for the driver to buy for Alan.

It was not long before she was telling stories about him, often in his presence at parties. As an actor, she said, he had been "one of those people who would come in during the second act of a play, carrying a tennis racket with rhinestone strings, and ask the assembled company, 'Who's for tennis?' "

Once, while she and Alan were riding in an automobile with two friends, one of them asked Alan about his career as an actor.

"Did you ever see him on the stage?" Dorothy interrupted.

The friend said he had not.

"I wondered why you asked," she muttered. "Well, it was like watching a performance that Vassar girls would do, all dressed as men, and you'd expect their hair to fall down any minute."

Hearing his wife say these things about him, Alan Campbell would smile his actor's smile.

She told other lies about him. Appearing in public with a discolored lump on her forehead, she said Alan had hit her. Her friends found this statement somewhat bewildering, inasmuch as Alan at that time was in New York, negotiating a film contract. Actually, she had tripped over one of their six dogs, falling against a living-room coffee table.

Listening to the stories she told about Alan, everyone felt sorry for him—both Dorothy Parker's friends and his. They felt that he was wonderful for her, that he was doing everything he could for her, and that she had no right to be so cruel to him. Had Frank Sullivan been in Hollywood at the time, he might have expanded on his theory that Dorothy Parker always bitterly resented anyone who tried to help her. In any case, both Alan's friends and her friends were sad to think that what had at first seemed to be so strange a marriage, and then so complementary a marriage, was showing signs of strain. Dorothy Parker's oldest friends remembered the stories she had told about Edwin Parker, and what had happened after that.

It was another filmwriter who inadvertently suggested a possible path to salvation. He had been writing in New York when the Depression came, and like many another city dweller at that time, he thought that if he and his wife could find a cheap place in the country, where they could raise garden truck and chickens, they could save money. They had accordingly bought a farm in Bucks County, Pennsylvania, along with the first of what became a throng of New York writers and theater people to do so.

"When we were working on the Coast," the writer said, "in an effort to touch some kind of reality, we used to tell Dottie and Alan about this place, and pretty soon we began to hear this sort of threnody from Dottie:

" 'Alan, we've got to have roots. We've just got to have roots.' "

The more Dorothy Parker thought about this, the more reasonable the idea seemed—particularly with those royalty checks and all that Hollywood money now drifting so deep against the door. She and Alan could attend story conferences in Hollywood, take the resultant screen treatments away with them, catch the Super Chief east, and there, on a farm, far from the madding crowd, write their scripts together. They could go to New York on weekends to see the shows. They could have their New York friends come to stay at their farm. They could see only the people they wanted to see. They could get away from the nightmare of Hollywood, and they would have roots. She decided the roots they needed were early American ones. They would buy a Colonial farmhouse. Then she could have flowers and birdsong and dogs and write poems in the garden and help Alan with his silly scripts, and have roots, and share her private happiness with friends from New York when all this became too boring for words. Her new dream was a kind of Hollywood version of the old dream of the little white cottage with green shutters in the country, but it helped to make the many splendors and wonders of Hollywood bearable to her.

3

She was visiting in New York City because, like a female Antaeus, she needed to touch her mother earth. She was also in New York because her collection of short stories, *After Such Pleasures,* was to be adapted for the stage by Edward F. Gardner, whose wife, Shirley Booth, was to play the leading roles. The stories would be difficult to stage, and as matters turned out, the show lasted only twenty-three performances; but on the day that Alexander Woollcott telephoned her, he was not interested in discussing the theater, or her stories, or in chatting about the reasons why she was in town from the Coast. Mr. Woollcott was concerned about the fact that a number of Waldorf-Astoria Hotel waiters were on strike, and he wanted to help them. He wanted her to help, too. He said he had called Mr. Benchley that morning (it was the morning of February 6, 1934), and that Mr. Benchley had said he would try to be there.

Mr. Woollcott explained that Selden Rodman and Alfred Bingham, young staff members of the magazine *Common Sense,* would go to the Waldorf-Astoria's blue and gold Empire Room that evening, and as soon as the dance band paused, Mr. Rodman would make a speech calling on the diners to leave the hotel as a gesture of sympathy for the strikers. He said he and Mr. Rodman were notifying the hotel management and the town's newspapers that a demonstration would be made—but not by whom. He wanted Dorothy Parker and Mr. Benchley to be among the diners who would walk out. She told Mr. Woollcott that he could count on her.

If it should seem odd for the exquisite Mr. Woollcott and the elegant little Mrs. Parker to be championing the cause of labor, the reason was this: In 1934, the state of the Union was so moribund that a great many serious people believed the nation was close to revolution. "Comes the Revolution!" was a catch phrase of the day, and even the people who said this as they raised their glasses at "21" were not entirely sure they were joking.

What everyone did understand was that a new social order had to be found, and found soon, and very nearly all of the suggestions were radical ones. Huey Long, senator from Louisiana and the dictator of that state, said every man could be a king if the nation's wealth was equitably shared; and so many people believed him that he was taken seriously as a potential Presidential candidate.

Father Coughlin, a Catholic priest, acquired considerable national power by preaching, on radio, a simplistic nonsense filled with racial and class hatred that he called "Social Justice." Silver-shirted Nazis paraded in New York, and black-shirted Fascists surfaced in Michigan. Trotskyites, Townsendites, and Technocrats were also to be found in what President Franklin Roosevelt called this lunatic fringe of American politics, but taken all together the dissidents amounted to something more significant than a fringe.

Among the comparatively more responsible political elements were the Communists, the Socialists, and President Roosevelt's New Dealers—all of whose programs represented radical departures in politics and economics, if not revolutionary ones. Common to all the radical political groups, from far Right to far Left, was a concern for the toiling masses. Briefly, the Right wanted to rule the workingman, and the Left wanted the workingman to rule, and there was such a difference between the extremes that Right and Left were willing to fight about it.

In all this, Americans were caught up in the same arguments already virulent in the equally depressed Europe of the early thirties. The arguments were so bitter that those to right of center called those to the left of it Communists, whereas those to the left called those to the right Fascists. In America, as in Europe, the intellectual community marched briskly to the Left. A good many intellectuals went so far as to join the Communist Party; a large number were sympathetic to the Party's programs (particularly those dealing with labor's right to organize into trade unions and with those advocating an end to racial discrimination), and the largest number of all supported President Roosevelt's New Deal reforms.

One result of the intellectuals' enthusiasm for the Left was a spate of proletarian plays, poems, and novels with Marxist messages, and criticism of all works of art along Marxist lines. Another result was that many writers, actors, artists, and professors, believing themselves called upon to take social action, marched in union picket lines and otherwise lent their support to labor's battles. They felt they should show their solidarity, as they said —not just talk about it. Such was the context of Mr. Woollcott's February 6 telephone call to Dorothy Parker, and the following day, *The New York Times* reported its result:

"House detectives, scattered at various vantage points in the impressive dining hall, kept watching the faces of the customers, tensely waiting for the outbreak. They knew that something was going to happen, but none of them knew just what form the demonstration would take, nor did they know what person in the room would start it.

"Woollcott, beaming behind his glasses, came in with Miss [sic] Parker and took a table near the strike missionaries [Rodman and Bingham]. Benchley, bundled in a fur coat, came in with Miss Betty Starbuck [a young musical comedy actress] and sat with them. They ordered their food and then leaned back, ready to give all the moral support at their command.

"At eight o'clock the band stopped. Up jumped Rodman, clutching in his hand a thin sheet of manuscript.

" 'The people at our table,' he began, 'are in sympathy with the strike in which the waiters of this hotel are engaged and hope that every decent and self-respecting man and woman will leave this hotel when we do. The management of this hotel'—

"The house detectives reached Rodman before he could go on.

They came down on him en masse, tipping the table as they tried to start him for the door. Young Bingham grabbed his manuscript, mounted the gilded chairs, and carried on.

" 'We call upon not only the patrons to leave with us,' he shouted, 'but we call on the waiters too, to walk out in sym—'

"With a crash, the chair went from under him as the second wave of house detectives came charging up from remote corners of the dining room. The head waiter had ordered the door closed, and the flying squadron that had borne Rodman to the door was stymied.

"At this juncture the band leader leaped back on the bandstand, waved his baton, and his orchestra swept into the strains of 'Did You Ever See a Dream Walking?'

"By that time, Woollcott, Miss Parker and Benchley were departing. Miss Parker wondered out loud whether it was a private fight or whether anyone could get in on it. The remark was not wasted. Someone giggled.

"Rodman, his shirt front rumpled and his face whiter than ever, shouted:

" 'Help! Help!'

". . . Woollcott shrugged himself into his coat, adjusted his scarf, and summed the spectacle up in a single phrase.

" 'Just a swirl of ugly passion,' he said, and left with Miss Parker.

"Benchley got back into his fur-lined coat.

" 'Here I've been in bed all day with a cold,' he remarked, 'and Woollcott called me ten or twelve times to get to this thing. I come and do this thing for the waiters, and I suppose when I come out with this fur coat some striking waiter will sock me.' "

The *Times* reported that Mr. Benchley watched "with narrowed eyes" while the house detectives punched, kicked, and otherwise manhandled Mr. Rodman and Mr. Bingham out of the Empire Room. The newspaper said that Mr. Woollcott, Mr. Benchley, and Dorothy Parker "gibed at the detectives with a running fire of extemporaneous bon mots and 'wisecracks' as Rodman and his friend were mauled. They escaped unscathed."

Between his lines, the *Times'* anonymous reporter seemed to ask what in the world these wealthy wits thought they had in common with a union of waiters, and why they thought their *opéra bouffe* in the Empire Room would help the cause of labor. No doubt the *Times'* reporter thought these sophisticated people could not have been serious, particularly since they did little more than make jokes while their friends were being beaten.

But Dorothy Parker was quite serious—indeed, passionately so. Mr. Benchley might have gone to the Waldorf-Astoria more out of loyalty to Mr. Woollcott and Mrs. Parker than for any other reason, but her responses to the plight of the workingman were altogether genuine if not always well informed. She had just come from Hollywood where, at a supper party, she heard a guest complain that striking workers had vandalized his plant and beaten several of his employees. Knowing nothing more than this, she had taken after him, demanding to know why he had not met the workers' demands and avoided a strike in the first place. Everyone else at the party thought the manufacturer's reply was reasonable, but not she. She called him "a money-grubbing old poop" and would not believe a word he said. "To her," one of the supper guests said, "it was enough to know that the plant was struck: therefore, the strikers must be right." Her sympathies had always been for whatever dog seemed to be the under one, and whenever she made up her mind about this, she immediately closed it. In 1934, when the nation lay at the very bottom of the Depression, she strongly identified with the depressed, although she knew none of them personally.

She was not, however, wholly consistent, for shortly after taking part in the demonstration at the Waldorf-Astoria, she crossed a picket line of striking waiters in order to have a drink at "21" with Heywood Broun.

She tried to hide in the depths of her floppy black hat when Mr. Benchley saw them there. Mr. Benchley paused by the table and chided Mr. Broun, who crusaded for labor's causes in his newspaper column and who was the founder of the newspapermen's union, the American Newspaper Guild, for having committed the Left wing's cardinal sin—crossing a picket line.

"And don't blink those ingénue eyes at me," Mr. Benchley told Mrs. Parker, who was fluttering her eyelashes at him.

"What did he mean by saying I had ingénue eyes?" she asked Mr. Broun, now batting her lashes at him while Mr. Benchley chuckled and moved away.

Such inconsistencies made it difficult for many people, including not a few union men, to imagine that Dorothy Parker was sincere. Even some of her acquaintances wondered if she was not just being intellectually fashionable in taking a position on the Left. There did seem to be reasons for such a suspicion, because she had always moved on the crest of the wave of the moment. As a girl, she had found her way directly to *Vanity Fair* when that magazine set a style for the stylish. She had been early on the scene at the Algonquin. She was a part of the *New Yorker* group in its earliest days. She had gone to Paris and met the writers there just when the Paris group was being talked about in New York. She went to Hollywood when that was the thing that many successful writers were doing. No matter what group was in, she was in that group. Now, she was espousing the cause of "the little man" (as the New Dealers rather infuriatingly called the ordinary citizen) just at the time it was fashionable to do so.

"I am a Communist," Dorothy Parker declared in 1934, but everyone laughed, including bona fide Communists who could not take seriously anyone who wore John Frederics hats and lived in a Beverly Hills mansion with a butler and a cook and who openly adored Franklin and Eleanor Roosevelt. To the Communists, Roosevelt was an enemy, for his reforms were plainly delaying the Revolution. But Dorothy Parker thought President Roosevelt "was God; you didn't exactly feel you were slumming around him," while Eleanor Roosevelt impressed her as being decent and fair-minded. "It's hard to believe," she said of Mrs. Roosevelt, "but when you met her, she was the most beautiful woman you ever saw." So the bona fide Communists thought Dorothy Parker was naïve, but they did not let this thought dissuade them from making what use of her they could.

Her closest friends also thought she was politically naïve in calling herself a Communist, because if there was anything that typified the dedicated Communist, it was an unemotional, unswerving, and disciplined commitment to a singularly glum and tortuous body of thought. No one could envision Dorothy Parker subjecting herself to what the Communists called "Party discipline." No more could they imagine her plowing through the dense thickets of dialectical materialism as set forth by Marx and Engels. But they could very well agree with Beatrice Ames Stewart's remark that Dorothy Parker could never look critically at the Communist Party, once she had decided that the Party really wanted to help suffering humanity.

"She didn't get it, you know," Beatrice said, "but she was not a personal friend of the multitudes. She was a very, very *grande dame*, and contrariness was the wellspring of her Communism. She was anti. She was anti the Establishment."

Insofar as the Hollywood Establishment of 1934 consisted of those magnates who ordered the studios to confect silly and sugary dreams for a despairing populace, Dorothy Parker was certainly against *that*. Returned from her New York visit, she associated, ever more exclusively, with a Hollywood group that shared her disgust for what they were all doing in films, and who, like herself, entertained a somewhat romantic notion of what Communism was all about. This group included Donald Ogden Stewart, whose conversion to radical politics was set alongside Dorothy Parker's: none of their closest friends doubted their sincerity, but they thought it was misplaced, and joked about it. One story that went the rounds was that Mr. Stewart was hit by a truck as he crossed a street, suffered a concussion, and discovered when he woke up in hospital that he had become a Communist.

Another story, which Mr. Stewart said was not only funnier but true, was that he wondered what Communism was, and asked the doorman at Claridge's Hotel in London to suggest a book that might explain it. He said the doorman recommended John Strachey's best seller *The Coming Struggle for Power*, and that he read it on shipboard while returning to the United States, and by the time the Statue of Liberty hove into view, he was convinced. Beatrice added that, when they settled in their New York hotel, Mr. Stewart announced they were going to attend a Communist Party meeting in Union Square, and demanded that she turn her fur coat inside out, lest they be mistaken for capitalists. Mr. Stewart immediately disclaimed any memory of this, but Beatrice had a very clear one. "It was a mink cape with brown satin lining," she said, "and I turned it inside out."

What is not in dispute is that Mr. Stewart did embrace Left-wing causes, and shortly after his conversion, another story went the rounds in Hollywood and New York. It seems that Mr. Stewart attended a rich man's dinner party in Hollywood together with his old friend Mr. Benchley, and that at some time in the evening, someone said to Mr. Benchley, "I think you ought to look to your friend." Mr. Benchley looked, and there was Mr. Stewart in a corner, waving a glass of champagne in one hand and a piece of toast with caviar on it in the other, telling the party guests, "Comes the Revolution, none of you will have any of this; none of you will have anything. Join us while you can, because we are going to take this away from you."

Mr. Stewart does not remember this occasion, but those who tell the story, saying they were there at the time, all tell it the same way, even though some place it on a yacht and others at a Beverly Hills mansion. They add that no one could tell whether Mr. Stewart was serious or not. He was not laughing, they said, although he was saying that very kind of thing that would have sent him into gales of laughter had he heard someone else say it. Of course, what puzzled the guests was that Mr. Stewart was, and is, one of the gentlest men who ever lived, enormously civilized and full of gaiety, and the image of Mr. Stewart directing revolutionary workers to take champagne and caviar away from his rich friends just did not, somehow, come across. But he was not laughing. He was quite serious. He had "swung to the Left," as he said, and Mr. Stewart subsequently became sufficiently committed to radical causes to attract the attention of the United States government. And so did Dorothy Parker, who to everyone's astonishment showed herself to be just as capable of organizing committees and making speeches as she was able to appear to be a gently bred, demure, and rather helpless little woman who delighted in saying the most unexpected and hilariously appropriate things in the softest of voices.

Looking back on that chapter of their lives thirty years later, Mr. Stewart described his and Dorothy Parker's Left-wing activities as having been embraced "in absolute ignorance of what Stalin was doing." Nevertheless, even though Mr. Stewart could now perceive the real purposes of the Communist Party with the 20-20 vision of hindsight, he made no apologies for the causes he and Dorothy Parker espoused in the thirties. They *were* the right causes to have embraced, romantically or not, and no matter if instigated by professional Communist organizers working underground.

"It is very easy," he said, "to make fun of that Hollywood group in the light of what we have learned from Mr. Stalin, but it wouldn't be fair to judge the Left in Hollywood in terms of the Left of today. It would have been awfully easy for me to have made an awful lot of fun out of that whole Left swing in Hollywood, but in a way, it was so much better than the sham world of Hollywood. I think we all felt a bit guilty about making all that money and not doing anything with it."

In so saying, Mr. Stewart suggested a perfectly plausible reason for Dorothy Parker's turn to the Left, and one that may have escaped the attention of those who were unaware of her long-standing suspicion of wealthy people, and of her ambivalent attitude toward having money of her own. Then, too, she had been suspicious of the social contract since the day she watched the old men shoveling snow from her childhood sidewalk; she had been a feminist and a New Woman when she left Miss Dana's. Virtually every line she ever wrote had to do with the pain of living. In all those years of being a wisecracker and a party girl, bounding off to the Bowery to be tattooed, she had also been writing out of a deep sensitivity, with utter sincerity and disciplined artistry, within the framework of a tragic view of life. These qualities could not have been, and were not summoned up by, any kind of political Hey, Presto! of the nineteen-thirties. But the Depression, the public's agonized search for a better social contract, the emergence of the Roosevelts, the dialogue of the times, the dangers that Fascism and Nazism represented, the contrast between the irresponsible hedonism of Hollywood and the despair of the outside world, the plausible-seeming promises of the Communists, and Dorothy Parker's lifelong sentimentality for underdogs—all combined in 1934 to enhance her awareness of the pain of living and to give her emotions and abilities a different focus. So did they give a different focus to the lives of many others in Hollywood's never-never land, and if it might seem incongruous for so many wealthy actors and writers to play a part in radical politics, it did not seem so to them at the time.

They played such a role to save their honor and self-respect as much as to be of help to others. They may have seemed naïve, but history may one day say they were not wrong. Mr. Stewart said the time of the Hollywood radicals was Hollywood's proudest hour. Perhaps it was. In any case, when that hour struck, Dorothy Parker was there on the barricades, for all that she might have seemed better cast as Marie Antoinette than Madame Defarge.

"Dottie and I arrived at the politically conscious stage of our lives at about the same time," Mr. Stewart said, "and suddenly Hitler came into view. Dottie and Oscar Hammerstein, II, formed this Anti-Nazi League. I was the first president of it.

"Dottie was ready to do anything as far as fighting Hitler went. She made speeches and collected money. The Anti-Nazi League developed into quite a concern, because we could call on stars like Norma Shearer and Freddie March, and have them make speeches, and Dottie was always good, and I think she found a lot of pleasure in doing that sort of thing. But she was also terribly sincere."

She found something more than pleasure in radical politics. She found a sense of purpose. The conversation of the Hollywood radicals was not confined to salacious studio gossip. The talk was of issues, and the issues were important. She had believed her Hollywood life to be a rootless one, and she simultaneously perceived the nation to be as rootlessly adrift as she, or any tumbleweed. Radical politics promised roots of a sort, both for herself and for everyone else: the very word "radical" has to do with roots. The people in radical politics were not acquaintances or friends: they were more than that; they were comrades. They were comrades who brought meaning and purpose to the random chaos of existence. There was an excitement about this.

But political activity was helpful only to a degree. It gave her something to cling to and believe in, and this made Hollywood an easier place for her to endure. Still, she also felt a need for a private, personal holdfast—for a place of her own, far from Hollywood, where she and Alan Campbell could establish the roots of their marriage. The dream of a country place grew together with, but apart from, her increasing concern for politics.

So it was that late in 1934 she and Alan visited Bucks County, Pennsylvania, and there they found a beautifully proportioned Colonial house, and beside it a stone barn built in 1883, standing halfway down a gentle slope at the center of one hundred twelve acres of softly folded pasture and woodland. It was called Fox House Farm, and it was still in the possession of the original Fox family. The house itself was a slate-roofed, fieldstone ruin that had no bathrooms and only one fireplace. The fireplace was in the kitchen, and it was so large that Alan could stand in it.

Because all prices were low during the Depression, and because extensive remodeling would have to be done to make the farmhouse livable, the asking price for land and buildings was $4,500. Many a Bucks County native thought this was much too high, but to Dorothy and Alan it was less than one week's pay.

They spent some weeks at the nearby Water Wheel Inn while exploring the property and arranging for its purchase. An architect was engaged to rehabilitate the buildings, but many of the ideas were Alan's. The interior of the farmhouse would be gutted, then completely remodeled. The first floor would include the kitchen, a dining room, a living room lined with bookcases, a study that would also be lined with bookcases, a butler's pantry next to the kitchen, a bathroom, and a porch opening off the study. Upstairs there would be three bedrooms and three bathrooms. A five-room apartment for servants would be built in the stone barn. Next to the farmhouse there would be flowerbeds and an herb garden, and the slope before the house would be terraced and held in by stone retaining walls. Alan thought they needed a wrought-iron grillwork to frame the front door, after the New Orleans fashion, and that there should be Italian cupids and nymphs in the garden. Most important, they must have electricity and a telephone line. No farm in the area had either one, but their farm, which they would continue to call Fox House Farm, would have both. It would cost $3,000 to have electricity brought in—twice the average American family's annual income in those days—but they were content to pay this. Not counting a $2,600 swimming pool, which Dorothy would later give Alan for a Christmas present, they spent more than $98,000 to improve their $4,500 estate. And these were Depression dollars, worth thrice the dollars of today.

They employed a small army of carpenters, stonemasons, plumbers, and electricians, and they engaged a permanent staff to look after the farm during their absences. The staff consisted of a local farmer and jack-of-all-trades, Hiram Beer; his wife; and a sixteen-year-old boy, Louis Bohlman, who was to run errands, act as chauffeur at need, and help Mr. Beer with the lawns, gardens, flowerbeds, simple repairs, and carpentry.

With the farm bought, the work ordered, and the staff engaged, Dorothy and Alan returned to Hollywood in a much better frame of mind. Alan was happy because he was returning to Hollywood. She was happy because just having her farm, knowing she could always go to it whenever Hollywood became too much for her, was as comforting as a security blanket is to a child. She thought it marvelous fun to have a farmer whose real name was actually Hiram. She had never really believed that farmers were named Hiram. He was not to farm the property, however. She did not want livestock, nor did she wish to raise crops for market. She wanted to be able to look out over grassy fields and wooded hills. Hiram was under strict orders to keep everyone off the property. The land abounded in game birds and deer, and she could not bear the idea of anyone shooting them.

Hiram said he understood.

No one shot the birds and deer while Dorothy Parker and Alan Campbell were on the farm. Everyone waited till they left. Times were hard. In hard times, county people respect no posted lands or gunning seasons.

4

People noticed how particularly radiant Dorothy Parker looked when she returned to Beverly Hills following the purchase of her Bucks County farm. A reason for this was no doubt the pleasure she took in having at last that little house in the country she had once upon a time talked so much about. Her dream had come better than true: it was no little house, but a quite substantial one in the center of a considerable estate. But there was another reason for her apparent beauty, and Louella Parsons, a Hollywood newspaperwoman whose life was dedicated to spreading gossip about the people in pictures, learned what the reason was. It will be recalled that Dorothy Parker's original dream house in the country was to be replete with flowers, dogs, and babies. The great good news, which appeared at once in Louella's column, was that Dorothy was pregnant.

Now that she had roots, she was going to have her baby. Apparently, given a husband who took such care of her, and wealth beyond her prior experience, and given a place that, for the first time in her life, she could call home, she felt secure enough to allow her natural yearning for a child to overcome her earlier fear that nothing—particularly a child—could ever come to any good end in this worst of all possible worlds.

Her friends could scarcely believe Louella's good news. They immediately thought of Dorothy's notorious inabilities in all domestic affairs.

"Can you imagine her changing a diaper?" Beatrice asked Donald Ogden Stewart, and Mr. Stewart had to say "No," he could not.

The image of Dorothy Parker as a housewifely mother was just as difficult for everyone else to entertain, especially those who knew of all the elliptical things she had written and said about children, and how nervous she seemed in the presence of children.

But she was now as full of secret smiles and tenderness as any expectant mother of age twenty. She knitted tiny sweaters and boots and colored crib blankets, and to everyone's surprise, her needlework was quite beautiful. The idea of Dorothy Parker being good at this sort of thing had never occurred to anyone, either. All in all, this was a very pleasant Dorothy Parker—a rather sweet and girlish one who, like any very young mother-to-be, seemed wandering in a wholly delightful trance.

She grew sentimental over any mention of marriage and babies. Her great eyes filled with tears when, at a Hollywood party, she learned that one of the guests was to become a bride.

"Oh, it's so wonderful," she told the woman. "You're going to be married! You're going to have babies! What more wonderful than to have babies!"

The actress, who was about to become a bride true enough, but not by any means for the first time, could be forgiven for thinking that Dorothy Parker was being catty. But the pregnant Dorothy meant every word she said.

In the spring of 1935, in the third month of her pregnancy, she and Alan Campbell returned to Bucks County to see how work on their farmhouse was progressing, and they stayed again at the Water Wheel Inn. She visited with friends and her farm couple, the Hiram Beers. She talked with the Beer children about garden flowers, and about the wild flowers to be found in the woods, and Mrs. Beer was glad to see that the children "were crazy about her." Mrs. Beer thought Dorothy Parker was awfully kind, and that she knew an amazing lot about flowers and children.

While Alan discussed matters with the architect and watched the workmen, Dorothy had long conversations with Mrs. Beer. She said she had always planned on having six boys, all redheads.

Emboldened by this intimacy, Mrs. Beer asked Dorothy about her own childhood, but she refused to talk about that.

She puttered in her new garden, wearing rubber gloves, a big sombrero, a peasant blouse, and a dirndl that made her look something like a fat-stemmed mushroom. It was exactly what, in the thirties, the well-dressed country gentlewoman was expected to wear—but then, the country gentlewoman was also expected to be tall and slim.

"She never really gardened," Mr. Beer explained. "I did that. But she loved flowers. She used to play around digging in them, getting down on her hands and knees, trimming them up a little. She smoked all the time."

No doubt certain of the sophisticates of the Vicious Circle could have thought of clever things to say about Dorothy Parker in her role of fruitful Earth Mother, womb-heavy among the blossoms with her scissors, her basket, and her pack of Chesterfield cigarettes, but it is doubtful that their cruelest shafts could have pierced her new serenity.

She made it plain that she and Alan had planned this child. She left no doubt in her friends' minds as to how eagerly she looked forward to it. Some felt that, to listen to her, you would never think there had been a baby born before. But they were so glad to see her happy that they were not bored by this, and they were also touched by Alan's looking so brave and husbandly in his new role as father-to-be.

Any physician could have told her how the story would most probably end. Of course, any physician who *would* have told her this would have been a fool, but as a matter of medical fact, there is a strong possibility that a forty-two-year-old woman, experiencing her first full pregnancy, will miscarry during the third month.

Dorothy Parker's case was not exceptional. In the third month of the first pregnancy that she permitted to develop, she miscarried while she and Alan were staying at the Water Wheel Inn, making plans for the home that was to have sheltered a child.

And that was the end of that dream.

5

Her friends were sorry for her, but what could anyone say? Dorothy Parker did not speak of it. Mrs. Beer wished she could unburden herself, but it was not Mrs. Beer's place to suggest this. Without anyone having said a word, the layette, with its beautiful tiny sweaters and knitted blankets, disappeared. So did the photograph that showed Alan standing proudly behind her while Dorothy sat knitting baby clothes.

Slowly, life resumed its normal course, and normality for Dorothy Parker and Alan Campbell meant dividing their time among work on film scripts and Dorothy's political meetings and going to parties and entertaining friends and taking the Super Chief and the 20th Century Limited back and forth across the depressed country that lay between Beverly Hills and New York City. Their lives were busy, but a shadow obviously lay on Dorothy Parker's mind. Apart from helping Alan with his film scripts, she stopped writing in 1935, and Alan worried about this. It is too much to say that he knew that art was a form of catharsis, because to Alan writing was a job like any other. He did think that if she had work of her own to do, she would be happier. He also thought all one needed, in order to write, was a typewriter and free time. One afternoon at the farm, he took their house-guests on a long walk through the woods and fields in order to give her time to write a poem. He was disappointed when he returned to discover that she had filled an enormous silver bowl with violets, instead.

She neglected not only her talent but also her figure. While no one can remain lithe and beautiful forever, and while she was past forty, there is still a difference between being somewhat overweight and being fat. It may be presumed that she was aware of this; being so small a woman, she was doubtless acutely aware of it. But she seemed not to care anymore.

She did, however, care a great deal about her politics. She brought to her personal war against totalitarianism all the emotion she might otherwise have spent upon the child she never had. Within Hollywood's radical group, she formed a particular friendship with the playwright Lillian Hellman, a younger woman quite unlike herself in many respects. As Miss Hellman subsequently recalled in her autobiography, *An Unfinished Woman*, it was a strange friendship in that they did not like the same books or the same people. There was a difference in their ages, they led quite different lives, and were quite different sorts of writers. Miss Hellman's turn of mind was hard-driving, precise, and scarcely sentimental—an almost mirror image of Dorothy Parker's. In her book, Miss Hellman said she and Dorothy had met four years earlier in New York under conditions hardly conducive to further acquaintance: Miss Hellman had gone to a cocktail party with Dashiell Hammett, with whom she lived, and Dorothy Parker, on being introduced to a writer whose work she admired, fell to her knees and kissed Mr. Hammett's hand. This gesture, Miss Hellman recalled in her autobiography, was meant to be both funny and serious, but it was neither one to her. Nor was it to Mr. Hammett, who so detested Dorothy Parker from that time forth that he later refused to stay, not just in the same room, but in the same house with her. For her part, Miss Hellman found Alan Campbell difficult to stand.

Yet, meeting now in Hollywood in the winter of 1935, the two ladies were drawn to one another. One reason was that Miss Hellman's opinions on certain matters marched exactly with those forming in Dorothy Parker's mind. In her memoirs, Miss Hellman said that as a seventeen-year-old schoolgirl, she had walked out on Alexander Woollcott's New York University lectures whenever "he paraded the jibe-wit and shabby literary tastes of his world." She said she had no use for New York's wisecracks and witty insults behind the back. This view of New York's wit and taste was now Dorothy Parker's.

"Oh," she said, "the years I have wasted, being a party girl and a smartcracker, when I could have been helping all the unfortunate people in the world."

As if making up for that lost time, she renounced her New York past with all the fervor of a new convert confessing his misspent years; and again like the convert, she wished that everyone else would be converted, too. In this, Dorothy Parker was quite like many of the radicals of the thirties who disregarded the fact that their position was a minority one in the nation at large. They passionately believed in a better world and were as convinced as so many missionaries that they, alone, had the key to it. For whatever reasons, their advocacy was strident if not shrill. They believed together with Marx that the new world could be reached only after a class struggle. They were also convinced that anyone who did not agree with them was potentially, if not overtly, an enemy. Many people sympathetic to reforms that the radicals suggested were put off by this kind of contempt for others that the radicals so often expressed, and Dorothy Parker's older friends were sad to see an unintelligent intolerance growing within her.

"Dottie . . . set up a standard of political behavior with a stringent set of rules," her old friend George Oppenheimer said, "as had most of the members of the left-of-center group in Hollywood. If one of her friends failed to conform, Dottie stopped seeing him. She would be infinitely polite and overaffectionate when you met, but you were not admitted to her shifting inner circle. What's more, if you continued to see people with whose political viewpoints she disagreed, she found you guilty by association—a single standard which she applied, but resented bitterly when it was applied to her."

So Lillian Hellman and Fredric March and the Hollywood radicals were in, and Mr. Oppenheimer was out. And because he was a liberal too, and not a radical, Mr. Benchley was another victim of Dorothy Parker's new all-or-nothing single standard— for all that Mr. Benchley had been the first and best of her friends. Perhaps more by his choice than hers, they began to see less of one another. In New York, Harold Ross supposed that Dorothy Parker was now lost to *The New Yorker.*

Alan Campbell grew more and more concerned. He told Dorothy that her politics were dangerous. Being against Hitler might be all very well, but the kind of people who were most strongly against Hitler were also on the side of the labor unions, and the studios didn't like people who were on the side of unions. Making speeches in Hollywood couldn't hurt Hitler, Alan argued, but it could very well hurt Dorothy Parker and Alan Campbell with the studios. When she laughed at him, Alan grew angry, and Dorothy became angry in turn. She told him she thought he was nothing but "a fawn's ass."

For some time, she had been telling stories to his detriment, saying such things as "Alan can't even boil an egg," and "All Alan thinks about is parties, parties, parties"—even though the truth of it was, she could not boil an egg whereas he could, and she enjoyed parties every bit as much as he did, even if she wished to pretend she did not. When she had first said such things in his presence, Alan had smiled and said nothing, but that was before the farm, the miscarriage, and Dorothy's radicalism. Now, Alan was desperate. Pathetically enough, he called on one of Dorothy's new friends, another Hollywood writer, and asked if Dorothy couldn't be a Communist without making speeches.

"Dorothy cared terribly about politics," the writer said, "and Alan didn't know how to handle it; he wanted to get her out of it. She used to say the most frightful things about him."

One of the things Dorothy now said was that Alan was homosexual. She said this in his presence and out of it. She publicly accused him of a specific affair, turning to her friends and saying, "How do you like that for competition?" She referred to him as "the wickedest woman in Paris." One afternoon, she ended a party at her house by telling her guests she had to work on a film script. "You must excuse me," she said, "but I have to go to that fucking thing upstairs." Then, as if she remembered that Alan was upstairs in bed with a cold, she added, "And I don't mean Alan Campbell."

All this was worse than embarrassing: it was believed to be true. Her friends found it difficult to imagine that she had just made the discovery. Surely, they felt, she should have heard the gossip long before she married him. After all, there is no smaller town than the theater, and Dorothy Parker was well acquainted in the theater, and the gossip was that Alan was bisexual— AC/DC, New York brightly called it. This was one of the reasons why her marriage caused so much comment: people had wondered out loud whether the relationship was not that of the older woman and the young homosexual man, a relationship in many ways akin to that of doting mother and dutiful mama's boy. Some of Dorothy's friends had wondered how long it would be before she found this arrangement to be unsatisfactory, or if she ever would, for all that Alan might make heterosexual love to her. Alan, meanwhile, had done nothing to dispel the gossip. He had been, and continued to be, friends with a considerable number of male homosexuals.

But Dorothy Parker had not made this sort of attack on her husband prior to her interest in Left-wing causes. It was now as if she felt that the times called for men to act, and when Alan did not want to act as she wished, and moreover said he was afraid to do so, she simply wrote him off as a man.

Yet, there was no question of divorce. Their friends speculated that Dorothy Parker was much too important to Alan's career for him to think of divorcing her, no matter how she treated him, whereas Dorothy needed Alan's care far too much for her to think of leaving him. They remained together and quarreled constantly.

They also grew richer. In the two years, 1935–37, one of her publishers paid Dorothy Parker more than $32,000 in royalties— her collected poems, *Not So Deep as a Well*, appeared in 1936 to a chorus of critical praise—and the Hollywood money was pouring in. She promptly spent it. She regarded it all as ill-gotten. Everyone knew what she thought of the motion pictures she and Alan worked on, but now she said that the royalties from her books of stories and poems represented a kind of cheating: she said all of her work was meretricious.

Not unnaturally, the people who heard her say this sort of thing (while she fished around in an empty purse and someone else paid for the drinks) supposed that she was donating huge sums to Left-wing organizations. Her checkbooks do not indicate that she ever did. According to her checkbooks for those years, most of the money went into the farm, a great deal into personal luxuries. Insofar as her charitable donations are concerned, she gave more to the Los Angeles Boys Athletic League, the National Association for the Advancement of Colored People, the League of Women Voters, the Democratic Party, and a summer camp for slum children than she ever gave to a radical cause. There was only one radical organization listed on her balance sheets. It was the Friends of the Abraham Lincoln Brigade, an organization supporting those American volunteers who in 1937 were fighting for the Loyalist side in the Spanish Civil War. She sent them $120. At the same time, she sent $250 to the Democratic National Committee.

It is always possible that she could have made anonymous cash contributions to the Communist Party or Left-wing groups, but at that time it was not an American sin to be a Communist. So there was no reason why she should have needed to resort to duplicity, and in any event, her disorderly checkbooks do balance and do not reflect sizable cash withdrawals. What her books chiefly reflect is that she spent quite a great deal upon Alan and herself. Yet her conduct of her financial affairs should not be taken as evidence of a lack of a true humanitarian concern. If it is evidence of anything, it is only that she never did equate money and reality.

During the period 1935–37, she did very little writing of her own. She wrote no poems, and her prose was not particularly inspired. In 1937, *The New Yorker* published a story called "But the One on My Right," which glittered with such lines as these: "I'm here against my better judgment. That would be a good thing for them to cut on my tombstone. . . . I should have stayed home for dinner. I could have had something on a tray. The head of John the Baptist, or something." It is all done in interior monologue, and the slender burden of the story is that she is bored to death at a party, wishes to talk to the man on her right, but finds him taken up by the woman on his right. Eventually, she seizes a chance to talk with him, finds that he is as bored as she, and they make an arrangement to leave the party together as soon as possible. It is a wry, sad, and occasionally funny piece, but it is not much of a story. When Mr. Ross said he felt that Dorothy Parker was lost to *The New Yorker*, he might have had contributions like this in mind.

During these same two years of more politics and less writing, the Pennsylvania farm lent a measure of stability to a quarrelsome marriage. She had never done such a thing before, perhaps because she had never before owned a place of her own, but Dorothy Parker busied herself with interior decoration. She told Alan what they chiefly needed in their lives was color, and she decided to do their living room in nine shades of red: pink, rose, scarlet, magenta, vermilion, crimson, maroon, russet, and raspberry. There was strawberry wallpaper in the hall and in the dining room; the interior shelves of the bookcases were Paris green; the shutters and iron grillwork outside were pink; their bedroom was blue and white. Alan had the deep recesses of their windows lined with mirrors, so that the windows seemed wider than they were, and the trees on the lawn closer. Dorothy dipped a feather into a bucket of gray paint and traced arabesques with it on the living room mantlepiece to give the dark varnished wood an appearance (she thought) of marble. This so intrigued them that she and Alan painted their superb mahogany Duncan Phyfe dining room table gray, tracing curlicues on it with a feather dipped in white paint to simulate a gray and white marble surface. They purchased two crimson wingback chairs that each had but one wing, and set them on either side of the living room fireplace. A large, thick, deep cerise rug was bought for the living room but this, they realized, was a mistake. The rug was sent to New York, where they kept an apartment, and throw rugs were scattered on the living room floor instead. The dining room had a wall-to-wall carpet, and this and the lighting fixtures were startling novelties to the Bucks County natives who were doing the work under Alan's direction. The lighting was indirect, and the handyman, Louis Bohlman, thought that Dorothy and Alan had got the idea for it from the light fixtures in the recently opened Holland Tunnel.

So there were light and color everywhere in the house, and tall vases and copper bowls filled with flowers, but unfortunately, not everyone admired the total effect. Some of Dorothy's friends who visited the farm could no more recall the decor than they could recall that of the cheap furnished rooms she had lived in during the early days in New York. Others were appalled by the desecration of the Duncan Phyfe table and by the anachronism of a Colonial farmhouse furnished in other-than-Colonial style and taste. Worse, they had the bad manners to say so.

"We caused talk," Dorothy Parker later wrote in 1942 in an article for *House and Garden* magazine. "We even caused hard feelings. . . . There are no folk so jealous of countryside tradition as those who never before have lived below the twelfth floor of a New York building. They moved into their beautiful Pennsylvania stone houses, and they kept their magazines in antique cradles, and they rested their cocktail glasses on cobblers' benches. . . . Their walls were hung with representations of hydrocephalic little girls with scalloped pantalets and idiotic lambs, and their floors were spread with carpets that some farmer's wife, fifty years ago, must have hated the sight of, and saved her egg money to replace. Now, they can't *really* think such things are a delight to live with. Can they? They found us vandals. . . . Now only the natives speak to us. We feel all right."

It was perhaps just as well that when the natives spoke to her, they did not tell her what they thought.

"The furniture those people had was different from the kind ordinary people use," Mr. Bohlman said. "It didn't look comfortable."

Nor was it comfortable, said the farmer, Hiram Beer. The twin red fireplace chairs were not easy to sit in, he said, "and the dining-room chairs were all busted."

"I just never cared for her furnishings," Mrs. Beer said. "There were never any drapes on the windows."

The absence of shades, drapes, or curtains scandalized the country people, even though as Mr. Bohlman admitted, "of course, they were back in there, where there was nobody to bother them." Still, the countryfolk thought that not having curtains was suggestive, if not downright lewd—and Alan's mother thought so, too.

Hortense flatly told her daughter-in-law to put curtains across those windows. Even more flatly, Dorothy refused.

Hortense decided there was nothing for it but direct action, but she waited until Dorothy and Alan were away from the farm for a fortnight. Then she had the Beers install drapes, curtains, and shades on the windows. It was her little gift to the children. Dorothy, on her return to the farm, ordered the Beers to take those things down and throw them away.

"I don't know why Dottie hates me," Hortense told Mrs. Beer.

"I wish that woman would never come to this house," Dorothy Parker told Mrs. Beer.

She went on to say that she thought Richmond, Virginia, was not far enough away for Mrs. Campbell to be. Alan, however, wanted his mother to buy a house near them in Bucks County, and this raised serious doubts in Dorothy's mind as to Alan's good sense. She said she would never stay at the farm if Hortense was in the same county: Alan would have to choose between his wife and his mother. But Alan made no such choice, nor did Dorothy move out when Hortense came to visit. She was particularly gleeful whenever Alan quarreled with his mother. Lillian Hellman was a visitor to the farm on one of those occasions. In her memoirs, Miss Hellman said she and Dorothy Parker were knitting by the fireplace while Alan and his mother quarreled loudly and angrily upstairs.

"When the voices finally ceased," Miss Hellman wrote, "Alan appeared in the living room.

"He said, immediately, irritably, 'It's hot as hell in here.'

" 'Not for orphans,' Dottie said, and I laughed for so long that Alan went for a walk and Dottie patted my hand occasionally and said, 'There, there, dear, you'll choke if you're not careful.' "

In later years, Dorothy Parker spoke of the times she spent on the farm as being the happiest of her life, and while this may well have been true, there was always an atmosphere of tension about the household even when Hortense was not there to add to it.

"You knew things weren't going good," Mr. Bohlman said, "but you didn't know why, or what, because you tried to stay clear of those things. If they knew you knew things weren't going good, that wasn't good. So you just tried to stay clear of them."

He said something seemed to be annoying Alan. Dorothy and Alan had facing typewriters on a table in the study, and Mr. Bohlman said that from time to time they would argue over the work they were jointly doing.

"She'd be very calm and nice about it, but he had this quick temper," Mr. Bohlman said, "He could be the sweetest person you'd know, and next minute he'd take a poke at you. He could explode in a split second. I can remember him booting the dogs in the rear end, he'd get so mad.

"If you want my honest opinion," Mr. Bohlman went on, "I think he was just a spoiled brat. I think he found himself a pocketful of money when he married her: she was always paying the bills. He was always being introduced as 'This is Dorothy Parker's husband, Alan Campbell,' and I guess this made him pretty tense. I think he felt she was a better writer, and it bothered him. I felt she bought a nice-looking, strong young man, and she had the power to get one. He tried to hold himself down as much as he could, but at times I guess he just had to let go. He just built up so much steam inside, that after a while —bingo!"

The one employee with whom Alan had no trouble was Hiram Beer. One day Alan blew up at Hiram, whereupon the solid, square, tough-muscled and independent Pennsylvania Dutch farmer stared contemptuously at the handsome actor and told him where to go.

"After that," Mr. Beer said, "'I had no more Alan Campbell trouble."

In addition to the Beers and Mr. Bohlman, the domestic staff included a Negro couple from Richmond and a Filipino. The Negro man served as butler, his wife as cook, and the Filipino (whose stay was short) as the houseboy. To these people, Alan presented another kind of problem. He loved to cook, and was particularly proud of his liver loaf, and he amused himself in the kitchen during the servants' day off. But as Mrs. Beer said, "Oh, the kitchen when the help came back! Oh, the pots and pans! The help were about to quit so many times!"

Presumably it was Dorothy who persuaded them to stay on, for the servants found her to be as delightful to work for as Alan was difficult. Mrs. Beer said Dorothy was gentle and generous to them, that she might forget to pay them and they would have to remind her, but then she would have Alan write out a check with the amount left blank. This was also her practice with respect to Mr. Bohlman and the Beers. She trusted them all to write in the amount that would cover their monthly pay, plus whatever the Beers or Mr. Bohlman might have purchased for Alan and Dorothy at the local village store. Beyond this, there was one other thing about her that commanded the respect of the country-bred Beers:

"When she sat down to work, she was all business," Mr. Beer said. "She'd really work hard, late at night, get up early in the morning and get to it, no fooling around. And when she played at gardening, she was serious about that, too, and very orderly, keeping a place for every tool, and every tool in its place."

Since the work she did on film scripts was hateful to her, the fact that she went so diligently about it suggests loyalty to Alan, for all that she might think him a fawn's ass; perhaps a realization that the chore must be done if the bills were to be paid; and possibly a respect for work itself even if she detested the task to which she had been set. But her disciplined attitude about work and her fastidiousness with respect to tools did not carry over into all else in her life, and the fact that it did not fed the tension that clung about the farm.

There were, according to one of her Hollywood friends, twelve dogs and five cats. Perhaps there just seemed to be that many. Mr. Bohlman remembers only "six or seven dogs," but no matter what the number, they were always in the house, on the rugs, and on the furniture and underfoot, and whenever the staff had its day off and Dorothy and Alan also spent that day away, Dorothy would simply lock the animals indoors. "When they'd come back," her Hollywood friend said, "the house would be a shambles. You could skid on the floor. It was sickening."

Then too, Alan kept his clothing and personal articles in as neat a fashion as his military college would have liked, whereas Dorothy resented this and complained about it to her friends. She took no such care of her own expensive clothing. She had a habit of putting her soiled underclothing back in the drawer with the clean; this irritated Alan and faintly disgusted Mrs. Beer, who did the laundry. Mrs. Beer said that Dorothy had "lovely things, all the slips were handmade," but that she did not like having to sort through Dorothy's bureau to separate the dirty from the clean. Moreover, it did her no good to remonstrate.

She did so just once, and the hitherto-gracious Dorothy Parker icily asked Mrs. Beer whether she wanted her job or not.

It also seemed to the staff that Dorothy and Alan differed in their choice of friends. They said that Dorothy enjoyed the company of her friends to a far greater extent than she did Alan's. What the staff did not know was that many of Dorothy's friends were her political colleagues, whereas Alan's were not. All they knew was that famous theatrical and motion picture people called on Dorothy; when Fredric March came to the farm and put his hand on Mr. Beer's mother, that astounded and delighted woman was careful for a month not to wash the place his hand had briefly rested. Either out of hero worship or genuine feeling, the staff felt that Dorothy's guests were "more refined" than Alan's were. This, they said, made relations rather strained at times, but there was a further source of disagreement: Dorothy liked the farm more than Alan did.

The Beers remember Dorothy Parker walking alone across her fields with her dogs on warm, sunny late afternoons—a little woman in a huge Mexican sombrero, her full skirt bright-colored against the green. And Alan would be posing on the terrace in slacks, sports jacket, and turtleneck sweater, a drink in his hand. When Dorothy gave him a swimming pool as a Christmas present, it was to give him a reason for finding life in the country bearable.

The staff wondered what good their employers got out of the farm. They would come only in dry weather for a few weeks at a time, seldom in winter. They did not hunt, ride, keep cattle, or grow crops (although in her *House and Garden* article, Dorothy said they farmed their land), and it seemed to the Beers that Dorothy and Alan wasted the days they spent in the country.

"They never got up early," Mr. Beer said. "If they were out of bed by eleven o'clock, you were lucky. Dinners at nine P.M. would be real early; it was more like eleven, and they'd stay up 'way late, sometimes until four in the morning."

There were a great many parties, and on party occasions Mr. Beer, who had already put in a full, early-morning countryman's day, would be pressed into service as the bartender until predawn hours. He was amazed at the drinking that went on. He said

Dorothy drank Manhattans, and Alan, Scotch on the rocks, and when not this, they shared pitchers of Martinis.

"They'd bring it in by the cases, and both of them used to run around with drinks in their hands even when there was no company there," Mr. Beer said. "When they had people there, they had people who felt they had to drink just because they were there, and that's what there was to do. They'd all get up past noon, and after their lunch, or breakfast as it might have been, they'd start drinking until late at night."

The Beers, who were meeting New York and Hollywood theatrical people for the first time in their lives, and deeply impressed as they were by the famous names, could not understand anyone who could sleep through the best part of a country day, nor could they imagine what the city people found to be so amusing about just sitting around drinking and talking. Everyone seemed to be having fun, but the Beers wondered if they really were. They knew that Dorothy Parker was famous for saying funny things, but they never heard her say anything that seemed funny to them, and when Mrs. Beer overheard Dorothy telling jokes to the guests, she marveled at the response.

"To me," she said, "her jokes were nothing." Mrs. Beer blushed. "I thought they were vulgar, but the dinner guests would just roar at them."

If the staff found Dorothy's ménage incomprehensible, so to a certain extent did at least one of Dorothy's Bucks County neighbors.

"I think in terms of those evenings when we used to sit and wait and wonder whether dinner ever would be served, while Alan was saying, 'Dottie, don't you think we could have just one more pitcher of Martinis?' " her neighbor said.

"We would chew our fingernails down to the quick, wondering what horror Alan would be serving," he went on. "By the time anybody ate, it wasn't a casserole bubbling on a hot stove—the stove would have been turned off at nine P.M. It was now past midnight and still no one had had anything to eat, and what was on the stove was a congealed morass. By two thirty A.M. they would be pleading with you not to go home, but to have another pitcher of Martinis."

By this time in the morning, Alan, Dorothy and their unfed

company would all be well in their cups, but despite this, her neighbors would have had a good time because the company assembled at the farm was always a brilliant and witty one. The conversations were never serious, nor did anyone expect them to be: that was not the point of a drinking occasion. There was no talk of writing, nor of books, painting, music, nor even of current political events, nor of anything else that bespoke the slightest concern for affairs of the mind. What there was, was funny gossip about people, and often about the Bucks County natives. Dorothy and Alan were endlessly amused by the shortcomings, naïveté, gaucheries, attitudes, and beliefs of the country people, including their staff. They would refer to louts and peasants, and have a great deal of fun making fun of them. And all the guests would laugh, as people at cocktail parties always do, loudly and more loudly, while Hiram made their drinks.

But, like virtually everyone who entered Dorothy Parker's circle, one neighboring couple found that it was not all laughter, that she was an uneasy friend. For a time, he and his wife were banished from her house.

"One day they invited us to dinner," he said, "and we drove down that long lane that leads to the farm. The house looked so completely different that we both thought we had gone down the wrong lane, because we remembered having seen three huge Norway maples that used to stand in front of the house, and here was this house that had all been done up like something out of *House Beautiful*, with all the Charleston, South Carolina, trimming. We got out of the car and they both came out of the house and greeted us and said, 'What do you think of it?'

" 'The trees,' I said. I was absolutely floored.

" 'Oh, we chopped them down,' Alan said. 'It was too dark; they overshadowed the whole house.' "

At this point, Dorothy's neighbor was so flabbergasted that he forgot his company manners. "You must have needed the wood awful bad," he said—and Dorothy and Alan stopped speaking to him for two and a half years.

"Well," he said, "two and a half years later we had a party and invited them as well as a playwright and a man who lives here who was dying to meet Dottie, and after a while I asked Dottie what she thought of him. She said, 'You must have needed the wood awful bad.' I thought this was so funny I screamed with laughter, but that mysteriously angered her, and they didn't speak to us for another whole year."

Like all of Dorothy Parker's friends, however, this man and his wife were willing to accept the penalties of her friendship, including occasional ostracism, for the value they found in her. But again like so many of her friends, they felt a concern for her.

"When you ask whether she was a happy woman," the husband said, "the answer is, she most definitely was not. She was rejecting her work and she felt unfulfilled—not unfulfilled at not having children so much as that she was naturally a despairing person. Her short stories were the thing that she should have been doing, but they lived at the farm as though they were in Beverly Hills."

So the farm was Hollywood without the politics. In Hollywood it was possible to see the sham and the stupidity of the parties and the studio gossip, and to crusade on behalf of the little man against his oppressors; and Hollywood was so hateful that it was necessary to escape from time to time to the open fields, the woods, and the birdsong where the pattern was to joke about the peasants and go wobbling off to bed near dawn, choking down two sleeping pills, waking out of a wet sleep late in the afternoon, and beginning to drink in another day. When this was not the pattern and there was work to do on motion picture scripts that simply had to be written, then it was a matter of grinding away at a job that was not worth doing at all, except in terms of the money it produced.

Lillian Hellman, who knew Dorothy Parker as well as anyone at this time, wrote that she saw in her a woman of great pride who virtually begged others to wound that pride: she saw this in Dorothy Parker's relationships with "everybody and anybody." But the one person who most grievously wounded that pride was Dorothy herself. She lived with a fretful husband in a rather oddly furnished house, quarreling with her friends, allowing herself to grow dumpy in barren middle age, wasting her time on silly scripts, stunning herself with alcohol and sleeping pills, loving the workingman in general while despising him in particular, ridiculing as meretricious the artistry that had enabled her to become the mistress of a New York apartment, a California mansion, and a country estate. Between 1935 and 1937, she spent herself as she spent her money: as if she hated both. And she made jokes and laughed.

Perhaps the story would be different if she had not lost her child. Perhaps not. Montaigne suggests that the traveler takes himself wherever he goes.

6

"The only group I have ever been affiliated with is that not particularly brave little band that hid its nakedness of heart and mind under the out-of-date garment of a sense of humor," Dorothy Parker wrote from Spain in 1937. "I heard someone say, and so I said it too, that ridicule is the most effective weapon. Well, now I know. I know that there are things that never have been funny, and never will be. And I know that ridicule may be a shield, but it is not a weapon."

She wrote this for the Left-wing newspaper *The New Masses*. In addition to disclaiming adherence to any political group, she assured her readers she had come to Spain "without any axe to grind"—although she was in Spain to cover the Loyalist side of the war, and not the Falangist one. The Loyalist government was supported by the trade unions, dominated by Communists, and given military support by the Soviet Union. The rebellious Falange was supported by the Spanish aristocracy, the large landowners, Spain's Catholic Church, and the Spanish military; it was dominated by Fascists and was given troops, tanks, guns, and airplanes by Fascist Italy and Nazi Germany. As many thoughtful people knew and feared at the time, the Spanish Civil War was the opening engagement of a war to the knife between the military dictatorships of the far Right and all the world to the Left, including the democracies. There could be no doubt where Dorothy Parker's sympathies lay. The only truth in her reporter's disclaimer was that sometimes humor could conceal an emptiness.

From Madrid, she sent *The New Masses* a fairly straight, mostly hard-news report, although her account of a child day-care center might have impressed any but Left-wing enthusiasts as being unduly roseate. Madrid was being shelled and bombed. The children were, as children in a war zone always are, the victims of an incomprehensible terror. But she chose to see them as happy and healthy, and to find the quality of their education at this center to be "as good as American children at a progressive school" receive. And *that* was either propaganda or wishful thinking.

She resorted to bathos to describe the results of an aerial bombardment of Valencia by Fascist aircraft: "There was a great pile of rubble, and on top of it a broken doll and a dead kitten. It was a good job to get these. They were ruthless enemies of fascism."

But then she wiped out all this nonsense by writing a marvelous short story, "Soldiers of the Republic." It contains no lies about unground axes, unbelievably happy children, or symbolic dead kittens. The story is quite simple:

Dorothy goes to a café in Valencia with a Swedish girl, and there they see Spanish families taking what pleasure they can, drinking small cups of coffee or glasses of wine, in a moment stolen from the midst of a holocaust. Spanish soldiers join Dorothy and her friend at a table.

> One of them, some six months before, had heard of his wife and his three children—they had such beautiful eyes, he said—from a brother-in-law in France. They were all alive then, he was told, and had a bowl of beans a day. But his wife had not complained of the food, he heard. What had troubled her was that she had no thread to mend the children's ragged clothes. So that troubled him, too.
>
> "She has no thread," he kept telling us. "My wife has no thread to mend with. No thread."

One of the soldiers suddenly discovers what time it is—time to return to the war and go to their probable deaths. They all jump up and leave, having had a brief moment to talk of homely things, and when they had gone, the Swedish girl signals the waiter. The waiter shakes his head and his hand: the soldiers had paid for the wine.

Perhaps "Soldiers of the Republic" is not fiction, although it was published as a short story. It is told in the first person, and this, plus the entirely credible account, leads us to believe we are reading a report. But it is a report on the human condition, not on Spain or Valencia. In a very few words, Dorothy Parker created men, women, and children alive in a believable time and place and gave them a universal, timeless quality. In this writing, she did what Hemingway tried all his life to do: she created literature more true than fact. Her "Soldiers of the Republic" could be placed exactly alongside Hemingway's "Old Man at the Bridge" (which Hemingway filed as a straight news story out of the Spanish Civil War, and then republished as a short story). Both stories are examples of an attitude and a technique employed by two contemporary and very similar masters during the golden age of the short story.

Her story was significant in another sense. In virtually all of her other stories, Dorothy Parker had rather bleakly disparaged the fatuity of the lives she saw about her, or had created fictional characters who disclosed that which she saw in herself and despised. But in "Soldiers of the Republic" she indicated that the author was going to correct, rather than simply disparage, the faults she saw in herself, now that she had found in others human values worthy of emulation—and well worth protecting. As different from the bulk of her work, "Soldiers of the Republic" was an affirmative statement. She had enlisted for the duration in the good cause, instead of sheltering on the sidelines behind the shield of ridicule.

She returned to the United States to be widely misunderstood. *Newsweek* magazine, reporting on what it called "the startling conversion to the Loyalist cause of hitherto class-unconscious intellectuals," said:

"Most surprising of those hearing the call of the proletariat was the bitter-sweet wit and poetess Dorothy Parker. A visit to

Valencia unhinged her renowned flippancy on a subject it had never touched before: 'Darling of me to have shared my cigarettes with the men on their way back to the trenches. Little Lady Bountiful. The prize sow.' "

The lines *Newsweek* quoted were from "Soldiers of the Republic," not from Dorothy Parker in conversation, but the magazine pried them out of context and imagined them to be flippant. This is surely a monument to journalistic callousness. The "startling conversion" of the intellectuals to the Left was, in 1937, already a story some four years old. Self-disparagement was hardly something she had "never touched before." No doubt *Newsweek* was a prisoner of its clipping files; no doubt Dorothy Parker's early reputation as a flippant and funny girl prevented the magazine from believing that she could be, at age forty-four, a mature woman and a mature artist who meant every word she said.

Newsweek's skepticism marched with that of others who thought the pro-Communist activities of Hollywood radicals were bogus. Some of the Hollywood people believed that the radicals among them, Dorothy Parker included, were just pretending to be pro-Communist so that in case there *was* a revolution, the wealthy radicals would claim to have been revolutionaries, too. This kind of suspicion was maddening. She had tried to support a waiters' strike in the Waldorf and the *Times* implied she was silly; she helped form a league against Nazism and some of her friends drew away from her, and her husband became angry and frightened; she wrote a passionate truth from the ruins of Valencia, and now *Newsweek* thought this represented a startling change in her. She beat her head against the walls of her reputation. She told all who would listen that she wished she had never written a humorous line. She wanted everyone to forget her wit and listen to the alarm she was trying to sound. But Harold Ross wanted her to be funny, and Alan Campbell wanted her to shut up, and Metro-Goldwyn-Mayer wanted her to write film fantasies that would entertain a public that possessed (so Hollywood producers believed) the mind of a twelve-year-old. MGM wanted her to work on *Sweethearts* with Jeanette MacDonald and Nelson Eddy and all those teeth and all those moony eyes and all those cotton-candy plot situations—while the world was burning down. It was enough to give a vulture indigestion.

Somehow, she managed to come out of Spain and into Hollywood again; in the two years, 1937–38, she worked with Alan on five film scripts; she conducted a social life in Hollywood, in New York, and on the farm; she found time to work on another short story, "Clothe the Naked," which *Scribner's* magazine published in 1938. The story dealt with the horrible distance that separated the nation's whites and Negroes, and showed how the white middle class knew nothing about Negroes nor much more about itself. But her principal activity during those two years was political. She attended radical meetings in Hollywood and made speeches up and down the nation, pleading for support of the Spanish Loyalist government and for relief of the victims of the Spanish war. When Ernest Hemingway came to Hollywood in 1938 to show the film *The Spanish Earth*, to raise money for the purchase of ambulances for the Loyalists, she helped make the arrangements. The film was shown at the house of Fredric and Florence March to a selected group of wealthy actors and writers, who that night contributed $13,000; and afterward Dorothy Parker suggested that everyone come to her house for a nightcap. In her memoirs, Lillian Hellman said she gathered the impression that Dorothy and Ernest did not like one another, but the circumstances of the occasion were, she said, pleasant enough to make both of them feel affectionate. Of course, the circumstances of this meeting were such that the characters "Wisecracking Dottie" and "Old Dr. Hemingstein" were absent.

Unfortunately for herself and all the world, Dorothy Parker campaigned for a losing cause. For two years, she sought to arouse Americans to the Fascist threat and persuade them to support the legitimate Spanish government. She derided, as only she could, the isolationists; the fence-sitters. Finally, speaking at a party in Washington, D.C., held to raise money for the relief of refugee Spanish children, she broke down and wept.

Life, no longer a humor magazine, but now under the auspices of Henry Luce a news magazine, printed a photograph of that occasion. It showed Dorothy Parker in a fur jacket, seated on a piano, holding forth her arms, tears glinting on her cheeks. They could well have been tears of vexation, as much as those of compassion, for on the same page of that *Life* issue of January 30, 1939, that showed Dorothy crying, there was a photograph of young Senator Henry Cabot Lodge contemplating eight thousand telegrams sent him by Catholics who did not want the nation's Neutrality Act amended to permit the United States to send arms to the Spanish government. *Life* also reported that former New York Governor Alfred E. Smith, Archbishop Curley of Baltimore, two former ambassadors to Spain, Father Coughlin, and at least half of all the rest of America's Catholics wanted a Fascist victory in Spain, where Fascist troops were now closing in on Barcelona. *Life* printed a photograph of Philadelphia's Cardinal Dougherty shaking hands with the Imperial Wizard of the Ku Klux Klan; the magazine further reported that Mussolini's newspapers had praised Father Coughlin for that priest's anti-Roosevelt, anti-Semitic speeches and for his propaganda against the Spanish Loyalist government. The clear purport of *Life*'s coverage was that Dorothy Parker's position was a minority one.

Time magazine picked up the picture of Dorothy Parker on the piano. Its caption said that "famed Writer & Wit Dorothy Parker nervously swore off humor: 'I don't see how you can help being unhappy now. The humorist had never been happy, anyhow. Today he's whistling past worse graveyards to worse tunes. If you had seen what I saw in Spain, you'd be serious, too. And you'd be up on this piano, trying to help those people.'"

Time's decision that she was nervous may be placed beside *Newsweek*'s notion that she was flippant. But worse, those of her friends who thought she had often been acting in the past, now thought she was overacting.

Much worse yet, as the quality of her prose improved, the demand for it dropped. True, she sold "Clothe the Naked" to *Scribner's* magazine in 1938, but magazine editors did not want her to speak to the condition of man. They wanted the wry, witty, and sophisticated Dorothy Parker to amuse them, and this enraged her. She found an opportunity to express her anger when asked to address the Left-wing Congress of American Writers in that portentous year, 1939. She entitled her paper, "Sophisticated Verse and the Hell with It."

"Out in Hollywood," she told the Congress, "where the streets are paved with Goldwyn, the word 'sophisticate' means, very simply, 'obscene.' A sophisticated story is a dirty story. Some of that meaning was wafted eastward and got itself mixed up into the present definition. So that a 'sophisticate' means: one who dwells in a tower made of a DuPont substitute for ivory and holds a glass of flat champagne in one hand and an album of dirty post cards in the other."

She returned to Hollywood in this bitter mood to hear the end of the Spanish war. Of course, there had never been much hope for the last year or so—but the end was so miserable, and the United States recognized the new Fascist government with such indecent speed. The fighting ended when Madrid fell on March 28, 1939, and the last bodies had not been cleared from the wreckage before the United States recognized the Franco dictatorship—on April Fool's Day.

To be sure, there was no other government in Spain for anyone to recognize, and there was always that chance that by shaking hands with Franco the United States might be able to draw him a bit away from Mussolini and Hitler, but reflections of this sort would not have commended themselves to Dorothy Parker. More than one million people had died in Spain, and neither she nor anyone else on the American Left regarded that war as having been simply a Spanish one. So the American Left did not want the United States to shake hands with Fascist dictators; it wanted the United States to oppose them. No one today can doubt that the Left was quite correct, and Franklin Roosevelt's administration felt so at the time, but in 1939 the United States was in no position to oppose anyone. It had an antiquated, one-ocean Navy, an Army (including an Air Corps) of 125,000 men, and nearly half its citizens were ardent isolationists.

Dorothy continued to do what she could. She helped to raise money for the relief of Spaniards who fled from the tyranny that so swiftly and inevitably followed the Falangist victory. And she went doggedly ahead making speeches on behalf of the Anti-Nazi League. Her audiences included those who were compiling lists of names that would later be made available to studio managements, to the Federal Bureau of Investigation, and to the

House Committee on Un-American Activities. At least some people were taking her seriously. Once she stepped out from behind the shield of ridicule, there were those who described what they saw, writing it all down in the form of a dossier.

7

Alan Campbell was frantic. Didn't she know about studio spies? About the possibility of blacklists?

Dorothy Parker could scarcely not have known. Nor could she have cared. She was always frightened of being hurt, but she always put herself in a position that invited hurt, and she was always ready to return measure for measure. This, her friends said, had characterized her relationships with lovers, and it seemed to characterize her growing love affair with causes she believed to be humanitarian ones. So there were spies? Let them spy.

This, too, was the attitude in early 1939 of the Hollywood radicals, who regarded being spied upon as a compliment to their effectiveness. They felt no particular fears then, for it seemed as if the nation was coming to agree with them, even though they had not been able to influence events in Spain. They could see that many of the radical proposals of 1933–34 were now the law of the land; that the Administration was solidly pro-labor and anti-Fascist even if the same could not be said of the citizenry or of the Congress; that President Roosevelt's New Deal was by no means unresponsive to radical suggestions; that Roosevelt had recognized the Soviet Union and that relationships between the two nations were, if guarded, at least amicable; that the worst of the Depression was past, although a good bit of it certainly remained; that the nation was belatedly looking to its defenses and was selling arms to England, Holland, and France.

Nor were the Communists, the most radical of the Left-wingers, unduly worried about being spied upon. Their doctrine assured them that they would be. But meanwhile the Communist Party of the United States had legal status like any other political party, and its members felt that the Constitution protected their right to belong to it. The Communists could take some pride in the success of what they called their transmission belts, or front organizations, by which they meant political action groups they either controlled or strongly influenced, such as the anti-Fascist groups to which Dorothy Parker belonged. The Communists accounted it a solid victory that Hollywood stars and intellectuals like Dorothy Parker had been brought into camp. Very well, there were spies about. Let the capitalist bosses spy all they pleased. The world was moving to the Left, and the days of the bosses were numbered.

Actually, it was the Left whose days were numbered, and the death blow came from a source the radicals least suspected. In the last week of August 1939, the Soviet Union made a treaty of peace and friendship with Hitler's Germany. Each nation pledged not to attack the other for a period of ten years. Exactly one week later, Hitler invaded Poland. England and France took up the cause of the Poles, and the second World War began, with the Soviet Union standing aloof. But not for long. Three weeks after Hitler invaded Poland from the west, the Soviets invaded Poland from the east, meeting the Germans in the center of that unfortunate country and, with a mutual show of peace and friendship, dividing Poland between them.

Heretofore the Communists had been the stoutest of America's anti-Fascists. American Communists had fought in the Abraham Lincoln Brigade. They had supported the Anti-Nazi League, to which Dorothy Parker gave so much of her time. The Communist newspaper, The Daily Worker, had portrayed the Soviet Union as the implacable enemy of Fascism, making much of the fact that Soviet aviators had fought Fascist ones in Spain. American Communists were therefore poleaxed when the Soviets signed their nonaggression pact with Hitler, and they writhed helplessly when the word shortly came from Moscow that they should regard the signing of this pact to be a positive blow for peace. Everyone else in the world, if not the American Communists too, quite properly regarded it to be a guarantee that war would ensue, as it promptly did.

Next and worse, the American Communists were required to say that Russia's invasion of Poland was a purely humanitarian act, undertaken to safeguard the rights and lives of the Polish workers. But worst of all, the American Communists were required to accept the Party line that the war between England and France on one side and Germany on the other was *not* a fight against Fascism. Rather, the Party line said, it was just another imperialist war between capitalistic nations, and therefor the Communists would have nothing to do with it. Communists must, however, oppose America's possible entry into the war, and oppose, too, America's sale of arms to the western allies, because Communists should never serve the ends of a capitalist war.

Obediently, the United States Communist Party dropped its pre-August anti-Fascist flags and raised new placards that said, "Let God Save the King," and "The Yanks Aren't Coming," and Dorothy Parker and all other members of Hollywood's radical group were trapped.

If they continued to oppose Hitler and Fascism, urging support for France and England, their Communist friends would attack them as being tools of capitalistic imperialism. If they did not continue to oppose Fascism, everyone else would assume they were pawns of Moscow.

Dorothy Parker wanted to think of herself as being a Communist, even if no one else could think that she was, but she could not go along with the new Party line, and neither could many other intellectuals in Hollywood or elsewhere. Many of the intellectuals who had joined the Party during the Depression felt betrayed and quit the party in angry disgust; many a fellow-traveler would no longer go an inch of the way, because they began to see the Communist Party as simply an agent of Soviet foreign policy.

A problem was that the Party line with respect to the war was only a part of the line. Hollywood Communists also wanted to help build unions of writers, actors, stagehands, musicians and electricians, and they backed many another cause with which a good many people were in full agreement. But now because Communists were viewed with profound suspicion, a suspicion also attached to anyone believed to be the friend of Communists, or who agreed with any of the Communists' aims and goals. Since the Party kept its membership rolls secret, the suspicion was enhanced: Who could tell who was, or was not, a Party member? "If it looks like a duck, flies like a duck, and quacks like a duck, then it is a duck," became a popular expression, and the United States government was shortly to work out a set of criteria to determine whether a person might be a Communist. These criteria were based on the Party's avowed programs and beliefs, and if anyone subscribed to a large number of these programs and beliefs, then that person was suspect.

Under these suspicious circumstances, the nation's move toward the Left lost momentum, for the Communist Party's loss of credibility jeopardized the credibility of any Left-wing cause they had supported—and the Communists had supported very nearly all of them.

As the atmosphere of suspicion deepened in Hollywood, Dorothy Parker found herself being judged, as Mr. Oppenheimer said, by that single standard she had applied to others. Nor was she alone, for suspicion fell also on people entirely innocent of any sort of political activity: there were those in Hollywood who sought to curry favor with studio managements (and assignments for themselves) by denouncing their friends as Communists. Social relationships became somewhat more than uneasy, and as if this were not bad enough, some studios began to demand that actors, writers, and others employed in the film industry prove their political innocence to the studio's satisfaction before being assigned to a film.

Fox House Farm was one refuge from a world suddenly turned disastrous, and an apartment in the Algonquin was another, but Dorothy Parker did no work at either place during 1940. It would seem that there were so many frustrations in her public life, and so many tensions in her private one with Alan, that she could not write—that once again she suffered from writer's block, this time for an entire year. Her only publication in 1939–

40 was *Here Lies,* collecting all her fiction published till that time. A reviewer, William Plomer, writing in the *Spectator,* described the stories and guessed as to the author's state of mind:

"The urbanity of these stories is that of a worldly, witty person with a place in a complex and highly-developed society, their ruthlessness that of an expert critical intelligence, about which there is something clinical, something of the probing adroitness of a dentist: the fine-pointed instrument unerringly discovers the carious cavity behind the smile.

"Mrs. Parker may be amused," he wrote, "but it is plain that she is really horrified. Her bantering revelations are inspired by a respect for decency, and her pity and sympathy are ready when needed."

What her critical intelligence told her had, indeed, horrified her, but now as the nation drifted more and more quickly toward the whirlpool of Hitler's war, and she had abandoned banter as a means of revelation, and as her pity and sympathy became politically suspect, Dorothy Parker was unable to write, even though stories published just before this year-long drought showed her to be at the very height of her powers.

Nor, during the two years 1939–40, did she and Alan work on a single film, although she said she did. She listed as her screen credit for 1939 work on *Five Little Peppers and How They Grew.* Anyone looking up Dorothy Parker's film credits in the Lincoln Center's theater library in New York will find that entry, and Dorothy's friends today go faint with laughter when asked about it. That, they will explain, was her little joke. It was her way of stating what she thought of Hollywood.

It was not much of a joke, but then it was not much of a time, and Hollywood (never much of a place for an artist at any time) was a singularly poor place for an artist with a social conscience in 1939–40.

It would also seem that no one in Hollywood asked Alan Campbell to write a script during those years, despite the fact that he and Dorothy Parker had worked on fifteen successful films in the past, and despite the fact that his political disagreement with Dorothy was well known. He might very well have suspected why no one wanted to sign a contract with him now, and quite probably knew why.

8

When the United States entered the war, many of Hollywood's screenwriters, directors, actors and technicians volunteered to produce training films for the United States Army. They were ordered to report to the Hal Roach Studios, which the Army had requisitioned, and there they learned to make their beds, sweep their floors, and salute. Sentries were posted about the grounds, which everyone now called Fort Roach. It is recorded that, when one of Fort Roach's new garrison saluted his equally new lieutenant, whom he had known for years, that officer affectionately licked the fellow's nose in return and presented him with a package containing one white feather, rubber ducks for use in the bathtub, a Japanese compass, a Tyrolean hat with an enormous plume, a yo-yo, and a file of *House Beautiful* magazines. A sentry, witnessing this scene, and not understanding the private joke, was so startled that he nearly dropped his rifle.

It would have been perfectly possible for Alan Campbell to have joined this happy band of warriors, but he felt called to other duties. He had been graduated from a military college, and he volunteered for retraining as an officer. The Army sent him to its Air Force ground school at Miami Beach, from which, three months later, he emerged as a new lieutenant.

At age forty, Alan was embarrassingly old for so low a rank, particularly in the Army Air Forces, where fliers in their early twenties became colonels, but Alan looked far younger than his years. When he left Florida, he was in hard physical shape, bronzed from sun and sea wind. He was so happy and handsome in his carefully tailored uniform that Dorothy wept.

Of course, Dorothy Parker passionately believed in the war against the military dictatorships. She was proud of Alan's having volunteered, proud that he wanted to serve overseas instead of at Fort Roach. She loved being able to say, "my husband, Lieutenant Campbell." At the same time, she hated those words, knowing that a man cannot be both a husband and a soldier. Twenty-five years earlier, she had seen a young husband go off to fight Germans; she felt she was living in a recurrent nightmare. She asked Alan why he couldn't wait to be drafted. She accused him of deserting her by enlisting. She refused to be consoled; she would not believe a word he said. She quarreled with him up to the moment of his leaving, but when he was gone she was proud of him, and it seemed to her that they had never been closer than at the moment of their parting. Their purposes finally ran together.

This same feeling, that everyone was in the same lifeboat, pulling hopefully through a tempest, brought a kind of truce to Hollywood. The Right was still suspicious of the Left, but when Hitler invaded Russia it became more fashionable to regard the Soviet Union as a brave ally than as the potential destroyer of the American way of life. As the Arab proverb says, "The enemy of my enemy is my friend," and all the enemies of the enemy agreed to be at least civil to one another as they made their common cause.

It was also a time for everyone to do what he could, and the advent of war created a climate in which serious writing was far more acceptable than sophisticated witticism. Perhaps these two facts helped to remove the block: in any case, Dorothy Parker returned to her typewriter and sold *The New Yorker* a short story, "Song of the Shirt, 1941." It ridiculed the well-meant efforts of one type of society woman to be of use in the war, and it seemed to have been written with her left hand exclusively, but *The New Yorker*'s acceptance of it was indicative of the new national climate. Then, for *Mademoiselle*, Dorothy Parker wrote an article called "Are We Women or Are We Mice?"—urging women to stop acting as if the war were a charity bazaar. She said there *was* something intelligent and effective that upper-class women could do. They could take on all the sorts of work that had been done by the men who had gone to war: they could drive buses and taxicabs and work in factories. Much as her friends may have been tempted to imagine Dorothy Parker trotting off in her little high heels, wearing her John Frederics hat and her Valentina gown, carrying her lunchpail through the factory gate in the wake of Rosie the Riveter, the fact was, she was doing the thing she could do best. She was writing—this time, urging ways and means of action.

In 1942, Universal Pictures asked her to work on the film *Saboteur*. The film had no particular significance, beyond a possible implication that so many scriptwriters were in uniform that the studios were willing, during the war, to hire radicals from the blacklists. She accepted the assignment, writing a film about sabotage was war work, of a sort.

Yet it seemed to her that writing articles and propaganda was not enough. While Alan was in training camps in 1943, she presented herself to the Army recruiting office as a candidate for the Women's Army Corps. All went well enough until it came to the matter of her age. Women who had passed age fifty by a date specified in the regulations could not be accepted. She explained that she had been a premature baby and that had she been a full-term one, she would not have passed her fiftieth birthday by the critical date. An application was made to waive the age regulation; the Army was granting such waivers in the cases of a great many men. In due course, Dorothy Parker received the Army's answer.

It was No.

She hated the Army for being so stupid about this. She hated being too old; she did not think of herself as old; she refused to think of herself as ever becoming old. The Army had taken Alan, although he was too old to have been drafted. It made no sense to her that the Army should have taken him and refused her.

Then it occurred to her that there was another way she could fit herself into the war. It was an even better way than by being

234 / you might as well live

a woman soldier, for if she had joined the WAC, she doubtless would have been confined to duty in the United States, whereas if she became a war correspondent, she could serve overseas. Very likely, she could make her way to wherever Alan might be serving. Obtaining a newspaper or a magazine contract would hardly be a problem. So she applied for her passport, entirely unaware that the government had for some time been keeping careful track of its citizens.

In every military company there was at least one soldier whose duty it was to spy on his fellows and report to the Army Counter-intelligence Department whichever of them seemed to him to be a Communist, Fascist, Nazi, or other sort of subversive. The civilian population was likewise under surveillance by local and federal police who, among other things, watched the citizens' mail and maintained files of photographs taken of persons who attended Communist Party meetings and/or patronized book-shops operated by Communists. It will be recalled that spies attended gatherings of Hollywood's Anti-Nazi League, and that the government worked up a set of criteria against which to measure a citizen's political loyalties.

High on the list of criteria of suspicion was the category PAF, or premature anti-Fascist. This included all those who had thought Hitler was a monster before the government officially declared him to be one. The category surely included all Communists, for Communists had been outspoken anti-Fascists in the days before the Hitler-Stalin nonaggression pact was signed and the war began.

The government did not charge Dorothy Parker with being a Communist: the Party was not an illegal one, and she would have committed no crime if she had joined it. But she was a PAF, and any PAF *might* be a Communist. Moreover, she wished to be a war correspondent, and such people were in a position to learn military secrets. The government felt that if a person might be a Communist, and might learn a secret, then he might betray that secret, if the opportunity ever arose, to our ally-by-sufferance but potential next enemy, the Soviet Union. The government also then believed that citizens could not claim passports as a matter of Constitutional right, but rather that the government could grant or deny passports to its citizens as it pleased. During the war, it was not granting passports to PAFs who were members of Left-wing organizations, and particularly not to such PAFs who wished to be war correspondents.

Dorothy Parker's immediate reaction was one of incredulous outrage. But with this, there came a sickening fear, and suddenly the Army's refusal to take her into the WAC was seen in a new light. It is one thing to imagine, but another to know, that one's name is lettered on a government dossier. From anger and fear, her mood passed into one of despair: a friend said at the time she seemed to be completely defeated—defenseless, vulnerable, and apathetic. She moved in a trance until the sense of shock was gradually replaced by one of sadness.

She worked on a film for Republic called A *Gentle Gangster*, which was released in 1943, and for Warner Brothers on the motion picture *Mr. Skeffington*, which appeared in 1944, but her heart was no more in this work than it had ever been, and she spent as little time in Hollywood as possible.

She followed Alan from camp to camp whenever she could, just as she had followed another husband from camp to camp in another war a quarter of a century earlier; and in the summer of 1943 she found herself the houseguest of Robeson Bailey, an instructor of English at Smith College in Northampton, Massachusetts. Mr. Bailey had met Alan at a cocktail party given at Smith by women Navy officers for officers attached to Alan's nearby Air Force base, and the Baileys invited Alan to spend a week in their house and to bring Dorothy Parker, whom they had not met.

"We figured if she was Alan's wife she must be pretty all right," Mr. Bailey said, "although because we had a household of three young children we were afraid she might not fit in very well."

Her appearance at once disarmed his fears. She arrived in Alan's old, ramshackle automobile, and to Mr. Bailey's astonishment, she seemed to be "small, dowdy, and timid." He said his first thought was, "What a nice, harmless little person!

"She had an awfully funny dress," Mr. Bailey said. "She looked somewhat like a beehive, and she was being awfully, very definitely Alan Campbell's wife. She was self-effacing; she was quiet. I wanted to protect her. She was so damned decent, and yet she had this legend of indecency about her, encrusted with this New York glamour. She was oversensitive, and wanted to be protected from being Dorothy Parker. I kept calling her 'Mrs. Campbell.'"

Both the Baileys immediately noticed how much older Dorothy Parker was than Alan Campbell, but Mrs. Bailey said, "They seemed to be just a very happily married couple despite the disparity in age. He obviously must have had a mother thing about her, I should think."

Dorothy and Alan handed the Baileys what Mrs. Bailey still remembers as "an enormous hoard of ration points" with which sugar and meat could be purchased, but other than this, Dorothy Parker pulled a fairly weak oar as a houseguest.

Mrs. Bailey shortly discovered that her famous guest had no feminine small-talk about keeping house or raising children. Nor did she ever speak of her family or of Alan's. Puzzled, Mrs. Bailey wondered if Dorothy Parker's silence on these matters had something to do with her being a barren woman, sadly envious of a fruitful one.

The Baileys waited for the Parker wit, in vain. One day Dorothy saw a rose bush thick with Japanese beetles, and she muttered, "The damned things are always making love, aren't they?" and Mr. Bailey clutched this to his memory for want of any other pearl. She did not talk about the war. Being a teacher of English, Mr. Bailey tried to talk with her about her works and about books, but she put him off. The only thing she said about books was that she and Alan had once tried to sort theirs. They had tried the Dewey decimal system, but gave it up because neither of them understood it, Dorothy said, "So we tried it by other things, by authors, by subjects, and then we tried it by Good and Crap. So our bookcases are divided only by Good and Crap."

Not unnaturally, Mr. Bailey wanted to introduce the author to the Smith College faculty, but he fought down this temptation, for it seemed to him that she wished to remain incognito— she was certainly playing everything in the lowest possible key, as if she had a need to withraw from the world. But one evening toward the end of her visit, Mr. Bailey could restrain himself no longer. He was, after all, entertaining a writer whose works the college generation greatly admired, and he asked if she would be willing to say something to a few members of his class.

"The students were very much taken with her," he said. "She talked with them forty to fifty minutes on the general problems of writing. I cannot recall what she said to them; she didn't have anything to say that was immediately helpful to them. It didn't seem to me that they'd got much out of her, although the girls seemed to think they had."

The moment the last of the girls left the Baileys' living room, Dorothy Parker fled upstairs, crying.

Thinking back on her tears, the Baileys wondered if the appearance of the young girls had evoked in Dorothy Parker a nostalgia for her own youth.

Following this brief experience in what might be called a normally intelligent middle-class household (certainly one of very few such experiences, if not the only one she had), Dorothy Parker returned to what Mr. Bailey presumed to be the glamour of New York. Alan left for England, where he presently wrote the good news that he was stationed in London, meeting the London theater people and having a marvelous time. She was not having a marvelous time. She moved fitfully through the days of being a soldier's wife. She did not go to the farm where, with her permission, Hiram Beer was now growing crops for the war effort. Everyone was involved in the war, it seemed, except herself; she was being kept out of it because she had joined the right side too soon. It seemed that everyone was out of town except for Beatrice Ames, who was living alone in a New York apartment. It was sad about Beatrice, who had resumed her maiden name. Donald Ogden Stewart had left her and married another woman. Beatrice and Don had had their troubles, but perhaps they would not have parted had Beatrice gone along with Don when he moved to the left.

An invitation came from Somerset Maugham, and Dorothy Parker accepted it. He was staying in the cottage made available to him by his publisher, Nelson Doubleday, on Mr. Doubleday's estate in South Carolina.

There ensued what Dorothy later told Beatrice were the longest three weeks of her life.

"That old lady," she said of Mr. Maugham, "is a crashing bore."

She had gone there, she said, hoping to find bright people around, but instead there was only Mr. Maugham and various handsome young men who were not interested in ladies but who were interested in Mr. Maugham. And for three long, long, long weeks Mr. Maugham had wanted to do nothing other than play bridge.

Since virtually everyone else in the sophisticated world paid tribute to Mr. Maugham's wit, intelligence, charm, and urbanity, her statement strikes a strangely discordant note. Even those intellectuals who disliked Mr. Maugham's writing never said he was boring. Perhaps she just said this for Beatrice's benefit. Yet at this time in Dorothy's life, Mr. Maugham could have quite unnerved her. He was British, and as Dorothy Parker said, "Whenever I meet one of those Britishers, I feel as if I have a papoose on my back." She tried to deal with the sense of inferiority that the British gave her by parodying their accents. She was fond of wrinkling her nose and saying that once an Englishwoman had introduced her as "the gret Ammeddican pwetess, Miss Doddothy Wadden"—probably, Dorothy said, confusing her with Mrs. Warren of *Mrs. Warren's Profession.*

So it was one strike against Mr. Maugham for being British; a second, for being rich. Next, his life was orderly and assured, whereas hers was something of a mess. Then, he was a prolific writer and she was not—and Dorothy Parker was always uncomfortably aware that she was wasting her talent by not using it. She was now given to judging people by their politics, and Mr. Maugham's politics were hardly radical ones. Finally, she had her own reasons to dislike homosexuality in men.

Her wail could, more simply, have welled up out of a sense of purposeless loneliness, and a conviction that playing bridge was a form of anesthesia. The loneliness was surely there, and she eventually got to the heart of it, if she did not exorcise it, when she returned to New York and wrote an altogether remarkable short story, "The Lovely Leave."

The story is that of a soldier and his wife who quarrel from the moment of their brief meeting until the moment of his return to the war. Each loves and understands the other, but as they reach toward one another, each does or says some selfish thing that triggers an angry, selfish response in the other. If the soldier's leave were longer, if they were not each so terribly conscious of swiftly passing time, the differences might have been understood and reconciled. But there is no time, and each fails to understand the other at the precise moments when it is imperative to do so, and there is no way to salvage these moments. Only at the instant of their parting do they find one another—and then it is too late.

It is possible to read into "The Lovely Leave" a parable for marriages in general. But for the reader who knows something of Dorothy Parker and Alan Campbell, there is more here than a despairing report on one aspect of the human condition. The lieutenant and his wife in the story are not literally Lieutenant and Mrs. Campbell, anymore than Hazel Morse in "Big Blonde" is literally Dorothy Parker. She has, however, given her characters certain mannerisms of Alan's and her own, as well as their styles of speech, and the source of the emotion in the story is certainly her own experience. While "The Lovely Leave" is fiction, it must (when it appeared in 1943) have told Dorothy's friends all they needed to know about her relationship with Alan. It must also have told Alan that she loved him.

The following year, she broke a decade's poetic silence to plead with Alan. In "War Song" she said:

Soldier, in a curious land
    All across a swaying sea,
Take her smile and lift her hand—
    Have no guilt of me.

Soldier, when were soldiers true?
    If she's kind and sweet and gay,
Use the wish I send to you—
    Lie not lone till day!

Only, for the nights that were,
    Soldier, and the dawns that came,
When in sleep you turn to her
    Call her by my name.

In that same year, she turned to another feminine problem with which she was also thoroughly familiar. In July 1944, the war was not yet won, but there could be no doubt that it was ending, and she thought it appropriate to speak to women whose husbands were fighting overseas. She wrote an article for *Vogue*, called "Who Is That Man?" in which she said:

"You say goodnight to your friends, and know that tomorrow you will meet them again, sound and safe as you will be. It is not like that where your husband is. There are the comrades, closer in friendship to him than you can ever be, whom he has seen comic or wild or thoughtful; and then broken or dead. There are some who have gone out with a wave of the hand and a gay obscenity, and have never come back. We do not know such things; prefer, and wisely, to close our minds against them. . . .

"I have been trying to say that women have the easier part in war. But when the war is over—then we must take up. The truth is that women's work begins when war ends, begins on the day their men come home to them. For who is that man, who will come back to you? You know him as he was; you have only to close your eyes to see him sharp and clear. You can hear his voice whenever there is silence. But what will he be, this stranger who comes back? How are you to throw a bridge across the gap that has separated you—and that is not the little gap of months and miles? He has seen the world aflame; he comes back to your new red dress. He has known glory and horror and filth and dignity; he will listen to you tell of the success of the canteen dance, the upholsterer who disappointed, the arthritis of your aunt. What have you to offer this man? . . . There have been people you never knew with whom he has had jokes you could not comprehend and talks that would be foreign to your ear. There are pictures hanging in his memory that he can never show to you. Of this great part of his life, you have no share. . . . things forever out of your reach, far too many and too big for jealousy. That is where you start, and from there you go on to make a friend out of that stranger from across a world."

Insofar as Dorothy Parker was concerned, truer words were never set in movable type. Who indeed was the Edwin Parker who had come to her from the first World War? And had it ended because she had failed to "go on and make a friend" or be a friend to him? Her marriage with Alan had been going badly before this new war, and in "The Lovely Leave" she had, among other things, remarked on Alan's strangeness in uniform and his concern for comrades she had never met and for matters and events that had nothing whatsoever to do with her. In "War Song" she presumed that he, like other soldier husbands, would bed with foreign girls. In "Soldiers of the Republic" she recognized the fact that there are soldiers who deeply love their wives, and while she knew it to be true that men and women could resume their lives together when wars were done, she also knew it to be true that some could not. She knew what had once happened to her, and feared that it could happen again, and in her *Vogue* article she tried to acquaint women with what was, to her, one of the facts of feminine life.

All of this fell very ill upon the ears of Pleasantville, New York, where the editors of *The Reader's Digest* immediately bought the reprint rights to her article, condensed it, and sent copies of their condensed version to various public personages. The *Digest* printed the condensed version, and the comments of these personages, in its September 1944 issue.

"This sounds like nonsense to me," wrote the hero of the first World War, General John J. Pershing. "What do our men want most? To finish the war and come home! They will come back to that home, most of them, stronger wiser and more understanding men—with more to give to marriage than before they went away."

"Miss Parker reminds me of the mother who sends her child off to boarding school, lamenting that he will be a stranger when he returns," John Erskine, Columbia University professor and novelist, told the *Digest*. "If love of husband and wife is a reality, no superficial strangeness can keep them apart, once he is sheltered in her arms."

John LaFarge, a priest, said, "What is between man and woman is too deep to be altered by separation, or suffering, or new companions in danger. . . . I would remind Miss Parker of the song that Solomon sang, "Many waters cannot quench love.' "

Equally strong in the faith was a Protestant divine, Ralph W.

Sockman, who assured *Digest* readers that "Wives who strive from day to day for a richer and finer life may await the return of their lovers with confidence."

Bonnie Gay, a columnist for the *Baltimore Sun*, said *her* husband "writes me, 'Darling, I feel closer to you every day!' " and she said, "That's how I feel. Love is a shortcut to understanding —every wife knows that."

"Only the mentally ill like to brood on past unhappiness," a psychiatrist, Edwin G. Zabriskie, told the *Digest*. "Does Miss Parker mean that the majority of returning veterans will be mentally ill? If so, she is deeply mistaken. The majority . . . will no more want to live with the past than, having awakened from a bad dream, [they] would want to return to [the] nightmare."

The way the *Digest* set it up, the choice was at least clear: Either everyone else in the world was wrong, or there was something badly wrong with Dorothy Parker.

Of course, she and her sophisticated friends had nothing but contempt for the *Digest* and its Pollyanna view of life, and for them the asinine comments of the public personages would have been amusing, but it is not altogether funny to be ridiculed in public, even by fools. Moreover, she was past fifty and growing fat, and if her much-younger husband returned much more of a stranger than she feared he would, her second marriage could go the way of the first—although for different reasons.

The following year there was a famous victory, but to Dorothy Parker 1945 was, in all its important respects, 1918 revisited—for Alan was not coming directly home. Just as Edwin Parker had remained in the occupation forces in the Rhineland, now Alan Campbell was remaining overseas, occupying himself in London. Distraught and enraged, Dorothy told her friends that the reason for this was a homosexual affair—not the slightest military duty.

"As for his much-vaunted war record," she said, "he was over there playing hostess."

She went on to name the man she suspected; she said she had heard about it from London theater friends. Not everyone who knew Alan believed Dorothy. The consensus of Alan's friends was that he was "a very gentle soul, a sort of nonvirile man," as one of them said, but one who was much more interested in a social life than he was in a sexual one. Alan's friends pointed out that he had a great many platonic friendships with women, and they saw no reason why his friendships with homosexual men were not equally asexual. But it did no good to point out to Dorothy Parker that one can be the friend of a homosexual without being his lover. She was impressed by the fact that Alan was not coming straight home, and she believed the gossip. Mercilessly, she enumerated his shortcomings:

Alan couldn't act. He couldn't write anything but Hollywood trash. He never understood her; he couldn't cook; he was a political cretin; he was weak; he was afraid; he married for her money; all he thought about was parties; he couldn't hold his liquor; he deserted her; he wasn't a man, he was a pansy. She never wanted to see his weak face again.

She played the role of Woman Scorned, rather than to try to follow her own excellent advice: that wives must after the war throw a bridge across the gap that separates them from their soldier-husbands. She slammed down the portcullis and drew up the bridge: she advised Alan that she had had enough, and that she was going to obtain a divorce.

It must have seemed to her that life indeed had come full circle. At the end of a second war, she was once again estranged from a husband, living alone, with no visible means of support other than her typewriter. This time, unfortunately, she was not young, beautiful and smart, on the threshold of her career, the boon companion of the Round Table. She was aging, rather dowdy, drinking too much, and the Algonquin group had long since been dispersed. Mr. Sherwood was no more an intimate friend; Alexander Woollcott was dead. When in 1945 Robert Benchley died, she was numbed.

It was difficult to think that those days on *Vanity Fair* had been an age ago. Mr. Benchley had given up his job because of her. They had been arrested together at the time of the Sacco and Vanzetti trial. There had been the good times at the theater, at Tony's, at Jack and Charlie's, and in Europe. Of course, they had been devoted to each other, as they and everyone else well knew. There was Alexander Woollcott's story about the time he and a young college boy saw her and Mr. Benchley at the theater, and the boy asked Mr. Woollcott, "Would that be Mrs.

Benchley?" and Alec had said, "Yes, that would be Mrs. Benchley, were it not for the fact that there already is a Mrs. Benchley."
Once at "21," she and Mr. Benchley had joked about it. She had
asked, "Why don't we get married right now?"

"What would we do with Alan?" Mr. Benchley asked.

"Send him to military school," she suggested.

It had been like that with them for years—a friendship in
which there was a love so genuine that they could joke about it.
On hearing the news of Mr. Benchley's death, she was guiltily
aware that it was she who had been responsible for their not
having remained the friends they once had been. Politics, her
politics, had divided them. But there had never been another
man like Mr. Benchley in her life, and his death now brought
forcibly home to her the fact that their years of friendship had
also been the years of an era that was now quite as dead as he
was. "Isn't it a bit presumptuous of us to be alive, now that Mr.
Benchley is dead?" she asked or, rather, stated.

She tried to bury herself. She said none of her past had been
worthwhile. She denied authorship of the bon mots attributed
to her. She said there had never been anything good, or even
memorable, about the Round Table or its members. She dismissed her poems as being silly verses. It was as if she was contemptuously filling up the grave of a woman she had always
despised, so that she could go on living. She was at least right
in one respect: the wit and the writer of the poems and the
stories had indeed died. Her wit would henceforth be more sour
than comic. "War Song" had been her first poem in ten years,
but it was also the last one she ever published. She would never
write another story as good as "The Lovely Leave," nor any
magazine article of more than passing interest.

If one phase of her career had ended, so too the gay, innocent
insouciance of the twenties was dead, and so was the political
camaraderie and sense of adventure of the early thirties; and out
of the most recent and worst of wars there was already plainly
visible the humorless new age of giantism. In 1944 The Viking
Press had brought out her collected work, *The Portable Dorothy
Parker,* for which Somerset Maugham wrote the introduction for
$250. It was a popular success at the time and still sells well in
paperback today, but the more perceptive contemporary critics

realized that they were reading what in 1944 was already a period piece. "She is not Emily Brontë or Jane Austen," Edmund Wilson wrote in a *New Yorker* review of *The Portable Dorothy Parker*, "but she has been at some pains to write well, and she has put into what she has written a voice, a state of mind, an era, a few moments of human experience that nobody else has conveyed." And Edward Weeks, in the *Atlantic*, said, "As we see the work *in toto*, with its laughter, its wit, its silly sophistication, and its heartburn, we realize that there are limitations, the chief of them being a lack of depth and a lack of cordiality."

At the end of a second World War, life had brought her full circle, placing her once again at a starting line. But this time, no bright colors gleamed ahead. The present was gray, and the future obscure.

PART
FOUR

"Aesop pulled a thorn
from a lion's foot,
and the lion ate him up, and said,
'Now, write a fable about that!'"

—Dorothy Parker

1

"I went to call on her the day the divorce from Alan became final," Vincent Sheean said. "She was living alone in the Algonquin. The hotel had sent dinner up to her room, filet mignon, and she was sitting up in bed, the dinner uneaten, with no intention of eating, streaming tears.

"Thinking to make her feel better, I said I felt sorry for Alan.

" 'Oh, don't worry about Alan,' she said. 'Alan will always land on somebody's feet.' "

But it was not really that simple. For months after the divorce, she would spend half her time talking about Alan. In a letter to George Oppenheimer, who was back in her favor for reasons that were as mysterious to him as those that had led Dorothy to dismiss him, she said she was crouched in silence, trying to regain various kinds of health; that several thousand things had come up out of hell, due to a general mess and bewilderment. Throughout 1945 and 1946 there was no record of any sort of production by Dorothy Parker—no film, no poem, no article, no story. In 1947, when the divorce was granted, the Bucks County farm, on which she and Alan had lavished more than $100,000, was sold for $40,000. The word around Hollywood and New York was that Dorothy Parker was cracking up. Universal Pictures asked her to work on the script of *Smash Up, the Story of a Woman*. Hollywood insiders said *Smash Up* was actually the film version of the life of Dorothy Parker. It was in fact no such thing, but it could at least be said that when Universal took her on the project, they hired an experienced writer.

Some people believed that work on *Smash Up* helped to keep her from smashing up herself, but while this is debatable, what was not debatable was that something vital had gone out of her life; she was, as she wrote to Mr. Oppenheimer, in a state of general bewilderment. She at last decided to try to write her way out of it, this time with the help of Ross Evans.

Mr. Evans was a playwright, novelist, and motion picture scriptwriter whom she had taken up in 1947 before her divorce from Alan. He was, like so many of her beaux, a tall and handsome man—"a beautiful hunk of Victor Mature," Beatrice Ames said, while other of her friends, skeptical of Mr. Evans' intelligence, called him "Li'l Abner."

"Everybody thinks he's banging me every night," Dorothy Parker confided to a room full of people in Hollywood, "and I only wish to God he were."

As she and Mr. Evans left the party where she said this, someone complimented her on her new friend, saying he had such a wonderful sun tan.

"Yes," she agreed. "He has the hue of availability."

The catty compliment and her answer were very much to the point. Some of Dorothy's friends supposed that Mr. Evans' relationship to her was that of a gigolo. He was good-looking certainly, twenty-three years younger than she and hardly her intellectual or professional equal. Other of her friends guessed that she was using Mr. Evans as a way of displaying rage at Alan, or was using him in a desperate attempt to prove that she, at age fifty-four, still possessed an attractiveness that had nothing to do with her superficial appearance, that she was still alluring to young men. Still other friends supposed that she was so distraught over the divorce from Alan that she did not know what she was doing and that Mr. Evans had moved in on her. What no one was willing to suppose was that she and Mr. Evans could genuinely love one another. Nor could anyone suppose the relationship was a particularly satisfying one sexually, for in addition to her remark at the Hollywood party, there was the occasion given by the Sheeans in New York:

"We were then living in an apartment in Marion Davies' house at Fifty-fifth and Madison," Mr. Sheean said, "and Ross and Dorothy sat on our great, oversized, red-and-green tartan sofa.

"We drank—it was one of our main occupations—and about two or three in the morning, they began to make love."

Mr. Sheean said, "I tried to avert my eyes," and he took a great interest in the New York skyline at night. Later, as she and Mr. Evans were leaving the apartment, Dorothy Parker apologized.

"You know," she said, "this hasn't happened for about six months. Hope you don't mind." She paused. "We must have been awfully picturesque," she said.

So she was as aware as anyone else that a quality of pathos clung about the picture that she and Mr. Evans presented to the world. Even more pathetic was their joint literary production. Never before had she collaborated with anyone when writing a short story, but she apparently now felt the need of a collaborator, and decided that Mr. Evans was the one she needed. In December 1948, *Cosmopolitan* magazine published their story, "The Game." It describes the psychological warfare waged by a man and a woman against each other as they play charades at a party. It is long, it is boring, and it sprawls, as Dorothy Parker's stories never do.

Collaboration with Mr. Evans did at least help keep her busy in 1948, for in addition to their story, they (and a third writer) worked on a film called *The Fan*, based on Oscar Wilde's play *Lady Windermere's Fan*, and still in that year she and Mr. Evans wrote a play of their own for the theater. This was *The Coast of Illyria*, based on the life of Charles Lamb and his mad sister Mary. It opened in Dallas in the spring of 1949.

Reviewing the play, *Time* magazine identified Dorothy Parker as "wit, verse writer, and movie-scripter."

"Herself celebrated for claw-sharp quotes," *Time* said, "Dorothy surprised the cast with her gentleness. With Evans, she fled the theater between acts to avoid stares by the curious, acknowledged compliments with a mild, 'Bless you.' Said one actress, 'She's sweet. She's even shy. She's a love.'"

Time's comment showed how difficult it was for her to escape the pigeonholes of journalism. No matter what else she became, she would always be called a wit, and whenever she said anything that was not witty, journalism would always assure the public that this was surprising.

As for the play, *Time* said the Texas audience and critics liked it, calling it the best of Dallas' eight-play season, and thinking it to be a cinch for a Broadway run. "Though the authors refused to share in this prediction," *Time* reported, "collaborator Evans sounded cautiously optimistic: 'We've tasted blood. We don't want to do anything ever again except write for the theater.'"

The Coast of Illyria might have been the best play offered in Dallas that season, but Dallas is not New York. *Time*'s article recalled that Dorothy Parker's first play, *Close Harmony*, written with Elmer Rice a quarter-century earlier, had been a flop. This time, she was not confused by all those beating hands. She knew that she and Mr. Evans had produced nothing in particular; she was content that the play closed in Texas. It was put on again in London under the title *Strange Calamity*, and at the Edinburgh Festival of 1949 under a third name, *At Last*, but nowhere, under any name, was it successful. The problem, she said, was that the play "was just silly. Nothing happened at all. It didn't go over."

Ross Evans said that he and Dorothy Parker wanted only to write for the theater, but success in the theater was beyond their grasp. In his case, this may have been due to a lack of sufficient imagination, but in her case, matters were exactly different. She loved the stage, and was close to it all her life, and her theater reviews indicated her sound taste. But her most singular talent was the very one least adaptable to the theater. Throughout her personal life and in her writing, she constantly saw both comedy and tragedy in the same event, and she saw them both together.

Of course, it was the juxtaposition of comedy and tragedy in the same poem or story that made so much of her work seem bright and sophisticated; it was her ability to see herself in terms of simultaneous comedy and tragedy that gave rise to her wit. But the theater is not a printed page, or the bar at Tony's. It is an artificial world that lives in foreshortened time, and a thousand years of dramatic tradition have conditioned audiences to accept its terms. A play is a tragedy or it is a comedy. There is usually no time, in theatrical terms, to develop a simultaneous double vision, except at peril to the movement of the story line, and whenever anyone tries to do this, the audience is usually confused. They do not know whether they are supposed to laugh or cry, and if they should do both, they wonder what on earth that play was supposed to have been about.

Then, by habit and turn of mind, Dorothy Parker saw life in an unconnected series of sudden, piercing insights. She did not, as a novelist or a playwright might, see life as a sum of many connected parts. During her summer in Switzerland, she said she was writing a novel, and George Oppenheimer believed she actually started two—one about life in a girls' boarding school; the other about the Devil. She, however, joked about it. She showed a visitor a box full of paper, saying it was her manuscript, but the box contained unanswered letters and unpaid bills. That, she explained, was the story of her life. Anyway, she said, putting the thought of a novel aside, "I am a short-distance writer."

As a short-distance writer, she could certainly contribute lyrics to *No, Siree!* and *Shoot the Works;* she could write any number of scenes for motion picture scripts, but she could not dramatize the life of the Lambs. Nor, because of her tragic-comic double vision, could *Close Harmony* be a pure romp, nor could the stories in *After Such Pleasures* be brought successfully alive on the stage.

The fact that she lacked a playwright's talent did not diminish her desire to be a playwright, but it did suggest she would always need a collaborator who could keep the sense of the whole play in mind while she provided the sharp insights. Such a collaborator would need a mind as quick, strong and tough as her own; skin at least a foot thick; the serenity of a stone Buddha; Job's patience; Christ's compassion, and Talleyrand's diplomatic abilities in addition, of course, to a dramatic talent. Unfortunately, Ross Evans did not combine all these virtues in himself.

Following their qualified failure in Dallas, Dorothy Parker and her friend returned to Hollywood to deal with the practical matter of finding a film assignment that would provide them with money enough to afford the time to work on another play. But there were no jobs for them in Hollywood. Nor did anyone at the studios know when any jobs might be available in the future. Since Hollywood was no place for her to be unless there was work to be had, she and Mr. Evans decided to go to Mexico, where life was reputed to be cheap and easy. She told her friends she was going for two weeks with Mr. Evans, saying that they could certainly write there, if they could write at all, and besides, she had never been to Mexico and that seemed to her to be a good reason to go there.

The next person to hear from her was Beatrice Ames, to whose New York apartment a telegram was delivered:

HERE I COME DARLING IN DESPERATE TROUBLE. NEED YOU. PLEASE STAND BY. FLYING FROM MEXICO CITY NOW.

"I called every airline," Beatrice said. "I called everybody. I couldn't find out what time she was arriving. So I waited at my little room, and the next day I found she had a suite at the Plaza.

"She had two straw bags with her and a dirndl skirt, and four bedrooms and five baths at the Plaza at fifty-five bucks a day," Beatrice said. "She had been absolutely deserted by Ross, who had gone off with a woman who had a dress shop in Acapulco. He just dumped her off at the airport and drove off in the car with her dogs, and that was it. He did, I think, buy her ticket. She didn't have any money when she got here, none at all."

Beatrice said that Dorothy arrived in New York "all mixed up emotionally," and so far out of her senses as to suppose that Mr. Evans had discarded her because she was half a Jew. This sounded to Beatrice like something she had heard Dorothy say before. She was in any case a defeated woman, as any woman of fifty-six might be defeated by a young man's desertion of her, particularly if that woman happened to be something of a national celebrity, and her rival a shopkeeper.

She was also a demoralized writer. She told Beatrice that she had given up poetry and that she could not write short stories anymore. She wanted to write plays but she was a failure at that. There was no work for her in Hollywood, and she said she did not know what she would do or what would become of her.

She was vague as to how much money she had in the bank. During the war, a book publisher had paid her $20,109.51 in royalties. (This was the last large royalty check she would ever receive; in the years that remained to her, she would only once receive more than $4,500 in book royalties.) During the years they had worked in Hollywood, she and Alan Campbell had earned more than a quarter of a million dollars at the most conservative estimate; very likely, they had earned more than half a million. But there was little or nothing to show for this; as more than one of her friends said, she spent money as if she felt guilty about having any, and had sold the farm at a loss of more than $60,000. Presumably, she had put money into *The Coast of Illyria*—how much, if any, she never said.

Since she had no money in her purse when she arrived in New York, and no apparent idea as to what, if anything, she had in the bank, a question uppermost in Beatrice Ames' mind was how she would manage to pay her way out of the Plaza, but Beatrice never learned the answer. Dorothy Parker's finances were always the blackest of mysteries to her friends, who presumed that whenever she was in dire need, any of several people gave her money. The names of certain Wall Street bankers and brokers were usually mentioned. One romantic story was that early in her life, she had an affair with an enormously wealthy man who never forgot her, and who always came to her financial rescue. It was a very pleasant fiction.

In fact, her financial poverty was always more apparent than real, and in 1949 her essential poverty was an emotional one. She came to New York from Mexico City to touch familiar bases and regain faith in herself from the company of old New York friends. She checked into the Plaza as she had taken suites there at the ends of other affairs. The view of Central Park from a high window, the carriages waiting across the street below, the gold and cream and the potted plants in the high-ceilinged Palm Room, the name of the place, and the opulence of a suite to herself in this fashionable hotel, seemed a necessary salve for her wounded *amour propre*. Here, as she had said, she "could get away from it all," and the people who had laughed when she had moved from a hotel three blocks away and into the Plaza to "get away from it all" did not wholly understand what she meant. To her, the Plaza was always that world of wealth and fashion that ever fascinated her. A suite at the Plaza told her that she was a great lady. A week seemed to do the job. Then, the pride restored, the splurge was over, and it was on to more reasonable quarters in another hotel, and on again with the business of what she called "this living, this living."

She stayed on in New York until she had worked Ross Evans out of her system. She took lonely stock of herself. Then she put in a call to Hollywood.

Yes, Alan Campbell said, he was as lonely for her as she was for him. He agreed that being apart did nothing for either of them.

Yes, he said, of course he would, he would be at the airport.

2

"I've been given a second chance," she said, weeping. "I've been given a second chance—and who in life gets a second chance?"

The people around her told her how glad they were for her and for Alan, and it occurred to one of them to ask where she was staying in Hollywood.

"At Alan's," she said, brightening. "Isn't that disgraceful?"

In another corner of the living room, where a cocktail party was being given to celebrate the reconciliation, Alan Campbell explained that Dorothy Parker received an average of $10,000 a year in royalties.

"I never believed Alan, and no one else believed him either," one of the party guests said later, "but what a darling thing for him to say. He was saying, 'I'm not marrying her to try to make her work because she needs money, because she doesn't need money.' He was marrying her because he wanted to help take care of her. Alan was so wonderful for her, and she would crucify him, but she relied on him and he was lovely to her."

Naturally on this festive occasion there were those who wondered how long Dorothy and Alan would stay together. There are, after all, many married people whose happiness is found in quarreling; possibly Alan liked to be crucified, and possibly she sang as she hammered in the nails, except at times the game would get out of hand and there would be real anger between them. But they had been divorced for three years, and perhaps in that time each had learned something about himself with respect to the other. It seemed to at least one of Dorothy Parker's friends that her tears of gratitude about her "second chance" were quite genuine.

"You never had an idea when she really meant a thing," one of her friends said, "but in this case, I really think she meant it."

Grateful and happy, she was at her charming best at that cocktail party, and the mood of euphoria certainly persisted at least until the following morning, their second wedding day.

"No peeking," she told Alan as they waked.

She pulled the sheet up over her face, and from beneath it she said, "Mustn't see the bride before the wedding!"

The reception that afternoon was a somewhat curious occasion, for three years is a long time in Hollywood, and as someone remarked, most of the people at the wedding had not been speaking to one another for years.

"Including the bride and groom," Dorothy agreed.

In choosing to live with Alan again, she may not have completely understood that she was choosing to live in exile with Alan in Hollywood, as opposed to living without him in New York. Perhaps because she did not concern herself with money matters, the thought did not occur to her, but as Smollett said, marriage is often the state of wholly matter-money. It was doubtless plain enough to Alan that most of their money was now gone, as was the mansion in Beverly Hills and the farm in Bucks County, and that it was impossible for them to maintain an apartment in New York. Surely he also knew that by remarrying Dorothy Parker, he was putting an end to his chances to earn a living by writing for films, for when they remarried in 1950, the political climate of Hollywood was more than routinely hysterical.

The days of the cold war were at hand, and the witch hunters were abroad; a congressional investigative subcommittee of the House Committee on Un-American Activities would shortly come baying into Hollywood; the voice of Senator Joseph McCarthy would be heard in the land, and the nation was about to be delivered into the hands of improbable Inquisitors—and into a nightmare of the soul that visitors from other civilized Western nations found absolutely inexplicable and nonsensical. It all made sense to the Hollywood studios, however. The studios, ever acutely sensitive to public moods, and fearful of audience boycotts, were quick to prove themselves more red, white, and blue than anybody—lest someone cast a first stone in their direction. The studios had compiled a list of more than three hundred names of actors, artists, scriptwriters and directors suspected of being Communists, and this list included the name of Dorothy Parker.

The studios' official position was that if a Communist was hired on a film, he might somehow insert subversive propaganda into it. This hypothesis seemed to embrace the curious notion that the men who ruled the studios lacked the intelligence to recognize propaganda when they saw it in a script, and the power to eliminate it if they did see it, but the official position was really a mask for fears and other motives. A national fear of Communist conspirators gave the studios a marvelous chance to eliminate from their payrolls anyone they regarded as a troublemaker of any sort.

So the studios set up an investigative agency of their own, before which, as before the House Committee on Un-American Activities, suspected people were required to prove their innocence. Like wretches haled before the Inquisition or a Soviet tribunal, they were pressed to confess and repent in public, and then to betray the names of their friends to the investigators. In due course, one of Dorothy Parker's quite apolitical friends was required by his studio to say why he had been a member of the Anti-Nazi League.

"Because I was anti-Nazi," he told his interrogator. "Weren't you? Which side were you on?"

But his protest did him little good, and when he refused to "rat on his friends," as he put it, his days in Hollywood were at an end.

Alan Campbell was a victim of the Red hunt, despite his well-known objections to Dorothy Parker's prewar political activities and his refusal to have anything to do with them. Because her career in films was over, he could not offer himself and Dorothy Parker as a writing team to any studio, nor was any studio willing to employ him alone, because he was the husband of a suspected Communist.

To be unemployed in Hollywood is normally to be regarded as a pariah, but in these abnormal times it was something worse. No one knew who might be reported for his association with someone else, however slight that association might be; no one knew how suspect were the friends of his friends. There was no help for this: no one could say when, or whether, the terror would end. Before twelve months were out, the House Committee on Un-American Activities said it had evidence that Dorothy Parker was a Communist. She was angrily noncommittal when questioned by newspaper reporters. She refused to become one of those who went crawling to the Committee, or to the studios, to wear the guise of a penitent and seek redemption and good fortune by being traitorous. Her attitude toward the House Committee was that of a noblewoman observing, with an understanding disdain, the vulgarity of a swineherd.

Love does not always fly out the window when the wolf is at the door, but the wolf at the door, and the shapes and lolling tongues of the Red hunters moving round about, put an additional strain upon the volatile relationship she and Alan Campbell shared. A friend said they resumed their quarreling the day they remarried, but now as Alan hopefully knocked on studio doors he knew were closed to him, Dorothy Parker once again began to accuse him of infidelities that he, once again, denied.

As far as Alan Campbell was concerned, his one interest was to look after her. But Dorothy Parker never lacked the ability to fend off rescue with one hand while beckoning to disaster with the other. The terror of the witch hunt served only to confirm her in those radical beliefs that Alan did not share. The apartment in West Hollywood was not the mansion in Beverly Hills. Alan was not working and she was not writing. They were drinking far too much, and without gaiety. The fun had died, really, in 1937, and it was never wholly to return, and whenever Alan was full of fun and charm (as he could certainly be), she was not in a mood to match his. She wanted to return to New York. They quarreled together for more than two years after their remarriage before they separated. She said the proximate cause was another homosexual affair which he, again, denied.

3

"From now on," Dorothy Parker told Ward Morehouse, drama critic of *The New York World Telegram & Sun*, "New York is my home—oh, please! I was in Hollywood for fifteen years, off and on, and that's over forever.

"Hollywood smells like a laundry. The beautiful vegetables taste as if they were raised in trunks, and at those wonderful supermarkets you find that the vegetables are all wax. The flowers out there smell like dirty, old dollar bills.

"Sure, you make money writing on the coast," she said, "and God knows you earn it, but that money is like so much compressed snow. It goes so fast it melts in your hand."

They were talking together in New York in mid-October 1953, and she had been in and out of Hollywood for more than twenty years, not fifteen, and in the last four she had earned exactly nothing there. Mr. Morehouse said she spoke "in a half-whisper . . . looking at me with her soulful eyes" as she drank Scotch on the rocks and told him of her happiness to be back again in the city.

"You just don't know how I love it—how I get up every morning and want to kiss the pavement. I want to stay and stay and if our play is a success, I can eat and live and have a roof—and buy some dresses."

The play was *The Ladies of the Corridor*, then having its

Philadelphia tryout before opening in New York in the last week in October. Dorothy Parker had written it together with Arnaud d'Usseau, a playwright who had collaborated on three earlier plays, *Tomorrow the World, Deep Are the Roots,* and *Legend of Sarah.*

"I can't tell you of my great fortune in working with Arnaud," she breathed to Mr. Morehouse. "I knew him in Hollywood. One day he said to me, 'Let's write a play.' We were going to write a murder play and then later he asked if I ever thought of the great number of women who live alone in hotels. I'd lived in hotels for thirty years and went into that—the unwanted, wasted women who belong to American life. Strong and healthy —and wasted."

She told Mr. Morehouse that Mr. d'Usseau was "a rigid taskmaster. He'd work at the typewriter and then get up to pace and we'd meet each other in the middle of the room. He types well, but he punctuates so badly . . .

"We've put our guts into this play and we have a fine producer in Wally [Walter] Fried, who worries and worries and worries," she said. "And we have a wonderful cast—just plain wonderful. You'll hear those Belasco tones next Wednesday night."

She spoke bravely and happily about the play, sipping her whisky and talking both to Mr. Morehouse and to her toy silver poodle, Misty, nestled high on her shoulder. More to Misty than to Mr. Morehouse, she said, "Did you ever realize that there are just no dogs in Philadelphia? Oh, what an ugly place." Then, more to Mr. Morehouse than to Misty, she said, "I'm amazed that they can get the New York papers there the same day they're published. Oh, how I'd hate to die in Philadelphia. Those cobblestones, they hurt your feet. Such a tacky, tacky town . . ." It was show-business talk. New York theatrical people fear and hate the tryout towns, Philadelphia and Boston, because the audiences in those cities are serious and discriminating ones, not given to the uncritical applause of New York audiences which are largely composed of people come from the provinces to the big city, ready to think that whatever New York shows them must be good. Enjoying her role as co-author of a play coming to town, she made the obligatory show-business remarks about Philadelphia. It was wonderful to be back in New

York, she repeated. She was living at the Volney Hotel, off Madison Avenue in the East Seventies, where there were forty-three dogs for Misty to be friends with, she said.

She seemed to be on the threshold of a new beginning. She was all her life poised on such thresholds. At age sixty, she was looking forward as eagerly as any girl to a wonderful life in New York and a brilliant career as a playwright. She said that everything else that had happened to her had happened "a thousand years ago." She spoke of the past as a schoolgirl might speak of ancient history—airily and inaccurately.

Nor was she being precisely accurate when she led Mr. Morehouse to believe that all of a sudden Mr. d'Usseau had walked up to her out of a clear pavement and said, "Let's do a play"— just as if such an idea had never crossed her mind. The play itself suggests otherwise, for its characters happen to include a castoff wife who drinks too much and commits suicide, a seedy Southern gentlewoman, a widow who mismanages her last chance at love with a man twelve years younger than herself, and a monstrous mother who consumes her son. There are not only recognizable bits and pieces of herself, Alan Campbell, and Alan's mother in the play, but characters who closely resemble then-living inhabitants of the Volney Hotel.

Kindest of the critics was Dorothy Parker's former lover, John McClain, who over the years had been graduated from covering shipping news to reviewing plays for *The New York Journal American:*

"The fate of lonely women, living in faded luxury in side street New York hotels, had been woven by Dorothy Parker and Arnaud d'Usseau into a drama of enormous depth and emotional appeal. We see the full flower of Mrs. Parker's profound and incisive preoccupation with the frailties of her sex, the tragedy and desperation that assail a world of women without men. The ladies . . . suffer from the mutual malady of boredom: their hours are filled with the small details of destroying time. There are some who manage to escape the barrier, but there is always the suggestion that the corridor is waiting there to claim them in the end. The authors have told this story by means of unrelated episodes in the lives of a group of women living in a small hotel in the East Sixties . . . there are countless lines worth remembering, many exquisitely humorous in the best Parker rabbit-punch tradition. . . . This is another solid success—the season looks brighter."

Another point of view was John Chapman's in *The New York Daily News:*

"The hazard inherent in the slice-of-life technique of play writing is that the slices may turn out to be just so much salami —and this is what happened to 'The Ladies of the Corridor.' "

The other reviews were mixed. The staging was good, the acting was marvelous, the lines were deft—but those Belasco tones, which Dorothy Parker confidently told Mr. Morehouse to expect, were not heard. The play closed after forty-five performances.

"It was a play that should have been a success, but for an elementary mistake," producer Walter Fried said fifteen years later. "The play failed unnecessarily, and I've unconsciously put it out of my mind.

"Mrs. Parker," he said, "acted as a junior, shy associate to Arnaud d'Usseau, her more knowledgeable play collaborator. She was quiet—too quiet—since she was in a new field. She did know her characters all too well, since she lived at one of these residential East Side hotels. Her feeling for them was at once unflatteringly illuminating, but with great compassion for these people who feared loneliness so much that they were pushed to do things sadly, although they exposed their emptiness of spirit."

The "elementary mistake" was that it was not a play. It read much better than it could possibly play; Mr. McClain was right to speak of "unrelated episodes," and Mr. Chapman was right to say such episodes lacked dramatic unity. Another trouble was that Dorothy Parker's double vision was once again fatally at work; within the episodes, comedy sat oddly and distractingly in the lap of tragedy.

"The end was changed," Dorothy Parker explained. "I vehemently protested, but who was I against so many?" To her, the "whole point of the play" was that her protagonist, the widow enamored of the younger man, would wind up like all the other ladies of the hotel corridor, a prisoner of herself and a prey to boredom, condemned to live alone until she could die. But the end was changed to provide a note of hope for that woman and, as Dorothy Parker said, "It wasn't right, you see." She said she had written "a very bitter play, but true . . . [it was] the only thing I ever did that I was proud of."

Except that it was not a play. It failed because, instead of being a play, it was true.

A psychiatrist familiar with Dorothy Parker's life would have noticed that her first attempt in the theater, *Close Harmony*, followed closely the time she had an abortion, that *The Coast of Illyria* came shortly after her divorce from a man by whom she had a miscarriage, and that *The Ladies of the Corridor* followed her separation from the man she had remarried. It was as if she sought to create life (but only in fantasy) whenever she was adrift in an emotional storm; as if she subconsciously equated writing for the theater with giving birth; as if in a time of crisis, she murmured Hamlet's words to herself, "The play's the thing wherein I'll catch the conscience of the king." So she would create life on the stage which, for one reason and another, she had not created with a loved king in reality. In this, she invited failure, for she was not a master of the theater; if she had turned to the short story instead, she would have invited success. As if to ensure failure, she (with one exception) chose as collaborators men of no outstanding literary potency. Just as she had not had children, so the life she created for the stage always miscarried. This esoteric rationale has at least the virtue of a pattern; it is at least consistent with her lifelong self-fulfilling prediction that nothing could ever end well.

"Obviously," Mr. Fried said, she "made terribly little in the way of royalties."

So instead of embarking on a glittering new New York life as a successful playwright, eating and living well under a fashionable roof of her own, and buying all those new dresses, there was nothing for her and Misty but the Volney Hotel, and the company of all the other lonely, aging ladies and their forty-three dogs, and that very hopeless, airless state of suspended animation she had so poignantly described. In his review of *The Ladies of the Corridor*, Brooks Atkinson of *The New York Times* said that "the authors are entitled to credit for having written parts that can be acted so well." It now remained for her to act out the part. She had written both a description and a prophecy.

4

In his memoir "Remembering Dorothy Parker," written for *Esquire* magazine, the screenwriter and New York magazine editor Wyatt Cooper said he was surprised when, one day in 1956, Alan Campbell, a man he barely knew, suddenly pleaded for his help.

" 'I have to go see Dottie,' " Alan said. " 'Will you go with me?' "

He said this as he and Mr. Cooper were leaving a party together, and Mr. Cooper, who felt a bit wary of Alan, but who was strangely touched by the quality of despair in Alan's voice, hesitantly said yes.

"She lived then at the Volney," Mr. Cooper wrote, "and my memory is of a stark, bare, colorless, and impersonal room, with a large bone on the floor, dog toys on the gravy-colored sofa, a dog, of course, and an agonized Alan facing a stricken-looking Dottie, who was then, as incredible as it seems to me now, actually fat. My impression was of a sad, bewildered young girl, angrily trapped inside an inappropriate and almost grotesque body. Of the desolate conversation, I remember only that she apologized repeatedly; for the disorder of the room, for her own appearance, for the behavior of the dog, and for the absence of anything to drink. There was a sense of unreality about it; the darkened room, the sad and lost lady, the man ill at ease and poised for flight, and the stranger to them both, with no reason whatever for being present. It was painful to witness the estrangement of two people who were forever to be deeply involved with each other. Loneliness and guilt were almost like physical presences in the space between them, and they spoke in short, stilted, and polite sentences with terrible silences in between, and, yet, there was a tenderness in the exchange, a grief for old hurts, and a shared reluctance to turn loose."

They had been separated for nearly three years, during which neither had luck. Alan had no work in films; her play, "the only thing I ever did that I was proud of" and the most living writing she ever created with a man, had failed. Her closest approach to good fortune had been that *The New Yorker*, which had long since ceased to be merely a humorous magazine, had in 1955 bought two short stories, written out of the material that went into *The Ladies of the Corridor*. One was the story of a woman who sought to dominate her daughter; the other concerned a woman who tried to devour her son. In neither story was there the slightest suspicion of compassion. The two mothers were entirely monstrous, and worse, one of them in appearance and manner of speech seemed only too closely to resemble one of Dorothy Parker's most intimate friends.

For the past two years, she had seemed intent on burning her bridges and sitting alone in the smoke. Friends would telephone to invite her out for a drink, or to supper, or to the theater, and she would say, "Oh, if you'd only called five minutes ago . . . I'm so sorry, but if you had only called five minutes earlier." Then she would sit alone in her bare room at the Volney and drink and talk for hours to Misty. When friends came to call, they were often glad to leave. She was not always sober, and when she was not, she was repetitive and boring; when she was sober, she often gave her friends the impression she was not overjoyed to see them. After a time, fewer friends called, and they called less often. It was as Lillian Hellman wrote in her autobiography: "Dottie's middle age, old age, made rock of much that had been fluid, and eccentricities once charming became too strange for safety or comfort."

She was once summoned from her self-imposed exile at the Volney by a New York State legislative committee in February

1955, an occasion that gave *The New York Daily News* the opportunity to lead page five with the headline, "Dorothy Parker Mum on Red Ties at Fund Probe." "Verse-cracking satirist Dorothy Parker, testifying in a legislative probe of charity fund abuse, refused to say whether she had ever been a member of the Communist Party," the newspaper reported.

She refused to answer the question on grounds that she might incriminate herself if she did. She testified that she was the chairman of the Joint Anti-Fascist Refugee Committee, and said she helped to raise money for that organization, but she did not know how much money had been raised or how it had been spent. She did not know, she said, and never asked, whether the Committee was controlled by the Communist Party. Earlier testimony of other witnesses was that the Committee raised more than $1,500,000, but instead of using the money to succor refugees from Franco's Spain indiscriminately, it had devoted the funds exclusively to help refugees who were Communists.

Caught in the mood of those Red-hunting days, the public was left to speculate as to whether Dorothy Parker was a dupe or a traitor: it was a time of such either/or judgments. But she would not, like some, fawn, apologize, beg forgiveness, and betray. Nor did she, like Donald Ogden Stewart and a few other radicals of the thirties, fly into voluntary exile abroad. She looked on it all with stone eyes, and sat silent, and let people think of her what they would. The stories in *The New Yorker* were indicative of that mood: it was one of contempt, unrelieved by charity or by wit.

Yet, during these luckless years, when she was once again crouched in silence, writing virtually nothing and drinking more than she ate, talking more with her poodle than with those who would be her friends, discontent with her present and dissatisfied with her memories of the past, she never quite lost hope. As she said, she was the greatest little hoper that ever lived, even if she never did quite know what it was that she hoped for, and even if she always expected to be disappointed.

Just as she never lost all hope, so her friends never lost their hope for her. For all that she might seem now withdrawn and strange, she was still the woman who had written what she had written, and who had said what she had said, and who might, hopefully, regain her kingdom if she could just pull herself together and make the effort. Out of a mixture of faith, hope and charity, her friends in the following year sought to bring her once more to the center of New York life by involving her in an ambitious production, a musical comedy version of Voltaire's *Candide*.

Here, if anywhere, was her own bit of country; Voltaire's sardonic commentary was certainly akin to her own. The music would be written by Leonard Bernstein whose star of great magnitude was still a rising one; the staging and direction would be managed by the talented Tyrone Guthrie; the book would be written by Dorothy Parker's good friend and first-ranking playwright, Lillian Hellman. Dorothy was asked to help Richard Wilbur and John Latouche write the lyrics.

All the auspices were good: seldom in the history of the New York theater were so many major talents assembled to dramatize, in the form of the operetta, a piece of writing of such brilliance. The commercial auspices were equally pleasant, for the age of the lavish musical comedy had arrived: the only plays earning money were what New York called smash hits, and the rule now on Broadway was that only musicals could be smash hits. Everyone felt that, with all that talent packed into the most popular medium, *Candide* would run forever and make all that money for everyone.

Dorothy Parker's role in this was very minor. "I had only one lyric in it," she said later. "It didn't work out very well. There were too many geniuses in it, you know."

She blamed Leonard Bernstein for her personal trouble; she said he was responsible not only for the music but for some of the lyrics.

"Lenny Bernstein has to do everything, as you know, and do it better than anybody—which he does—except for lyrics."

Others close to the production said that Dorothy Parker's contribution was a limited one, not because of any interference with her work by Mr. Bernstein, but rather because her own worst enemy was herself. She either did not or could not contribute as much as she might have, and a reason for this, they said, was drink. However this may have been, *Candide* brought her no closer to a place in the theater than had any dramatic production with which she had ever been associated. On December 1, 1956, the curtain at the Martin Beck Theater parted to disclose what one critic called a truly notable event in the theater, and what another described as "a really spectacular disaster."

All the critics applauded the staging, the direction, the sets, the costumes, the singing, the acting, the music, and the lyrics. But even the kindest of them admitted that an eighteenth-century political satire was not the most promising of dramatic material. The result was a stunning but very long evening. *Candide* was not a hit; it was a near-miss. It lasted on the boards for seventy-three performances.

Dorothy Parker afterward said the operetta's fault was that it strayed too far from Voltaire—whereas the weight of criticism was that *Candide* succeeded as much as it did to the extent that it did *not* follow Voltaire exactly. Once again, comedy and tragedy had been indigestibly mixed on the stage, and once again Dorothy Parker failed to see that such a mix was, in fact, indigestible. This time she was in distinguished theatrical company in her error.

Candide was the last of her experiences in the theater, and after its brief, bright hope died at the Martin Beck, there was nothing for her except the corridors of the Volney.

But then there was Alan.

Somehow, there always was Alan. Even if he needed a total stranger to help him summon up the courage to see her, there was Alan, nevertheless.

Alan returned to the drab, rather dirty room at the Volney, this time alone, and bringing not only an offer of reconciliation but a message of hope. Charles Brackett, an old friend from the early Algonquin days, and now a Hollywood producer, was willing to stand against the sickness of the times. Specifically, he was ready to ignore the Hollywood blacklist, and he wanted Dorothy Parker and Alan Campbell to write the script of a motion picture to be called *The Good Soup*. The star, Alan said, would be Marilyn Monroe.

Three years earlier, Dorothy Parker had sworn that she was through with Hollywood forever, that nothing could ever take her away from her beloved New York. But the New York she had loved, with its intimate groups and its intimate bars, and its excited certainty that it was at the very center of life, had in some strange way become giant corporations of organization men eating the expense account lunch at overpriced and tricked-out restaurants staffed by surly waiters. New York was a choke of traffic, advertising men in Eisenhower black Homburgs, brassy musical comedies staged for the benefit of out-of-town clothing buyers, the lonely ladies and the dogs of the Volney, and aging people she no longer wished to see. Hollywood was of course obscene, but Alan wanted her back, and Alan clearly would need her help on the film script, and if Hollywood money melted like snow in the hand, it was still money, and Alan needed that. But more than anything else, she needed Alan to help her through this living, this living in the humorless stagnance of the Eisenhower years when a conforming generation was silent and when the nation filled fat with plenty of everything and the best of nothing, when the intellectual community was apathetic or terrified or despondent, and when it must have seemed to her that she was nearly a ghost that moved slowly, if at all, through the now-empty rooms of a house that had once been gay and beautiful. So many old friends were dead. She needed Alan, and he needed her, and it was perfectly clear to them that they could not live apart no matter how difficult it was for them to live together. If living in Hollywood was the price that had to be paid, very well, she would pay it. She had been given a second chance; now she was being given a third. Or, as it might have been, Alan had had his second chance and was now asking for a third. The alternative was the Volney. Perhaps it occurred to her that this time when she agreed to go back to Alan, it was she who was changing the ending of the script she had written for *The Ladies of the Corridor*—changing it to add a little note of hope.

5

They found a place in what Dorothy Parker later called Peyton Place West. Its proper name was Norma Place, so called because the actress Norma Talmadge once had a studio there. The street was one block long, and its little frame houses had been the homes of railroad workers. Nearby were a bank, a branch post office, a supermarket, a bar called the Four Star, and a laundromat.

The neighborhood was one of those backwaters that seem always to be inhabited by people who hope that they are on the way up, and by those who know they are on the way down, and she found her neighbors fascinating. There was a lady film writer whose custom it was to lie nude in her bedroom watching television while everyone gazed admiringly on her through her unshaded window. Another resident was the actress Estelle Winwood, whom Dorothy Parker knew from the Algonquin days ("she was creaking, even then," Dorothy said) and who could be seen at almost any time of day sitting alone in her front room window, pouring tea, carefully dressed and wearing a hat. When Tuesday Weld and her mother moved into the block, Dorothy Parker went about asking other Norma Placers, "Have you met Tuesday Weld's mother, Wednesday, yet?" One of the most popular residents was a man who invited everyone to inspect a portrait of himself. It showed him stark naked, seated, facing front; and Wyatt Cooper, who became a good friend to Alan and Dorothy, and whose memories of Norma Place these anecdotes are, said the fellow's "carefully drawn genitals seemed to tumble out at you."

"Dottie," Mr. Cooper said, "was most genteel and admiring, murmuring things like, 'It's so real, you almost feel he could speak to you, don't you?'"

In this somewhat raffish version of middle-class suburbia, Dorothy Parker and Alan Campbell settled into a kind of contented obscurity, working on the script for *The Good Soup*.

"We wrote a nice, little, innocent, bawdy French farce," she said, "but in this town, everybody's a writer and has ideas. So they [the studio] took our script and hoked it up with dope pushers, two murders and, straight out of Fannie Hurst, the harlot with the heart of goo."

So in the end, the script wasn't anything at all, and the film was never produced, and that was the last film assignment that Dorothy and Alan ever had.

When they were paid off for their ruined work, they were immediately faced with the problem of how to live in Norma Place, or anywhere else, without money. Mr. Cooper suggested that he was drawing unemployment compensation, and so should they. He explained that no one should feel the slightest shame about this, because when Hollywood people were employed, they were paid fantastic salaries, and then they paid out a great deal of tax money to support state and federal governments. So the unemployment compensation office was in a way a service that their tax money, paid out during their salad years, had helped to create. They would be merely taking a bit of their own back when they sought relief, which was just as much their right as it was the right of anyone else. All you had to do was go to the office once a week and fill out a card saying you were available for work, and if no studio gave you any work to do, you drew $75 a week, tax-free. For Dorothy and Alan, this would be $600 tax-free each month.

"It was," Mr. Cooper wrote in his *Esquire* memoir, "a pleasant and even rather chic thing to do; you not only caught sight of such stars as Marlon Brando from time to time, but you also ran into old chums you hadn't encountered for ages, and whom you were happy to see so long as you didn't have to spend a lot of time with them. The parking lot always had a Rolls or two along with an abundance of sporty Cadillacs, and we once decided that you saw just as many celebrities there as you would lunching at Romanoff's; furthermore, as Dottie was quick to comment, 'it's a much nicer set.' "

She must have enjoyed the pleasant irony that, while one arm of government was fundamentally responsible for the studio doors being closed to them, another arm of government was giving them money. But she approached the interviewing clerks shyly and guiltily, looking, Mr. Cooper said, variously like a perjurer about to be led to prison, or a lamb being led to slaughter. But then, Mr. Cooper wrote, she approached one desk and Alan said, " 'Ah, she'll be all right now, that one has glasses on.'

"Sure enough," Mr. Cooper wrote, "the lady with the glasses started to read Dottie's record, looked up, asked a question, grinned broadly, took off her spectacles, shook hands, and called several other girls over to touch the author of the familiar line. We were too far away to hear what was being said, but we could see several pairs of lips moving as they recited the poem to her, and Dottie's expression on this occasion was one of deep gratitude."

They lived on their compensatory $600 a month and on the $1,000 to $2,000 a year that her books of poems and short stories, written in the great days, were still bringing in; and if Dorothy Parker still regarded herself in Hollywood to be a visitor at a zoo, this time she seemed willing to accept it and enjoy it. She listened to the gossip of Norma Place and of the studios and she invented funny and bawdy stories of her own about her neighbors; she took (or feigned) a kind of schoolgirl fascination in the comings and goings of the currently famous stars. She and Alan also drank a good deal, and enjoyed the company of their new friend Mr. Cooper, who was as tall and young and handsome and full of fun as Dorothy Parker could have wished a young man to be, and it seemed to Mr. Cooper that Dorothy and Alan had great fun together "as they must have done in earlier and younger days." He was impressed that neither of them seemed to be old, because their spirits were so young, and that they seemed to understand one another so well and to take such pleasure in each other's company.

But he was also aware that Dorothy and Alan quarreled all the time, and that she would accuse Alan of infidelities which she perfectly well knew had not taken place, and she would complain about Alan's drinking. It seemed to Mr. Cooper that they took turns quarreling, for next day it would be Alan complaining about Dorothy's drinking or about her not writing anymore. She would say she wanted to write; she would say that she was writing when, in fact, she was not. She feared that whatever she wrote would be no good.

It would seem, however, that there was a kind of comfortable familiarity about these quarrels and mutual complaints. Life for them had settled into something very close to a well-loved and well-understood tension which they both knew to be necessary to the other. It was as if they were at once acting in and watching a play. Alan was meanwhile cast as the suburban householder. He puttered around the house, building a guest apartment in the garage, selecting new upholstery for the furniture, taking an enormous interest in choosing a proper rug; and Dorothy his good wife played with her new poodle Cliché, who chewed up the upholstery that Alan bought.

Their small life was made a bit more spacious when, in 1957, *The New Yorker* published her short story "The Banquet of Crow." It describes a woman imagining that her estranged husband will return to her because, she thinks, he cannot live without her. It was a story close to her experience, and it was the last she published. But then in that same year, *Esquire* magazine asked Dorothy Parker to review books for them for a fee of $750 an article.

Since *Esquire* was a monthly magazine, this meant $750 a month. It would also mean an end to Dorothy's unemployment compensation checks, but still it meant $450 more than she and Alan had been receiving. The offer did not come about because *Esquire*'s publisher, Arnold Gingrich, had known her in New York, admired her, and felt sorry for her now. The idea originated with a young editor, Harold Hayes, who as a college boy had been impressed by her writing, and who approached her on the basis of hiring one of America's great contemporary writers to review books for *Esquire*.

Mr. Hayes met her when, as New Yorkers say, she was in town from the Coast. She had come to visit the city and was staying at the Volney, the days of splurges at the Plaza now being over.

"I expected a wisecracking hotshot, a very old one," Mr. Hayes said, "but when I met a woman who was more insecure than I was—as a young editor—I was charmed.

"There was an extremely feminine quality about her. She was a genuinely warm woman with a sense of great dignity, an old-fashioned great lady. I was very much overawed by her. Despite her insistence, I could not bring myself to call her 'Dottie.' She was one of a very few individuals I had met in the New York literary world who impressed me as much in person as in print. No matter how bleak her circumstances—and she was living in a Hopper-like setting at the Volney—she managed to suggest a kind of courtesy and attentiveness that immediately put you at ease. She made you believe she sincerely hoped everything was going well for you."

In other words, Mr. Hayes appeared in Dorothy Parker's room looking very much like Lochinvar and/or Apollo. If her life was filled with an undue number of tall, quite good-looking young men, why here was yet another one come to pay court. The impression she made on Mr. Hayes indicated she had lost nothing of her ability to bolster a young man's pride in himself and to give him to believe that he was in the presence of a princess awaiting rescue by the very man who now stood before her. She took on a royal dignity to match a courtly mood, and in an instant Mr. Hayes became another captive to her spell.

Mr. Hayes' opinion of Dorothy Parker as a dignified, warm and genuinely concerned woman never changed, but he was shortly to find that she was not the most dependable of book reviewers, nor the easiest writer for an editor to handle. "Editing her was a terrifying experience," he said, and what was particularly terrifying was that a magazine issue would be closing and her copy would be missing. She began her column well enough and on time in the December 1957 issue, but there was no Parker column in January, February, March or April in 1958;

she missed the August issue in 1959; she missed three issues in
1960, two in 1961, and five in 1962. There were occasions during
these years when she was ill, but there were more frequent ones
when she was not, and when the work was not done for any of a
variety of reasons.

One reason was that she could not always bring herself to
work. Alan could never understand this. He could always get
work done, and therefore thought that anyone could. He once
put a hair on her typewriter keys, and left the house to give her
time alone to complete an *Esquire* piece, which was then five
days overdue in New York. When he returned, she assured him
she had finished the article and sent it off, but the hair was still
in place on the typewriter.

"She seemed sincerely to detest writing," Mr. Hayes said. "She
truly hated to write. She'd just lie about how far along she was
with a piece. She fled from the problem of doing anything."

Mr. Hayes felt her dread of writing arose from her fear of
failure. "Her standards were higher than those of many writers,
and she had a constant awareness of her deficiencies in meeting
them," Mr. Hayes said. "When finally she would turn in a piece,
she expressed great dismay about it. She thought there was little
value in anything she had done. When I would attempt to re-
assure her, she would hang onto my praise with the gratefulness
of a small child. Once, when I told her how much I liked a line
in one of her reviews, she said, 'Will you marry me?' "

He also found that her critical sense, when applied to the
work of others, was not always as demanding; she would, he
said, "excuse in the work of authors she liked a sentimentality
she would never permit in her own writing." An additional dif-
ficulty, and a recurring one, was her drinking problem. "It was
often difficult to tell whether she was stalling because she was
drinking or because she simply did not want to write. But my
daily calls got me nowhere."

"I can't imagine why it hasn't arrived," she would say. "I sent
it days ago."

And Mr. Hayes, gripping the telephone in New York and
hearing those too carefully pronounced words spoken two thousand miles away, would know she had not written it at all.

On some occasions, he would asked whether there was a carbon; could she dictate it over the telephone? Sometimes she would pretend there was a carbon, and dictate something "that had her voice," Mr. Hayes said, but "the dictated copy would be wandering, redundant, an idea in one paragraph would turn up four paragraphs later. Her last reviews show they must have been dictated over the phone."

The most chilling words of all, however, would be "Oh, yes, it is almost done," for this Mr. Hayes learned to interpret as meaning "the goddamned thing isn't even started," and there would be no use asking her to dictate from memory her opinions of the books *Esquire* had sent her, for she would not have read the books.

Perhaps, in some corner of her mind, she entertained the notion that all this was good fun, as it had seemed to be fun back in the twenties when everyone was young and gay, and when she and Mr. Benchley and Mr. Stewart had teased editors who were haunted by deadlines. Perhaps she still thought herself to be able to drink all night and go clear-eyed to the typewriter next day, as people in the twenties once thought they were able to do. But few people drink heavily just for fun, although a good many do so seeking exile or escape. Perhaps she wished to shut off the vision of the really rather pointless life she was leading out of town (as she might have thought in her New Yorker's terms) among the shapeless lives, the stucco buildings, and routine eccentricities of Peyton Place West.

But, as Mr. Hayes said, "she never lost her capacity as a writer. When she was able to force herself to the typewriter, she was marvelously precise and witty—her voice was as true and distinctive as in her writing in the twenties."

Each month *Esquire* would send its $750, whether she sent them any copy or not. They were willing to pay this price for the articles they knew she could write when she was not drinking.

Dorothy Parker and Alan Campbell lived quite modestly in Norma Place, supported by her slender royalties, her *Esquire* check, and Alan's unemployment compensation, living on gossip and comfortable quarrels, with Alan doing the housework and looking after her, and both of them drinking a good deal more than they should, she writing as little as she could, but nonetheless reading and reviewing 208 books for *Esquire*. They were years when she was often ill and Alan was worried for her, but she kept coming back as it seemed she was always able to come back, and always would be able to come back, and she and Alan were often merry together. She was a great lady living in a somewhat smaller, crumbling castle, but still a lady in a castle, and Alan was a somewhat older but still boyish page, doing his devoir to his lady.

As she always had, she seemed content to let life make her decisions for her. One of life's decisions was that she should now enter upon a time when she was not so much known as remembered. In 1962, a New York City local television station, WNEW, dramatized three of her short stories as part of a festival-of-the-arts series, and a phonograph record company, Verve, decided to capture the memory of Dorothy Parker while it was still a living one. Accordingly, Verve asked her to read certain of her poems and stories for a record called "The World of Dorothy Parker."

The voice on the record is soft and shy, but with a surprisingly youthful strength beneath it. Reviewing the record in the January 1962 issue of his magazine, *Esquire*'s publisher Arnold Gingrich pointed out that the record introduces three Dorothy Parkers: the poet, the wit, and the woman of compassion. The last of these three Dorothy Parkers, he said, was virtually unknown because of the glare of legend surrounding the first two, but it was the woman of compassion who impressed him. "It is in the poems, and some of the short stories, such as 'Big Blonde,'" he wrote, "that she will speak most tellingly to posterity, as a major writer of our time.

"She doesn't go about as much as she once did," Mr. Gingrich told *Esquire*'s readers. "Indeed of late she has been something of a recluse, so it's a privilege to be able to go to her, as this record lets us do. For among her many other talents, she has fully mastered the art of being alone. Possibly she was helped in this by the perfectly valid realization that, searching the wide world over, she couldn't have found better company."

Possibly so. But if she had not mastered the art of being alone, she seemed to have reconciled herself to the fact that she and Alan Campbell now lived before a carefully banked fire, as compared with the uncertain fires of other years. The voice on the

Verve record seems to issue from some quiet place outside of time.

She and Alan Campbell had seven years together in Norma Place before life made another decision for her—one that was as unforeseen as it was inevitable, and one that she and Alan had never really allowed themselves to contemplate.

On the night of June 13, 1963, there had been a considerable bit of drinking going on, and perhaps to keep the room from spinning, Alan and Dorothy each took sleeping pills before they went to bed. It was something they both had done many times before.

When she woke next morning, Alan was strangely inert and terribly cold. She tried to rouse him, and she knew she never would.

The newspapers said that Mr. Campbell had a history of heart attacks, but added that police were analyzing pills found on the bed table. A physician said it was not necessarily a case of suicide; it was not unusual for a drunken person, asleep under sedation by barbiturates, to strangle on his own vomit. It was decided that death had been caused by accident.

But nothing that the newspapers, or the policemen, or physicians, or coroners said really mattered to Dorothy. What really mattered, and mattered terribly, was that Alan had died sometime during the night while she slept beside him, and she had not been awake to do anything, and now there was nothing, nothing at all, that could be done.

She moved through the rest of that day in a trance. A shaken and emotional Wyatt Cooper telephoned from Alabama, and, he wrote in his *Esquire* memoir, to his utter bewilderment he heard her say, "The whole world thanks you for what you are doing. And let's face it, dear, it's not for yourself you're doing it; it's for all mankind. I think we can say that Alan died with your letters clutched in his hand."

Suddenly, Mr. Cooper understood. He had been visiting the University of Alabama, whose president was one of his relatives, when Governor George Wallace barred the doorway against the admission of Negro students. Mr. Cooper had been writing daily accounts to Dorothy and Alan of the events leading up to this dreadful performance by the Governor. He now saw what she was trying to do.

"She was removing herself from her grief by talking of something else, something untrue, and she was outrageously giving me credit for accomplishing the integration of the university."

Mr. Cooper could plainly hear the voices of others in Dorothy's living room in Norma Place, and he asked who was with her. She said no one was, and then "she gave me an account of her discovery of his body, speaking as one might to a newspaper reporter, getting the facts straight," Mr. Cooper wrote. "She said that he'd asked to be awakened at a certain time, and that when she touched him, 'rigor mortis had already set in.' This last she said with some coldness as if that condition were somehow his fault. A final affront."

She seemed as strange and remote to those who came to call at the little white clapboard bungalow that day. One of the callers was a local gossip and busybody whose admiration of Dorothy Parker was as transparently false as her admiration of Alan Campbell had been transparently real. The woman fussed importantly about and begged Dorothy to tell her what she could do to help.

"Get me a new husband," Dorothy Parker said.

For a moment, the woman could not believe she had heard what she heard. "I think that is the most callous and disgusting remark I ever heard in my life," she said. "With Alan not yet buried."

Dorothy Parker regarded the woman with weary patience. "Well, if that's the way you feel," she muttered. "So sorry. Then run down to the corner and get me a ham and cheese on rye and tell them to hold the mayo."

In Eliot's phrase, she prepared a face for the faces she had to meet and, meanwhile, as her physician said, moved in a state of deep shock. She sealed off her grief and held it tightly inside where no one could touch it and mar it, contemptuous of the presumption of others that they could imagine what Alan, and his death, meant to her.

In the same grim mood, she allowed Alan's mother, Hortense, to take charge of the funeral arrangements. Her physician told her not to attend the funeral, which she had no intention of doing, anyway. It would be held in Richmond; Alan's body would be sent there. And that, she said of Hortense, "will be her coming-out party, I believe."

A former rector of Virginia Military Institute and a rabbi officiated at the ceremonies, which were held in Richmond's small and crowded Hebrew cemetery. Dorothy Parker followed these events at a disdainful distance.

"Can you believe it," she said of Hortense, "that after all these years of her going to the Episcopal Church, she buried Alan in the Hebrew cemetery? I see you can believe it. I'd hoped you couldn't."

Everything about death impressed her as being obscene, but more particularly, the graveside emotions of the living. These were not only obscene to her but grotesque: no one should go to a grave except the corpse and the gravediggers. She had made so many jokes about death; she had given each of her books a macabre title. There was nothing funny now. All funerals were to her exercises in pretense, and she regarded the ceremonies for Alan to be the most disgustingly pretentious of all. Very nearly as insufferable to her were the well-meant ministrations of her friends who wanted to call on her, to look after her in what they believed to be a difficult time for her, to help her come to some decisions about what she would do next.

She very tiredly wished that people would simply let her alone.

PART
FIVE

"Did Ernest really like me?"

—Dorothy Parker

1

Dorothy Parker spent the summer of 1963 in Norma Place, going nowhere and seeing virtually no one, waiting only for Alan's affairs to be settled and to dispose of the house. She would not have been in Hollywood had it not been for Alan, and now there was no longer any reason for her to remain there. She would return to her beloved New York, there, she was sure, to stay forever. She had written nothing for *Esquire* since the past December. Each month, *Esquire* sent their check, and she sent nothing back; she felt guilty about that and thought that when she returned to New York, she might be able to write again, and do something for *Esquire*. But she could not write in Hollywood. She sat at home with two black French poodles, who ate more than she did. She chain-smoked cigarettes, which blunted the edge of hunger, and she drank neat whisky, which blunted the edges of many things.

On her birthday in August, an Associated Press reporter came to call. Rather to their mutual astonishment, Dorothy Parker and the reporter realized that she was seventy years old. Once this fact was examined and conceded, neither quite believed it— Dorothy because she said she felt as if she were ninety, instead, and the reporter not believing it because he saw before him a little woman in a polka-dot dress and pearls, the hair still dark, who had (he said) a small-girl smile and "a look of startled innocence" in her great, doe's eyes.

She smiled at him over her glass of whisky and murmured that she should have started lying about her age years ago, but now it was too late for that.

"If I had any decency, I'd be dead," she said. "Most of my friends are."

The reporter reminded her of a poem, "The Little Old Lady in Lavender Silk," that she had written thirty-two years earlier. In it, she had said:

"I was seventy-seven, come August,
    I shall shortly be losing my bloom:
I've experienced Zephyr and raw gust
    And (symbolical) flood and simoom.

"When you come to this time of abatement,
    To this passing from Summer to Fall,
It is manners to issue a statement
    As to what you got out of it all.

"So I'll say, though reflection unnerves me
    And pronouncements I dodge as I can,
That I think (if memory serves me)
    There was nothing more fun than a man!"

"There was," she told the reporter, "nothing more fun than a man. Alan and I had twenty-nine great years together."

She said this evenly, the reporter said, and they both ignored the fact that for twelve of those twenty-nine years, she and Alan had been separated by war, divorce, and choice.

Shifting to what he believed might be a happier subject for her—and one that would greatly interest the public—the reporter asked about the memorable days of the Algonquin Round Table and all the fun of the twenties. She favored him with a sour look. He was the first of a parade of interviewers, now that she was seventy, come to pick the bones of the past.

She told him, and she told all the others, what in retrospect those Algonquin days now seemed to be to her, and what she thought of the witty, clever friends of her youth. The sum of her remarks to the Associated Press man, and to the others who came to call, was this:

"People romanticize it," she said of the Algonquin Hotel. "It was no Mermaid Tavern, I promise you. These were no giants. Think of who was writing in those days—Lardner, Fitzgerald, Faulkner, and Hemingway. Those were the real giants. The Round Table was just a lot of people telling jokes and telling each other how good they were. Just a bunch of loudmouths showing off, saving their gags for days, waiting for a chance to spring them. 'Did you hear about my remark?' 'Did I tell you what I said?' And everybody hanging around, saying, 'What'd he say?' It was not legendary. I don't mean that—but it wasn't all that good. There was no truth in anything they said. It was the terrible day of the wisecrack, so there didn't have to be any truth, you know. There's nothing memorable about them. About any of them. So many of them died. My Lord, how people die.

"Oh," she said, "I think of the Round Table and I really get sick at all this fuss about them now. In the first place, it isn't far enough back to be picturesque, and so it isn't anything. My dear, there've been so many things written about it, spoken about it, and it was such a mutual admiration society. Please excuse me; I don't mean to be so rude as to contradict you. But those people at the Round Table didn't know a bloody thing. They thought we were fools to go up and demonstrate for Sacco and Vanzetti. Fools to do this! And they didn't know about anything. I think it was ignorance, largely. They didn't know, and they just didn't think about anything but the theater. By the theater, I mean the little comedy they put on last night—and you know, that isn't good enough.

"At first," Dorothy Parker said, "I was in awe of them because they were being published. But then I came to realize I wasn't hearing anything very stimulating. I remember hearing Woollcott say, 'reading Proust is like lying in someone else's dirty bath water.' And then he'd go into ecstasy about something called 'Valiant Is the Word for Carrie,' and I knew I'd had enough of the Round Table.

"Woollcott," she said reflectively, "was ridiculous. He had a good heart, for whatever that was worth, and it wasn't much. George Kaufman was a mess."

But, she said, Mr. Benchley was very funny and wonderful; FPA was a lovely man, disagreeable and rude—but lovely.

Harold Ross, she said, "was almost illiterate, wild and rough, never read anything, didn't know anything, but had a great gift as an editor and was awfully nice to the people who worked for him."

"I don't read *The New Yorker* much these days," she said in answer to a question. "It always seems to be the same old story about somebody's childhood in Pakistan.

"There just aren't any humorists today," she said. "I don't know why. I don't suppose there is much demand for humor, although there ought to be. S. J. Perelman is about the only one working at it, and he's rewriting himself. Humor now is too carefully planned. There is nothing of the old madness Mr. Benchley and some of the others had in my time, no leaping of minds."

When she spoke of her "time," it was with the calm assurance of one who no longer needs to prove a point. During the ardent days of her anti-Nazi crusades, it seemed necessary to her to say that the fun of the twenties and the fun of the Algonquin group had been silly and irresponsible, in order to make a contrast and to explain her position. But now at age seventy there was no such need. She had outlived the time of fun, and the time of the political wars, and the time of the Inquisition, and she had survived into the brave new world of Great Societies, giant government, giant institutions, and giant supermarkets that sold what were called giant quarts. Each of these times had called forth different kinds and moods of writing, each reflective of different styles of life. Dorothy Parker had never been one to cling to a style; instead, she had always moved not just with, but slightly ahead of, all the times of her life. It struck her oddly that in the strangely haunted and introspective new time of the sixties, there should be such a nostalgia for what were supposed to have been the great and innocent days of the twenties, and such interest in those who were believed to have lived such a glittering life in New York. Of course, the people who came to interview her had, as young college people, been brought up to believe in the mystique of the twenties, of the Paris group, of the Algonquin group, of *The New Yorker*, of the golden days of the stars in Hollywood. She did not, as she told them, mean to be so rude as to contradict them, but she did want to share with them the perspective of her years.

She could, however, have gone on to add, just as truthfully, that the bright people of that New York group made a major contribution to American life and letters. Their own work might have been less than immortal, but they did help to pioneer a way out of a dank and stuffy Victorian woods, and to clear a field in which the more important works of others could take root. She had been one of those pioneers, and her contribution had by no means been a minor one.

Inevitably her interviewers inquired as to her future plans. She brightened, and said she was counting the days until she could return to New York and return to decent writing, by which she meant short stories.

"I want to be taken seriously as a short story writer and, by God, I hope to make it," she would say.

She would look pleadingly at all the people who came to interview her. "Promise me," she would say, "promise me I won't get old."

It was easy for everyone to promise this. It was impossible for anyone to imagine that she would ever grow old. She was not a tiny old woman of seventy who had lived past her time, and lived alone and smoked too much and disturbingly drank a great deal of neat whisky and did not write anymore. Her hair was thick and dark and her eyes were bright and her smile was that of a young girl, and she was going to go to New York and write short stories. She was Dorothy Parker, standing once again upon the edge of a new beginning, now that most of her friends were dead.

2

In his *Esquire* article, "Remembering Dorothy Parker," Wyatt Cooper described a visit to the Volney.

"Do you know what they do when you die in this hotel?" he said Dorothy asked him as he entered her apartment. "They used to take them down on the big elevator in the back, but it's not running, and they take them down that front elevator, and you know how small it is. They have to stand you up."

But Mr. Cooper had come to talk about life, rather than about death, and he had brought a tape recorder with him. A publisher had asked Dorothy Parker to write her autobiography, but she said she could never do that, although she wanted to, in order to be able to call it *Mongrel*. Perhaps, Mr. Cooper suggested, she could just talk into a tape recorder, instead of writing, and she supposed she could do that.

"It would give me something to live for," she said. "Let's make it gay; if it's not fun, there's no point in telling it."

While Mr. Cooper prepared the machine, he reflected on the barrenness of her rooms. No attempt had been made at decoration; there was nothing in the apartment to hint at the character of its occupant. There were no photographs except for a Christmas card that had a picture of Mr. Cooper's son on it; the one souvenir of her marriage was a set of thirteen porcelain figures of Napoleon's generals. Mr. Cooper remembered the day when he, Alan Campbell, and Dorothy Parker had found them in an antique store in Santa Monica. Alan had set them up in their Norma Place living room, and had installed a special light over them. Now Napoleon and his generals stared down from a shelf built into a hotel room wall.

The machine ready, Mr. Cooper sat back to enjoy the gay and amusing story of Dorothy Parker's life, whereupon she cheerfully fell to work.

"I apologize for introducing nobody but dreadful characters," she said, and began to describe her father.

"On Sundays he'd take us on an outing. Some outing. We'd go to the cemetery to visit my mother's grave. All of us, including the second wife. That was his idea of a treat. Whenever he'd hear a crunch of gravel that meant an audience approaching, out would come the biggest handkerchief you ever saw, and in a lachrymose voice that had remarkable carrying power, he'd start wailing, 'We're all here, Eliza! I'm here. Dottie's here. Mrs. Rothschild is here!' "

And on she went, brightly recalling what Mr. Cooper soon found to be a rather more-than-Dickensian chronicle as wildly funny as it was hideously macabre. He presently found that facts meant little to her, once she was off and running in full cry. During the course of many recording sessions, Mr. Cooper filled many spools that, he said, made his hair stand on end. There were passages that simply could not possibly be true; others that were slanderous and libelous, and more that seemed to him to be violently anti-Semitic. She would say, he said, "the most outrageous things about Jews and about her father." In the end, Mr. Cooper realized that in all fairness to Dorothy Parker, he should suppress these tapes, rather than to try to make sense, much less a book, out of them, for they were replete with "things that, in a more collected moment, she would never have said."

No doubt she hugely enjoyed Mr. Cooper's visits, but there was now little else in her life anywhere near so pleasant. She had returned to New York in the fall of 1963, as she had told her interviewers in California that she would, but she had not been able to do the work she wished to do. *Esquire* kept sending her new books to review, and she gave them away. The magazine gave her money, and she wrote nothing for them. Nothing, that is, until she wrote a brief text to accompany reproductions of paintings by John Koch that appeared in the November 1964 issue of *Esquire*. The article was called "New York at 6:30 P.M.," and Mr. Koch's paintings, done in a quasi-photographic style that might be called Madison Avenue Flemish, were principally illustrative of genteel people, stately interiors, and fashionable parties.

"I am always a little sad when I see a John Koch painting," Dorothy Parker wrote, or possibly dictated. "It is nothing more than a bit of nostalgia that makes my heart beat slower—nostalgia for those rooms of lovely lights and lovelier shadows and loveliest people. And I really have no room for the sweet, soft feeling. Nor am I honest, perhaps, in referring to it. For it is the sort of nostalgia that is only a dreamy longing for some places you never were.

"And I never will be there. There is no such hour on the present clock as 6:30, New York time. Yet, as only New Yorkers know, if you can get through the twilight, you'll live through the night."

It was the last article she wrote.

She was trying to get through her personal twilight, and the New York she loved no longer existed. The city was a clatter of jackhammers, and street barricades said, "Dig we must for a greater New York." The sky was stained and police sirens moaned through a cacophonous world from which humor had fled. She had been a girl in this city when nearly all transport was horse-drawn, and life was gracious and fashionable, and people lived in Manhattan.

It did not seem as if anyone lived there anymore, and in a sense, Dorothy Parker no longer lived there, either. She existed instead within a drab hotel, very much a lady of the Volney's corridors, and not an altogether graceful one on all occasions. She was in her last years, and she was increasingly living out Robert Benchley's terrible prophecy—which she had not for a moment permitted herself to believe—that each of us becomes the thing he most despises. She had most despised boring and garrulous women who did nothing, but because of age and because of drink there were times when she was not lucid and when she was nothing more than a fuddled old woman.

There were intervals of decent lucidity, however, and then she was bright and mischievous, as she was when talking into Mr. Cooper's tape recorder, and the wit flowed as strong and clear as ever. She never lost interest in events. She passionately believed in the Kennedy family, taking pride in their glory and promise and in their conduct in the grip of tragedy. She was thrilled by Martin Luther King's crusade in the South; she had been an early and consistent champion of the cause of justice for the Negro. Although she could not bring herself to review the books that *Esquire* sent her, she closely followed the new writers with admiration or derision (she expressed no literary judgments that fell between these extremes). She particularly admired Truman Capote and Saul Bellow; she said she thought James Baldwin "can write like all hell"; and she was bored by Peter DeVries, completely uninterested in John Updike, and found Mary McCarthy's book *The Group* to be "really trying." She also followed events in Hollywood with sardonic glee. "Now John Huston is doing something called, very simply, *The Bible*," she said. "Now you must admit that's a big job. I think he's going to stop with Moses because he can't stand another moment—he is playing Moses, you see." She said this in the course of an interview with radio station WBAI's Richard Lamparski, and when Mr. Lamparski interrupted to murmur, "I'm sure there'll be a part for him in the sequel," Dorothy Parker immediately agreed. "Yes," she breathed, "Moses Junior at Yale."

In the course of that interview in the year before her death, she disclosed her continuing interest in the world of wealth and fashion—the world that had commanded her attention since her girlhood. She was particularly put off by the Jet Set, or The Beautiful People, the ultimate inheritors of what had once been the brilliance of the scene at Jack and Charley's "21." The Beautiful People made her sick, she said, and she was amazed that anyone could take them seriously. But, she said, "I love to read about them.

"The women and the men that will write about them start out by being flippant," she said. "But they get so envious. They're like the little boy with his nose pressed against the bake shop window, you know, wanting to get in. They're just terrible. I have a friend who sends me this glorious thing, *The Women's Wear Daily* . . . it's all about The Beautiful People. Very unhealthy, I think. I have, when I can't sleep, a vision of Miss Ann Ford and, I forget the name of the Italian she married, in that wedding dress. And I thought how sweet that will be. They'll undoubtedly have babies and she'll have a lovely little girl and she'll grow up to be an exquisite slender young woman and she'll marry and it'll be most romantic because she'll wear her mother's wedding dress. That picture of the bride sitting down in that dress! Well, how much of a hurry can you be in? Oh, dear. I wonder what they're really like. But I know what they're like, I'm sure."

So her mind was as youthful as it had ever been—whenever it was not clouded by age and by drink. Unfortunately, in the last three years there were too many times when it was. Joseph Bryan, III, came to call at the Volney, only to be called "a Jew-hating Fascist son of a bitch" by a drunken old woman. Another friend recalled that he and a motion picture actor had the same experience. He said they came to pay homage to a lady, only to find a crone sitting on the floor, surrounded by bottles, who looked up at them blearily from a rug strewn with dog feces. "You're Jew-Fascists," this apparition said. "Get out of here."

This was worse than grotesque; it was horrible; it was the vilest sort of travesty upon a great tragedy. Fearing what they might find at the Volney, some of Dorothy Parker's oldest friends did not want to call on her, and when they did not go to see her they guiltily felt that they were deserting her. But others steeled themselves, accepting the fact that if she were not herself, then she was not Dorothy Parker but was instead an old and very sick woman to whom all visitors were strangers.

One of those who did not call as frequently as she wished she could have was Lillian Hellman. In her autobiography, Miss Hellman said she "was not the good friend I had been. True, I was there in emergencies, but I was out the door immediately they were over." She said she had long ago decided to stop trying to find out whether Dorothy Parker was as badly off financially as she chronically insisted she was, but "the last sick years seemed no time to argue." So in those years, Miss Hellman gave Dorothy Parker money—or, rather, gave it back to her, for, she wrote, many years earlier Dorothy Parker had given her two paintings, a Picasso gouache and an Utrillo landscape. Believing that Dorothy needed money, Miss Hellman sold the Utrillo and sent Dorothy a check, which Dorothy never acknowledged receiving. In 1965, she sold the Picasso for ten thousand dollars and took the check to Dorothy. Two days later, Miss Hellman wrote, a woman "unknown to me" called to say that Dorothy Parker was in the hospital and would Miss Hellman guarantee the hospital bills. She went at once to the hospital, and after visiting Dorothy's bedside, asked, as she rose to leave, "Dottie, do you need money?" Reluctantly, Dorothy said she did. She said she was broke. Miss Hellman insisted that she could not possibly be. She had just given her ten thousand dollars two days ago, and where was that check?

"She stared at me and then turned her face away," Miss Hellman wrote. "She said, very softly, 'I don't know.' "

And that, Miss Hellman said, was the truth: she did not know. She had put the check away somewhere, wanting to be without money and wanting to forget she had any, Miss Hellman concluded.

She grew thin; there were deep lines in her face and heavy pouches beneath her eyes, and she cared less and less for food. Her physician told her she would kill herself if she did not stop drinking. She tried to stop.

In the last year of her life, she would go in the evenings to visit with Beatrice Ames, who had an apartment on East Eightieth Street.

"I would prepare dinner for her," Beatrice said. "I was feeding her in the last year, but we never said anything about it. I gave her money to go home with every night. She'd open her little purse and look up and say, 'What am I going to do about taxis?' and I'd say, 'Well, I have a dollar and a half—take it.' And she'd say, 'Oh, but you musn't do that. But I haven't any money for the weekend.' "

They would talk about the past, and the good times on the Riviera with the Murphys, and about the new people on the stage, and gossip together. It was a terrible thing for Beatrice to see the disintegration of the woman who had been her best friend for more than forty years, but she was proud that Dorothy

Parker came to her for comfort. To her, it was proof that, of all the people Dorothy knew, she was the one Dorothy relied on.

"She was going blind, you know," Beatrice said. "Two Sundays before she died, I telephoned her to call her attention to an article in the *Times*, and she said, 'Oh, but I can't carry it in the door.' I said, 'Have the maid bring it in to you,' but the thing was, she couldn't see to read. I said, 'What the devil have you done with your glasses?' and she said, "There's no point in having them; I can't see, anyway.' "

In the week before she died, Dorothy wanted to make certain of a matter that troubled her.

"I want you to tell me the truth," she told Beatrice Ames. "Did Ernest really like me?"

Beatrice, who had her own memories of Hemingway, and who had never forgiven or forgotten the poem he had written about Dorothy, and the way he had turned on her husband Donald Ogden Stewart, found the question momentarily difficult to answer. But she also knew that Dorothy Parker wished to be remembered for her short stories, and had always looked to Hemingway as the master in that field. It was important to her to have Hemingway's good opinion.

Yes, Beatrice told her friend, Hemingway really had always liked her very much. He truly had.

She said Dorothy thought about this, and nodded, and seemed content.

3

On Wednesday, June 7, 1967, police were called to the Volney Hotel, where a woman had been found dead in her room. The next morning, *The New York Times* published the obituary, signed by Alden Whitman, on page one.

"Dorothy Parker, the sardonic humorist who purveyed her wit in conversation, short stories, verse and criticism, died of a heart attack yesterday in her suite at the Volney Hotel, 23 East 74th Street. She was 73 years old and had been in frail health in recent years.

"In print and in person, Miss Parker sparkled with a word or a phrase, for she honed her humor to its most economical size. Her rapier wit, much of it spontaneous, gained its early renown for her membership in the Algonquin Round Table, an informal luncheon club at the Algonquin Hotel in the nineteen-twenties, where some of . . ."

The obituary jumped to page 38, where it took up virtually all of the page—a matter that acutely irritated a survivor of the Round Table days who had, years ago, been pinked in the pride by that rapier. "You have no idea," he bitterly said, "how many people in New York were surprised by the space the *Times* gave Dorothy Parker."

Two days later, the *Times* devoted an additional column to

her, heading its report of the funeral services, "Dorothy Parker Recalled As Wit."

So it was the wit that people wished to remember, for worse or for better, and respect was paid to it at the services held at a funeral home at Madison Avenue and Eighty-first Street. The service was opened by a violinist playing Bach's "Air for the G String"—a title that Dorothy Parker had always found amusing. Then the actor Zero Mostel rose to tell the one hundred fifty literary and theatrical people who had come to say good-bye that it was Dorothy's express wish that there be no formal ceremonies.

"If she had her way," he said, "I suspect she would not be here at all."

But, he said, after she had written her will, she remarked that the least she could do now was die.

Lillian Hellman's eulogy also touched on Dorothy Parker's oblique sense of humor.

"Late at night," she said, "gulping what we called a watered extract of Scotch, she would put aside the gentle manner and let fly. Then I would roar with laughter that always ended in sober recognition that the joke hid a brilliant diagnosis of people, or places, or customs, or life." She said the remarkable quality of Dorothy Parker's wit "was that it stayed in no place, and was of no time."

Miss Hellman remembered her friend as a woman whose mind and spirit "were, until the very end, young and sparkling." But she also remembered her as having been an essentially brave woman who "never spoke of old glories, never repented old defeats, never rested on times long ago." She said Dorothy Parker had been "brave in deprivation, in the chivying she took during the McCarthy days, in the isolation of the last bad, sick years.

"She was part of nothing and nobody except herself," Miss Hellman said, and "it was this independence of mind and spirit that was her true distinction."

When the two brief eulogies had been spoken, the mourners slowly dispersed. One of them remarked that, for all the brevity of the service, he was certain that Dorothy's foot was tapping all the time. He, too, reflected on her humor. Some of the brightest things she ever said, "the real gems," he said, "were unprintable."

He seemed to be speculating, pleasantly, as to what she might have said about her funeral.

At the time of Dorothy Parker's death, it seemed both necessary and appropriate to remember her bravery and her gaiety, for to remember these aspects was, in a way, to keep her alive and well. But it was a very complicated woman who had died alone in a small hotel. When the police searched through her effects, they found Miss Hellman's $10,000 check in a bureau drawer, together with three other uncashed checks. Elsewhere four more uncashed checks, seven years old, come to light. Her will left $20,000 to Martin Luther King. One of her friends sought to explain the uncashed checks by saying that, once Dorothy Parker had decided on such a bequest, she would regard the gift to be pledged and sancrosanct, and she would not have touched the money those checks represented, no matter how desperate her personal need. But why had she not deposited the checks in a bank account? This brought up once again the matter of Dorothy Parker's curious attitude toward money, and none of the suggested explanations seemed satisfactory. The mystery of the money called up further mysteries, and stories of old loves, and despair, and questions as to who this woman had really been; this sardonic humorist as the *Times* called her, whose principal concern at the very end of her life was whether Ernest Hemingway had really liked her.

Thirty-five years earlier, a young Swedish newspaperwoman, Gunilla Wettergren, had interviewed Dorothy Parker. At that time she had written, "She is curled up in an easy chair, with a huge English sheepdog at her feet, a toy given her by a friend to replace her dog, which is in a hospital. She is in navy blue and her black, whirling hair makes her look like a Japanese doll. She is vivid, witty and impulsive, but now and then she suddenly seems so shy and helpless, and you would not be astonished if tears slipped out of her big brown eyes. Not by sentimentality, but by utter, trembling sensitiveness."

Then, aware of the impossibility of accounting for all this, Miss Wettergren rather helplessly added, "She is not like anybody else."

But another way of looking at Dorothy Parker is to say that

she was more like anybody else than anybody else is ever apt to be. This is because, to a greater extent than others, she permitted herself to be herself. And because she did, she became aware of a truth about the human condition, and so she was able, as Edmund Wilson said, to put down on paper "a few moments of human experience that no one else has conveyed."

EPILOGUE

Three be the things I shall have till I die:
Laughter and hope and a sock in the eye.

—Dorothy Parker

Three volumes of poetry and two of short stories are not an enormous literary legacy. Yet Dorothy Parker deserves a place in American literature for all that her total output was small, and despite the fact that its quality is uneven.

She was quite right to think that her literary position would be based on her short stories, and not on her poems. Her importance as a short story writer is that she was one of the first to report on the gathering tragedy of twentieth-century anomic.

Her generation was the first to enter upon the new world that began to emerge after the 1914–18 war. This was essentially an urban world, formless, messy, full of slippery values. More perceptive than most of the people around her, she saw more clearly than they the absurdity and pointlessness of their lives—her own included.

The time through which she moved would seem to be those of an awakening national intellectual maturity. The twenties, of course, were the most adolescent of times, when it seemed important to have irresponsible fun, and the people Dorothy Parker knew then were, for the most part, bright lightweights. "They were small-timers, most insecure people, very self-conscious, and addicted to big-shotism," an informant said. They were, like Alexander Woollcott, garrulous provincials who invested New York City with bogus glamour and "wanted to be smart." They were also, for the most part, young people on the way up; they would become successful popular entertainers and writers of coy ephemera for the magazines, including *The New Yorker*, and the writers of inconsequential plays. That is, the plays would be funny and bright, but hardly to be mistaken for theater of any real weight. So it was a smart set that she fell in with—one that had little to do with those who were making serious contributions in literature and the dramatic arts, most probably because the serious contributors had very little to do with New York City: Hemingway, Faulkner, and Dos Passos were, for example, based elsewhere.

More than the others in her circle, she appreciated the loneliness of Everyman as he drifted along in the impersonal, aimless urban throng. So, she began to search for meaning, and this search led her to become one of the first American short story writers to try to let carefully selected facts speak directly to the reader. What she wrote about in the twenties, and the way she wrote about it, became the prevalent subject matter and conventional style of the thirties. She was therefore one of those who contributed to the development of the American short story; Hemingway was another. It is perhaps unfortunate for Dorothy Parker's literary reputation that Hemingway was her contemporary, for his influence on a generation of writers was far greater than hers: nevertheless, her contribution was felt. The facts she chose to select from experience added up to very bleak meanings indeed, but none can say that what she chose to report about the human condition was inaccurate, and a great many college students of the thirties believed that what she had to say was precisely applicable to their circumstance.

Like many intellectuals, she loved mankind in general and despised her neighbor in particular. She had a strongly masochistic nature but was quite sentimental—and yet coldly perceptive. She sometimes let her sentiment submerge her critical intelligence; she ran scared all her life, and her life was in many ways a desperate one. For all her generosity, and for all that she devoted no small part of herself and her money to worthwhile politics, something always held her back from full commitment. Possibly, commitment would have made her happy, and happy was, probably, what she never wanted to be.

This tiny, big-eyed, feminine woman with the mind of a man; this truth-teller who told some of the damnedest lies; this lover who was terrified of the responsibility of being loved; this user of four-letter words who once coupled with a man in the presence of party guests; this "sour little girl who always went about slashing her wrists and having abortions"; this excellent poet and short story writer "who was a genius"; this mixed-up person who said if she wrote an autobiography she would call it *Mongrel* was, as a mourner at her funeral said, "a great lady." Perhaps any woman who lives her life all the way up qualifies for the epithet, just as a man may be defined as one who actually lives his life. Dorothy Parker lived in a love-hate tension. But she did live intensely all the loving-loathing while, and whenever she could bring herself to do so, she made very competent use of a first-rate talent. A pity that she could not have gone to the typewriter more often, but then, if she had, she might not have been Dorothy Parker.

So she had a life that was pretty much of a mess, as any existentialist's life is apt to be, and yet she did several things. She wrote poetry that was at least as good as the best of Millay and Housman. She wrote some stories that are easily as good as some of O'Hara and Hemingway. She gave a voice and an attitude to each time through which she moved, and which, to a certain extent, she also mirrored. She had a far better talent than most of her friends had, and she respected it and wasted it and seemed all the while to stand outside herself, watching herself kill the thing she called a gift from God.

Bibliography

PERIODICALS

Should the reader wish to examine Mrs. Parker's poems, stories, dramatic criticisms, and book reviews in the context of the times of their appearance, and to read contemporary evaluations of Mrs. Parker's work, the author regretfully refers him to the *Readers Guide to Periodical Literature* and to the *Essay and General Literature Index*—regretfully, because these are the only guides there are, and they are incomplete. Nevertheless, the author believes the reader may obtain a fairly comprehensive view of Mrs. Parker's work by looking up references cited by these two standard guides, particularly by looking up those in the *Readers Guide* for the years 1922 to 1963.

Her dramatic criticism and book reviews can be found in copies of *Vanity Fair, The New Yorker,* and *Esquire* magazines. Poems, stories, and articles were printed in *The Saturday Evening Post; American Mercury; Current Opinion; Colliers; The Bookman; The Literary Digest; The Golden Book; The New Republic; The Nation; New Masses; Pictorial Review; The Yale Review; The Readers Digest; Scholastic; The Saturday Review of Literature; House and Garden; The New Yorker; Harpers; Mademoiselle; Vogue; Cosmopolitan; Vanity Fair;* and *Esquire.*

Articles about Mrs. Parker appeared in *Arts and Decoration; The Saturday Review of Literature; Women's Journal; Colliers; The Literary Digest; Ladies Home Journal; Esquire; Time; Newsweek; Life; The New Yorker; Theater Arts; Catholic World; Commonweal; The Nation; The New Republic; America;* and *McCall's.*

BOOKS

In attempting to re-create the life and times of Dorothy Parker, the author found the following books to be particularly useful:

S. H. ADAMS, A. Woollcott. Hamish Hamilton, London, 1946.

F. L. ALLEN, Only Yesterday. Perennial Library, Harper & Bros., New York, 1931.

————— Since Yesterday. Bantam Books, Harper & Bros., New York, 1939.

————— The Big Change. Bantam Books, Harper & Bros., New York, 1952.

J. W. BEACH, American Fiction. Macmillan, New York, 1941.

NATHANIEL BENCHLEY, Robert Benchley. McGraw-Hill, New York, 1953.

E. R. BENTLEY, The Dramatic Event. Beacon Press, Boston, 1954.

MALCOLM COWLEY, Think Back on Us. Southern Illinois University Press, Carbondale, 1967.

M. CURTI, The Growth of American Thought. Harper & Row, New York, 1964.

JOHN DOS PASSOS, USA. Modern Library, New York, 1937.

R. E. DRENNAN, The Algonquin Wits. The Citadel Press, New York, 1968.

C. FORD, The Time of Laughter. Little, Brown, Boston, 1967.

W. GIBBS, More in Sorrow. Henry Holt & Co., New York, 1958.

J. Grant, Ross, The New Yorker, and Me. Reynal & Co., New York, 1968.

J. GRAY, On Second Thought. University of Minnesota Press, Minneapolis, 1946.

M. C. HARRIMAN, The Vicious Circle. Rinehart, New York, 1951.

ERNEST HEMINGWAY, Green Hills of Africa. Charles Schribner's Sons, New York, 1935.

————— A Moveable Feast. Charles Scribner's Sons, New York, 1964.

————— The Sun Also Rises. Charles Scribner's Sons, New York, 1926.

M. LAWRENCE, School of Femininity. Stokes, New York, 1936.

SINCLAIR LEWIS, Babbitt. Signet Classic, New American Library, New York, 1961.

V. LOGGINS, I Hear America. Biblo and Tannen, New York, 1937.

ANITA LOOS, But Gentlemen Marry Brunettes. Boni & Liveright, New York, 1928.

T. L. MASSON, Our American Humorists. Moffatt, New York, 1922.

W. MOREHOUSE, Matinee Tomorrow. McGraw-Hill, New York, 1949.

JOHN O'HARA, *Butterfield Eight*. Harcourt, Brace & Co., New York, 1935.

G. OPPENHEIMER, *Here Today* (play). Samuel French, New York, 1931.

———— *The Passionate Playgoer*. The Viking Press, New York, 1958.

———— *The View from the Sixties*. David McKay, New York, 1966.

DOROTHY PARKER, *Not So Deep as a Well*. Viking Press, New York, 1936.

———— *Here Lies*. Viking Press, New York, 1939.

———— *After Such Pleasures*. Viking Press, New York, 1933.

———— *Death and Taxes*. Viking Press, New York, 1931.

———— *Enough Rope*. Boni & Liveright, New York, 1927.

———— *Laments for the Living*. Viking Press, New York, 1930.

———— *Sunset Gun*. Viking Press, New York, 1928.

———— *The Portable Dorothy Parker*. Viking Press, New York, 1944.

RASCOE and CONKLIN, *The Smart Set Anthology*. Reynal and Hitchcock, New York, 1934.

G. SELDES, *The Seven Lively Arts*. Sagamore Press, New York, 1957.

D. A. SHANNON, *Between the Wars: America, 1919–1941*. Houghton Mifflin, Boston, 1965.

VINCENT SHEEAN, *Personal History*. Modern Library, New York, 1940.

H. A. SMITH, *Desert Island Decameron*. The Blakiston Co., Philadelphia, 1947.

H. STEARNS, *America Now*. Charles Scribner's Sons, New York, 1938.

M. THORP, *America at the Movies*. Yale University Press, New Haven, 1939.

JAMES THURBER, *The Years with Ross*. Signet Books, New American Library, New York, 1962.

E. B. WHITE, *The Second Tree from the Corner*. Harper & Row, New York, 1965.

EDMUND WILSON, *The American Earthquake*. Garden City, New York, 1958.

———— *Classics & Commercials*. Farrar, New York, 1950.

———— *A Literary Chronicle*. Garden City, New York, 1952.

THOMAS WOLFE, *You Can't Go Home Again*. Garden City, New York, 1942.

ALEXANDER WOOLLCOTT, *The Portable Woollcott*. Viking Press, New York, 1946.

Writers at Work, The Paris Review Interviews; Compass Books, New York, 1959.

N. W. YATES, *The American Humorist*. Iowa State University Press, Ames, 1964.

INDEX